T0301425

How to be an Academic Superhero

How to be an Academic Superhero

Establishing and Sustaining a Successful Career in the Social Sciences, Arts and Humanities

SECOND EDITION

Iain Hay

Academic Dean, Australian Institute of Business

Matthew Flinders Emeritus Distinguished Professor, Flinders University, Australia

Edward Elgar
PUBLISHING

Cheltenham, UK • Northampton, MA, USA

Published by
Edward Elgar Publishing Limited
The Lypiatts
15 Lansdown Road
Cheltenham
Glos GL50 2JA
UK

Edward Elgar Publishing, Inc.
William Pratt House
9 Dewey Court
Northampton
Massachusetts 01060
USA

A catalogue record for this book
is available from the British Library

Library of Congress Control Number: 2023945128

This book is available electronically in the **Elgar**online
Geography, Planning and Tourism subject collection
http://dx.doi.org/10.4337/9781803929439

ISBN 978 1 80392 942 2 (cased)
ISBN 978 1 80392 943 9 (eBook)
ISBN 978 1 80392 944 6 (paperback)

Printed and bound in Great Britain by
TJ Books Limited, Padstow, Cornwall

Contents

Tables

Boxes

1.   Making academic superheroes

Faced with the tangle of uncertain employment arrangements, rapid intensification of work, diminishing resources, performance-based cultures, overworked professional role models, problematic paradigms of success, and fearful of making a wrong career move in the demanding, unforgiving university culture of which they are a part, many scholars struggle to establish and sustain academic careers, let alone satisfy institutional demands for so-called 'academic superheroes' (Pitt and Mewburn, 2016, p. 99). This volume is a research-informed response to the challenge, intended to help those contemplating or developing an academic career in the arts, social sciences or humanities navigate their way through a successful, sustainable and rewarding vocation, balanced thoughtfully with personal and professional needs.

Precariousness and fear characterize the careers of many contemporary academics. For some time now widespread redundancies, high and growing levels of casual employment, unrelenting pressures from an increasingly global marketplace, new forms of professional surveillance, accelerating use of online technologies, and mounting institutional 'productivity' demands have placed increasingly apprehensive scholars in perilous professional positions (see, for example, Dyer et al., 2016; Fitzgerald et al., 2012; Gornall et al., 2014; Grove, 2016; Jones and Oakley, 2018; Patfield et al. 2022; Simpson et al. 2022; Spina et al., 2022). Evidence of anxiety can be seen by the growing attention being given to mentoring, staff development programmes, and other forms of personal and career support (e.g., Debowski, 2022; Ferguson and Wheat, 2015; Hemmings, 2015; Massner et al. 2022). Academics have less and less room for ineffective work on their personal high road to academic success. While this book can do little about the structural circumstances underpinning unstable university employment, on the basis of its ethnographic work clarifying the 'lived expectations, complexities, contradictions, possibilities, and ground' (McGranahan, 2014, p. 23) of academics as a cultural group, it is intended to go some way to minimize anxieties felt by early-career, as well as more senior scholars.

The fact that we work today in ever more competitive academic environments is evidenced by the growing significance attached to national and international institutional rankings (e.g. Times Higher Education World University Rankings, US News and World Report college and university rankings, Academic Ranking of World Universities (ARWU), and the QS

World Universities Rankings); individuals' publication numbers and research grant values (Musselin, 2018; Rhein and Nanni, 2021; *The Economist*, 2015); the heightened importance of publicly available online markers of scholarly productivity (e.g., Google Scholar's h-index [or Hirsch index] and i-10 index citation scores; ResearchGate's impact points); and the growth of online teaching quality evaluations (e.g., Rate My Professors, Uloop). Despite the development of teaching-related measures, academia's intensifying competitive, performance-based culture remains led largely by numerical measures of research activity. In the flurry of numbers, qualities such as influencing students, teaching effectiveness or community engagement, which cannot be simply quantified or easily compared across disciplines, have tended to be marginalized. Neoliberal, managerialist influences that underpin and sustain this cultural shift have also marginalized more diverse understandings of academic success (e.g., Bostock, 2014; Sutherland, 2015) that embrace matters such as life satisfaction and useful societal contributions. Rather than protesting continuing neoliberalizing tendencies, through its attention to 'objective' and 'subjective' measures of career success, this second edition continues to acknowledge the material characteristics and contexts of contemporary universities while endeavouring to support the human needs of the academic staff who sustain them.

Competition and the consequential emergence of institutional hierarchies point to another enduring foundation for this book. In an ever more competitive and stratified academic environment, and over and above their other advantages, postgraduate students, early-career academics (ECAs), and established scholars in high-status, wealthy universities arguably have access to high-flying, well-connected mentors and colleagues. This affords them greater support and competitive opportunities than those available to equally gifted colleagues at other institutions. By laying out publicly some new as well as more established ideas and perspectives on approaches to career success, this volume is intended to help level that playing field.

Notwithstanding the possibility that the claim about differential access to high-quality mentors is flawed, there is certainly broad worth in codifying the kind of advice or counsel increasingly busy senior academics may take for granted or be unwilling or unable to share in detail because of their own escalating professional commitments or because they believe that '"good" students find their way on their own, while the remainder cannot be helped' (Feibelman, 2011, p. xi). As Daniel Nehring (2013) has pointed out, while many emerging scholars do all the right things – teaching well, publishing in the right journals, securing grants – they still do not have stable academic careers. He suggests that the 'informal rules and techniques of academic labour often remain opaque to … early-career scholars' because postgraduate programmes are too large and senior academics are too busy to offer the kind of support that 'might have worked at Oxbridge in 1900'. The problem is worse now as online technologies simultaneously, and somewhat ironically, facilitate increasing physical distance between academic colleagues whilst reducing opportunities for informal and critical career development moments.

By setting out advice that some institutions and senior colleagues mistakenly assume 'everyone knows'; describing behaviours and actions successful academics have made without necessarily being aware of their importance or significance until much later; and recounting lessons learned from bitter experience, this book may help smooth some academics' career paths. Feibelman (2011, p. 142) reminds us: 'It is far better to learn from the bad experiences of others than from your own'.

National and international university competition is accompanied by heightened – if not extraordinary – expectations of staff. Though not new, government and public exhortations for universities to do more with less have intensified and academic staff bear the brunt of that. For example, in their disturbing analysis of academic job descriptions in Australian universities, Pitt and Mewburn (2016) refer to the institutional demand for 'academic super-heroes'. These are junior to mid-career scholars who, in their quest for a job, can satisfy up to 21 *essential* selection criteria, embracing discipline-specific knowledge, research performance, administrative duties, teaching prowess, networking and continuing professional development, interpersonal skills, corporate citizenship – and more – listed in a single position description! As Pitt and Mewburn (2016, p. 99) put it so colourfully:

> This new academic ... is a multi-talented, always ready and available worker that we have started to label the 'academic super-hero', capable of being everything to everyone and leaping over 24 KSC [key selection criteria] in a single job application.
> The academic super-hero conforms to university strategic priorities (including in directing their research focus and undertaking pastoral care for students and colleagues) and is always alert, if not alarmed. At any moment our hero must be ready to deal with the multiple uncertainties that beset the higher education sector ... all the while collecting business cards for that next round of student placements, soothing hurt feelings and smiling graciously at the crowds of prospective students at Open Day while publishing prodigiously and creating innovative learning opportunities for their students across multiple media.

The challenge for contemporary academics (aspiring academic superheroes) is to respond as fruitfully as possible to growing expectations but in ways that allow them to work sustainably and well, while remaining healthy and sane. This book is about achieving those ends. But let me make quite clear that this volume is not some form of apologist response to the apparently unceasing and escalating demands of contemporary universities on academic staff. It is intended instead to assist scholars to prioritize and manage effectively the various demands they encounter, in ways that are humane as well as personally and professionally viable.[1]

Finally, although it begins from a broader conception of success than the customary trinity of teaching, research and service, this book is not a detailed examination of the meaning and constituents of the concept. That research is left for others (Almeida et al., 2022; Archer, 2008; Arthur et al., 2005; Debowski, 2022; Kern et al., 2014; Laud and Johnson, 2012; Van der Heijden et al., 2022). Instead, starting from work such as Sutherland's (2015) expanded conception of academic success, this book offers a discussion of pathways through success, being informed by extant literature, extensive discussions with colleagues, and over 35 years of observation and experience around the world.

Some evidence that there is a need for volumes such as this is apparent from the emergence over the past 15–20 years of systematic initiatives to support scholars in the early stages of their career. These include the Preparing Future Faculty (PFF) programme offered by over 300 higher education institutions in the United States under the sponsorship of the Association of American Colleges & Universities and the Council of Graduate Schools; the wonderful US-based Geography Faculty Development Alliance (GFDA); Australia's institutional Graduate Certificates in University Teaching; Postgraduate Certificates in Higher Education Teaching and Graduate Teaching Assistant courses in most UK universities as well as the various initiatives of AdvanceHE, plus a range of more ad hoc face-to-face and online academic development and mentoring arrangements. Those projects have been accompanied by helpful volumes on academic career development, with notable examples including Robert Boice's (2000) classic *Advice for New Faculty Members*; Wendy Crone's (2010) *Survive and Thrive*; Shelda Debowski's (2012) *The New Academic*; and Solem et al.'s (2009) edited collection *Aspiring Academics*. Others include Boden et al. (2007), Cantwell and Scevak (2010), Clark and Sousa (2018), Furstenberg (2013), Gasman (2021), Goldsmith et al. (2001), Grant and Sherrington (2006) and Johnson (2011) as well as volumes focused more finely on specific aspects of securing and performing academic work (e.g., Belcher, 2019; Blumberg, 2014; Vick et al., 2016). This book is part of that swell of activity. Drawing on decades of observation and experience, it offers accessible support to university scholars on effective ways of developing and sustaining a successful academic career.

A focal point of this book is holistic academic career development. Following Sutherland et al. (2013, p. 55), scholars who understand themselves to be researchers, teachers and academic citizens are more likely to thrive than their more single-minded colleagues. But there is actually more to a truly successful academic career than the scholarly trinity of teaching, research and service. On the basis of international research, Sutherland (2015) reveals broader conceptions of academic career success (Table 1.1), which embrace a range of objective (e.g., research productivity, teaching performance, salary) and subjective markers (e.g., life satisfaction, freedom, influencing students). She notes that while objective indicators remain dominant in the literature – as well as in professional and institutional discussions of success – they are often ill defined in the minds of (early-career) academics to whom the measures are applied. And she goes on to observe that the subjective markers call for more research and practical consideration. To that call this book is a response.

Table 1.1 provides a helpful and comprehensive picture of the various faces of academic career success. On the basis of extensive investigation and experience, one purpose of this book is to discuss the ways those markers of success can be achieved. For the sake of comprehensibility – and with important caveats about the diversity of individuals, their personal, social, institutional and national contexts, and academic career progression as a 'pipeline'[2] (Frølich et al., 2018; League of European Research Universities, 2023; Spina et al., 2022, p. 534; Stringer et al., 2018) – it does this by providing advice and guidance structured in a loose progression, setting out strategies that may be useful as one engages with a 'balanced' academic career (i.e., involving both research and teaching) in the HASS (humanities, arts and social sciences) disciplines. Having said this, much of the book's content should still be of relevance to those who find themselves in 'teaching-focused' or 'research-focused' roles.

The book comprises five main parts. The first covers foundational material on getting qualified and securing good initial advice on career planning and development. The second is very much about making an important initial impact, including getting known in relevant scholarly circles and learning about academic cultures. The third deals with the very important subject of securing good employment. The fourth covers work-related aspects of everyday performance as an 'academic superhero', including publishing, teaching, securing funding and engaging with work-related communities. The book's final part is one of the most important: how to preserve your academic superpowers. The material in this part of the book covers such matters as keeping refreshed and staying happy and healthy. While these issues are located last in the book, a sustainable career requires that they be accounted for throughout that career.

Acknowledging that academic careers have multiple entry and exit points (Spina et al., 2022, p. 534) and a range of forms, the chapters that follow are not intended to suggest there is any specific, inviolable sequence of events or steps you must proceed through to have a successful career. This volume is not intended to be a textbook-like representation of some form of standard career development. The layout is an organizational device for the book and one that presents advice in accord with a pattern many people aspiring to become 'academic superheroes' follow. Issues and challenges discussed in this book need

Table 1.1   *Constructions of academic career success, as perceived by*
early-career academics

Objective Career Success in Academia	Subcategories Generated from the Data	Subjective Career Success in Academia	Subcategories Generated from the Data
Research productivity	External grant funding Publishing in high-profile journals/ with reputable publishing houses/ presses Generating more postgraduate students Launching a research programme/leading a research team First/last/sole authorship	Life satisfaction	Happiness Balancing work, family and leisure Keeping stress under control Staying healthy
Promotion and tenure	Early promotion or tenure Meeting requirements in research, teaching and service (all rounder) Promotion to professor/a personal chair	Contribution to society	Making a lasting contribution to human knowledge Influencing people's behaviour or thinking Connecting with/ changing the local community
Status	Disciplinary reputation International invitations to collaborate on research Working in a reputable university Research and teaching awards Being given departmental (or wider university) responsibilities	Freedom	To choose one's own research direction To work collectively not just individually To buy out teaching to focus on research To do interdisciplinary work To teach in one's speciality area/s

Objective Career Success in Academia	Subcategories Generated from the Data	Subjective Career Success in Academia	Subcategories Generated from the Data
Teaching performance	High student evaluation scores	Job satisfaction	Feeling confident as a researcher and teacher
	Teaching large classes		Receiving positive, unsolicited feedback on teaching from students and colleagues
			Maintaining balance in all academic roles
			Building a research niche/moulding the field
			Mentoring/inspiring colleagues
Salary	Adequate salary important, but not a key marker of success	Influencing students	Influencing postgraduate students' opportunities
			Challenging students' thinking
			Inspiring indigenous and/or female students[a]
			'Grandparenting' as an adviser

Note: [a]To this I would add inspiring students from underrepresented backgrounds.
Source: Sutherland (2015).

to be addressed continuously and sometimes simultaneously across a career. Some will have more or less significance at different times.[3]

It is envisioned that this volume will be of use to prospective, early-career and more senior scholars, or indeed to the same scholar passing through these different occupational stages. The pages that follow focus on HASS, though my own career background as a social scientist means that there may be embedded in the book some unintentional partiality as well as some blindness to the needs and requirements of, say, some scholars in the humanities. However, being conscious of this latter possibility, I have made a specific point of seeking out additional counsel and ideas from senior scholars in the research for this book.

The book is based primarily on informal but deeply interested participant observation (Gold, 1958; Ingold, 2014; Watson, 2021) conducted over a successful 35-year career as a teaching and research academic. Observations have been made during experiences as a postgraduate student in Australia, New Zealand and the United States; as a visiting fellow in China, England, Malaysia, New Zealand, Scotland, Singapore and the United States; and as a lecturer and professor in New Zealand and Australia.

As Kawulich (2005) notes, participant observation 'is the process enabling researchers to learn about the activities of the people under study in the natural setting through observing and participating in those activities'. It involves being physically and socially close to participants, experiencing activities and incidents first hand (Sandiford, 2015, pp. 414–15), and 'establishing a place in some natural setting on a relatively long-term basis in order to investigate, experience and represent the social life and social processes that occur in that setting' (Emerson et al., 2001, p. 352). While some scholars (e.g., Bernard, 1994) have argued that participant observation requires removing oneself from the observational setting or community and immersing oneself in the observational data to comprehend and write about it, that removal or distancing may not be possible in theory or practice given the various networks and sets of relationships researchers have with their 'field'. Nonetheless, careful reflection on one's observations is both possible and requisite. While my observations, deliberations and recommendations are inevitably incomplete, partial and biased, founded on my position as a middle-class, white, heterosexual male who has worked as a human geographer in English-speaking institutions almost exclusively, they have been facilitated and tempered by frequent public outings. To empower contemplation and to expose its outcomes to daylight's harsh reality, parts of this book have been used as discussion and resource material for students and ECAs in Australia, China, Malaysia, New Zealand, Singapore, the United Kingdom and the United States. The first edition of the book has also been reviewed formally by numerous thoughtful and well-informed critics. Through those outings, many of the ideas here have been exposed to a form of highly critical participant checking involving diverse others (for a discussion, see Stratford and Bradshaw, 2021). Nonetheless, while the book is intended to have broad geographical value it is inevitable that it will be characterized to some extent by a degree of insularity.

Around the world, university scholars are struggling to satisfy the many and often growing demands placed upon them. Teaching, community service and contributions to university administration are important and pressing components of these demands, and everywhere it seems there are new and more strident expectations to teach more students better; to more fully engage with professional and social communities; to publish high-quality books and papers, and more of them; to get more grant money; and to otherwise develop and then maintain ceaselessly a stellar career. These pressures come at considerable, and commonly acknowledged, costs that may include loneliness, divorce, stress, unhappiness, ill health and career abandonment. It is to the many scholars facing these challenges that this book is dedicated.

NOTES

1. I should note my sense that Lauren Berlant's (2011) seminal notion of 'cruel optimism' is apt within contemporary neoliberal universities: 'A relation of cruel optimism exists when something you desire is actually an obstacle to your flourishing' (p. 1). Berlant suggests that cruel optimism has prevailed since the 1980s, with people (including university workers) remaining attached to unattainable fantasies of the 'good life' and its promises of, for instance, upward mobility and job security, even when neoliberal societies – and their universities – can no longer be counted on to provide opportunities for individuals to achieve their ambitions.
2. Frølich et al. (2018, p. 13) observe that in the UK the linear path from lecturer to senior lecturer to reader to professor 'is no longer the reality for most academics' and the phase between PhD completion and a position as a lecturer has grown longer over the years. While similar patterns are emerging in other educational systems, as Frølich et al. themselves demonstrate this trend is by no means universal.
3. Despite these aspirations to fluidity the book's focus means that it may – unfortunately – fall into that class of cultural stories that Dyer et al. (2016, p. 309) suggest 'reify a standard career path and "other" those not willing or able to access such a path'.

PART I

SETTING OUT AS AN ACADEMIC
SUPERHERO

2. Get qualified

To set out as an academic superhero in the humanities, arts and social sciences (HASS) disciplines, you will almost certainly need a research doctorate (e.g., PhD, DPhil). But not all doctorates are equal. So many scholars have such a degree (Else, 2015; *The Economist*, 2010) that it is becoming more and more useful, if not critical, to get this qualification from a well-regarded university in a department with a strong research culture and a large, well-regarded and long-standing doctoral programme. Aside from prestige, such places offer a valuable array of resources and opportunities, for as Merton observed as long ago as 1968 (p. 62): 'centers of demonstrated excellence are allocated far larger resources for investigation than centers which have yet to make their mark. In turn, their prestige attracts a disproportionate share of the truly promising graduate students.'

Although your doctorate is intended to provide you with core research training and serve as a starting point for your career, a depressing reality is that the institution you graduate from will, to some extent, mark you for life in terms of academic status. Perhaps unjustified as it may seem, a degree from Oxford or Harvard will almost assuredly be regarded better than one from a newer, smaller, or provincial university and position you better in the academic job market (Clauset et al., 2015; Kerr, 2020; Oprisko, 2012). And as the competition between universities becomes more intense, the challenges of stratification and prestige are likely to increase. Moreover, the associations a specific programme has with your discipline's subfields may be critical. For instance, Berkeley's geography programme is known widely for its work on human–environment relations; Cambridge for history; Georgetown for foreign studies; London School of Economics for economics; Melbourne for psychology; and European Institute of Business Administration (INSEAD) for business education. Select your graduate programme wisely.

It is important to ensure that any doctoral programme you enter has acknowledged strengths in your preferred field, so do your homework on this: checking university websites; contacting programme coordinators, potential advisers and current doctoral candidates; consulting with learned friends and colleagues; and reviewing university subject rankings (e.g., QS World University Rankings by Subject). Your academic focus may change as you move through a degree but you would be well advised to be working in a programme aligned with your broad interests. For instance, as a budding scholar of the transferability of Japanese fashion to Western societies, you might choose a programme with specialists in social anthropology, rather than one that focuses on European history.

While some high-status, research-intensive universities may not offer a particularly strong commitment to teaching or formal mechanisms for student development, they will almost certainly immerse you in a research culture. This may test your commitment to an academic career, but it also promises to invigorate your work and offer valuable insights into contemporary research processes. A dynamic, well-resourced department should allow you to tap into a deep and broad reservoir of professional connections. Affiliations with a particular institution may allow you to more easily develop networks with alumni (e.g., some major conferences incorporate social events hosted by particular departments that offer an immediate networking mechanism) and of course, enable extensive connections with your own doctoral cohort. In a longstanding well-regarded programme, your postgraduate group might be quite large and very talented, offering the possibilities of constructive criticism of your work; models of good – and bad – research and scholarly practice; valuable insights into work aligned quite closely to your own; as well as access to a sizeable network of future colleagues.

Over and above providing and proving your research training, your doctorate will serve as a foundation for your early academic career work. You will probably need to build directly on the research you completed in it or to expand its scope in the early postdoctoral stages of your academic career. Consider carefully the specific directions you want your work to go and the fields you wish to work in. Be aware in your deliberations that research areas come and go in and out of favour, so bear in mind that this year's 'hot topic' may be 'cold' and unappealing in the next two to three years. As with so many professional decisions, it will almost assuredly be helpful to speak with colleagues and supervisors to get a few extra insights.

As a foundation for scholarly work, a doctoral experience that also includes teaching, research and service opportunities has been shown to result in more confident early-career academics (Sutherland et al., 2013, p. 58). Your graduate experience will be pivotal to the development of good scholarly habits and will serve as a platform for building confidence. And confidence plays a very important role in an academic's career (Hemmings, 2012, pp. 172–3). While gaining a broad academic experience has been the dominant model in North American doctorate-granting institutions, where many students secure teaching assistantships to help cover tuition and living costs, opportunities for part-time teaching experience and service roles are also available in other jurisdictions. In your inquiries about institution-specific PhD opportunities, check out the prospects of gaining teaching experience as a tutor, laboratory demonstrator, or seminar leader, for example. Service roles including committee memberships may appear in the course of events or you may need to seek some out. For advice on this, see Chapter 26.

Not only is it vital to get appropriately qualified if you wish to develop a successful academic career, but in most cases it is important to get qualified early and as swiftly as possible. Some people seem to do all they can to prevent this, turning their thesis into an unachievable conquest, posing monstrously large, if not unanswerable, research questions, setting out enormous data collection procedures, exploring limitless new and 'relevant' literatures, or finding endless ways to procrastinate.[1] These all extend indefinitely the delicious days of being a graduate student, but also push back and diminish your chances of a successful academic career. Note well that prospective employers may question an apparently inexplicably drawn-out doctoral programme, concerned about your scholarly commitment and capability. So remember, your PhD is not your life's work. It is not intended to be your magnum opus. It is simply about demonstrating your tenacity and capacity to conduct significant independent research successfully. Part of that is satisfying the requirements of the degree in a timely fashion.

Part-time study presents challenges to speedy completion. It is characteristically marked by time-consuming tensions between the urgent everyday requirements of work or other responsibilities (e.g., caring for children – discussed in Chapter 35) and the silent insistence of a calendar marking the relentless passage of time through your doctorate. Even if you are aware of these pressures and their consequences, the financial costs of a doctoral education often means that part-time employment or some other source of income is required to pay for food, tuition, transport and clothing. If you can, find scholarships that will cover some of those costs. Not only will these ease your financial plight and your path through your degree, but they will also add impressively to your CV. Seek out employment that is aligned with your study (e.g., as a research assistant or tutor) or with an employer who is very supportive of your studies and its demands. And, of course, move through your degree as quickly as possible so you can devote yourself completely to the pursuit of a steady income.

Part-time study commonly has a problematic 'geography' – it is often associated with part-time attendance on campus, part-time engagement with peers, and ultimately with less than part-time commitment to your degree as other 'more pressing' family, social and work matters intrude on your study. So, even if technology allows you to work away, make a commitment to be physically present on campus frequently, regularly, and for lengthy periods. It is important that in your mind, as well as in the minds of family, friends and colleagues, there are inviolable times for study. During those times you are first and foremost a student, not an employee, not a father or mother, not a golf partner, not a drinking buddy. To the extent that it is possible, set aside and make known to relevant others your opportunities for those life pursuits. By apportioning time and space for study (see Chapter 17), you will be better able to engage, connect and communicate with scholarly colleagues and you will find your mind freed to respond to the demands of your PhD.

Getting qualified early may be especially challenging for women also wishing to have children. Vital reproductive years for women coincide with the key academic career period in which PhDs are typically obtained, first jobs secured and academic trajectories begun. As O'Shaughnessy (2012) notes, in the United States the average PhD student is 33 years old before earning that qualification. Many women postpone childbearing until completion of their PhD, often in their late twenties or early thirties. This presents its own self-evident problems. And for those who have children and then try to complete a higher degree there is a different set of challenges!

> Over the past four years I have carried a full teaching load (with over 350 students), while doing my PhD on a full-time basis. My husband has been in the same situation and we have two teenagers. What work–life balance? (Lecturer, female, 45–49 years, cited in Sutherland et al., 2013, p. 25)

As several authors make clear (Mason and Ekman, 2007; Mason et al., 2013; Philipsen and Bostic, 2008; Tree and Vaid 2022; Tower et al., 2015), there really is no clear or simple way of resolving the clash of study, career and children. Much depends on your specific personal, family and relationship circumstances as well as on your individual priorities. These matters are taken up more fully in Chapter 35.

It may be possible to find a good academic appointment following a late doctorate if you have spent time securing relevant workforce or community experience. Some business leaders and politicians, for example, seem able to find senior positions teaching business or politics, although this is a phenomenon some commentators take exception to. Phil Honeywood, who in a former life was a deputy leader of the Victorian Liberals (an Australian state political party), said while there was a strong temptation for vice-chancellors to gather a cadre of VIPs (as professors), 'it's a temptation that should be resisted'. 'Genuine academics spend many years acquiring the skills and knowledge to have the right to be called professor', Mr Honeywood said. 'But to hand out the title to VIPs who might have graduated in the school of life but never taught a graduate class or written a research paper that has been peer reviewed is just wrong' (Hare, 2013). Irrespective of any merits, appointing academic staff in HASS who have achieved a doctorate later in life and/or who bring substantial external experience appears to be becoming a less and less common practice as universities underscore research track records.

North American and other doctoral programmes that include a signifi-cant coursework component prior to the dissertation present a number of career-disrupting challenges. First, the transition from structured coursework with its clear deadlines, intra-class competition and collegial classmates to the dissertation component sees some students fall by the wayside, unable to cope with the dissertation's more laissez-faire character. Second, on the strength of successfully completed coursework, and in the midst of their dissertation, some people take on full-time teaching or another job, hoping to be able to satisfy the requirements of both job and dissertation adequately. This often fails. If you do find yourself in this kind of ABD (all but dissertation) situation, think very carefully. Is the job on offer one that is unlikely to come around again? Just how much do you need the money? How much teaching, marking and administration is expected? Unless the position is rare and of especial value to you (e.g., at an institution you particularly want to work at or one that is close to family) or if you are living in poverty or somewhere near to that, it is probably a good idea to disregard these sorts of opportunities, focussing first on completing your PhD.

British-model PhD programmes present a different set of challenges, one of the most notable being the personal and intellectual isolation associated with working independently and full-time for three to four years on a topic that many of your friends and family may find mysterious and esoteric. Although good personal and professional networks can sometimes overcome isolation, it continues to result in some students failing to complete and others unpro-ductively chasing many ideas down many rabbit holes. Good doctoral advisers (also known as supervisors) can help deal with the latter problem – as well as with many others.

NOTE

1. According to Gray and Drew (2012, p. 16), Richard J. Gelles (2006) of the University of Pennsylvania, termed this kind of procrastination Watson's Syndrome. Their solution is to find a mentor who will help you circumvent the distractions and push you to complete, or else you run the risk of being one of the 43 per cent of (US) doctoral students who do *not* get their PhD within ten years of starting graduate school (O'Shaughnessy, 2012). But the issue is not all about procrastination. As discussed in Chapter 35 other significant challenges such as pregnancy and childrearing sometimes intervene.

3.   Find a good adviser

Good doctoral advisers (or supervisors) can make a significant difference to the development of your academic career, either nurturing it carefully or failing to support it usefully. So, if you are able, choose your academic guides carefully.[1] Bear in mind when you consider advisers (see Box 3.1) that the relationship you have with them is likely to outlast the duration of your graduate study. They may act as key referees for your first job applications and conceivably as mentors or confidants for many years after the completion of your degree.

If you are looking for a doctoral adviser in the university you are already attending, you have the advantage of being able to meet with them (if you have not already) and finding out a great deal about their approach to supervision. However, if you are applying to study at another university with which you are not familiar, the task of finding a prospective supervisor is more challenging. Some universities offer a 'find a supervisor' or 'search for a supervisor' facility through their website. Generally, these try to connect you with relevant academic staff on the basis of shared research interests. They can be more or less useful. An alternative or supplementary way of finding someone to help guide you through your doctoral process is by an intensive search of relevant web resources (e.g. departmental websites, Google Scholar) to check out the credentials of people working in the area you are interested in. Once you have narrowed down some likely candidates, consider communicating with them with any specific questions or concerns have (see Box 3.1 for some helpful cues).

The advisory relationship is personal as well as academic. The patterns of practice of some advisers will not suit all students equally well. Some advisers like to keep a tight rein on students, monitoring research activity carefully and providing written comments assiduously, whereas others may be happy to let students find their own way, stepping in only when they feel intervention is required. Depending on your preferences, certain practices may or may not be welcome, so when you are considering prospective advisers, ask them about their philosophy and performance of supervision. It may also pay to see if you can confirm their self-assessments informally through the opinions of some of their current (or recent past) students. If there appear to be discrepancies between the adviser's views and those of their students, probe a little further.

BOX 3.1   SELECTING A GOOD DOCTORAL ADVISER/SUPERVISOR: SOME MATTERS TO CONSIDER

Like finding a suitable spouse or partner, discovering a good adviser can be much more a matter of good luck than good management, depending on where you wish to study, scholarship or sponsorship opportunities, or your personal networks. Irrespective of how it happens, there are some matters to consider in your search for an adviser. Just as institutions and advisers have their own criteria for evaluating prospective students, the following lists offer a starting point to guide your own search for the perfect match. To answer these questions search the web and speak to your potential adviser as well as to some of their students. There are some additional useful tips available at Jabre et al. (2021), though these tend to focus on the physical sciences and laboratory environments.

Scholarly credentials

- *Does your prospective adviser have a good reputation as a scholar?* An Internet search will usually help you get some appreciation of this. Google Scholar, LinkedIn, ResearchGate, Scopus and Academia.edu, as well as the adviser's own professional or personal website, can offer helpful insights into their academic productivity and standing. If they have a limited online profile you may wish to exercise a little caution. In contemporary academic environments a low Internet profile sometimes signals a low scholarly profile. A good adviser is well regarded and networked in their field. And their associations may make it easier for you to find an academic position when you have completed your degree. If you have the opportunity try to attend conferences or seminars where your prospective supervisor is speaking and if possible speak to them. Let them know what you're thinking and see how they respond.
- *What are your prospective adviser's areas of research and do these align with your own directions?* Although you may not know the precise area in which you expect to conduct your research, you will probably be able to match your general interests with those of potential advisers.
- *At what stage of their career is your potential adviser?* While a very senior scholar may have credibility and experience in abundance, will they be around to serve as a mentor in the early years of your career? On the other hand, a more junior scholar may be enthusiastic but they may not have the same measure of professional authority. There can be value in having scholars at different career stages as advisers so you can draw from their various levels of experience and standing.

Advisory practices

- *What is the person's reputation as an adviser?* Who are their current students and what are they working on? Do the adviser's students work together or are their endeavours isolated? Why? Does that match your own way of working?
- *Do they have a track record of successful supervision?* How many students finish? How quickly? What about other measures of advisory success (e.g., students' publications, awards, conference presentations)? What are the explanations behind the answers to each of these? And what are the prospective adviser's former students doing? Do they still serve as a mentor to those individuals?
- *Does the adviser have a personality and work style that is compatible with your personal and academic needs?* For example, some advisers treat their role as a 9–5 job, exercising careful time management and placing strict boundaries around work and personal lives; others regard their work as a vocation that they are ceaselessly and, perhaps you may find, tiringly passionate about. They may expect you to share these characteristics, irrespective of your personal circumstances (e.g., in part-time paid employment while caring for a small child). How do these quite different approaches suit you? If you are able, speak with some of the adviser's current students to get some sense of their experiences.
- *How do students working with this adviser select their thesis project?* In some fields and with some advisers, teams work on cognate projects with a student's research being linked very closely to that of their adviser. In others, the connection is often less direct, with students expected to devise their own project. It is important that you understand how things work with your proposed adviser: if you are not academically prepared to develop your own topic and work out how best to pursue it, you may find the latter approach insuperable. If you crave intellectual autonomy, the former approach may not be to your liking.
- *Just how does this adviser engage with their current students?* Does this adviser challenge students' opinions constructively, forcing them to defend and strengthen their thinking? How, and how well, do they communicate? Do they have frequent, regular student meetings or are things done on a more ad hoc basis, with meetings being held only as 'need' arises? Is communication face to face, by email, or by some other means? How do these patterns of activity suit you? How do other students get along with this adviser? Why?

- *How is feedback on progress provided and how are decisions about satisfactory progress made?* Does the adviser prefer to see frequent drafts of work or do they prefer to offer comments on a near-final version of each student's thesis? How long does it take to receive feedback on drafts of preliminary chapters or journal manuscripts in preparation and what is the character and quality of that feedback? Who determines when a student has actually done enough work to complete their thesis and on what basis is that decision made?

Advisory support and research environment

- *Is this adviser available and accessible?* Some high-profile scholars who may otherwise make great advisers are simply unavailable to students because of the many demands on their time. Others may have periods of sabbatical, secondment, or long-service leave on the horizon, which means they will be away for substantial and important parts of students' work (e.g., developing a thesis proposal).
- *Will you have access to the physical resources you need to support your work?* Will you have an office or will you be expected to 'hot-desk' with another student? Some universities have policies on minimum resources for postgraduate students (e.g., office space, computer, library access, printing) so find out about these and check to see if those policies are actually honoured. Confirm that there is institutional or adviser support to conduct fieldwork required for your study.
- *What career development opportunities are available?* Is there encouragement and resources that will allow you to attend relevant conferences and to take up professional development opportunities? Do joint publication opportunities exist with your prospective adviser and how are these managed?

The personal element

- *Do you get on with your potential adviser?* This is very important. If you have the opportunity, meet with your prospective supervisor to see if you get on with them. Are they the kind of person with whom you think you can work closely for the intense years of study to come? Do they seem like the kind of person who will support you in tough times and good?

Regardless of their style of interaction, a good adviser will take an active interest in your work and scholarly well-being. All this takes time and some advisers with a high profile have so many students on top of their other commitments that they cannot offer the personalized support you may require (Johnson, 2011, p. 20). So, while you may secure a superhero adviser, be aware that you *may* not get superhero supervision. But of course the converse may apply, as actress Lucille Ball suggested in her aphorism, 'If you want to get a job done, ask a busy person'. A busy adviser may just be a great adviser.

Finally, despite all of your efforts to ensure a good match between you and your supervisor you may find that the relationship just does not work (e.g. personality clashes, supervisor unable to meet with you or fails to provide timely feedback, supervisor does not seem interested in your work) you may need to see if alternative arrangements can be made. To do this, consider raising your concerns directly and tactfully with your supervisor. Some universities also have regular (typically annual) formal review mechanisms that provide an opportunity to make your worries known. Alternatively, or subsequently, make some preliminary (perhaps confidential) enquiries with your doctoral programme coordinator, head of department, or dean of graduate research to work out how, and if, to proceed.

NOTE

1.   Universities increasingly require that graduate students have a supervisory team, rather than a single supervisor. This can be a strength and a liability. Too large a team (say four to five) can cause delays in your work as you struggle to communicate with each of them; may be characterized by divisions and tensions between supervisors, with you, the student, caught in the middle; or may see you receiving contradictory advice from different members of the team. Smaller teams (say two) tend to be more nimble, but you may not get the breadth of input and opinion you desire.

4. Get mentors; get advice

Sternberg (2013) asserts that 'successful academics, early in their careers, look for several mentors, including from departments other than their own'. Having good advice – and heeding it – can be of immense value throughout your academic career. Sound guidance and psychosocial support can facilitate the future success of early career scholars, support more productive research careers and networking within the profession, as well as aiding in stress management (Debowski, 2012, pp. 36–7; Detsky and Baerlocher, 2007, p. 2134). Mentors can offer valuable assistance on matters as diverse as balancing family and work; setting short- and long-term goals; getting more out of your PhD adviser; dealing with departmental politics and conflict; understanding disciplinary cultures; communicating with journal editors; and negotiating employment. For such reasons more and more institutions are convening formal mentoring arrangements, aligning early career staff with more senior colleagues, thereby helping to sustain the personal and professional advantages that can accrue to both mentor and mentee markets (see Box 4.1). One example is the Academic Mentoring in Learning and Teaching initiative at the University of New South Wales discussed in Harvey et al. (2016). Typically, these programmes are intra-institutional but some embrace external, and even international participants depending on participants' career stage, as well as their ambitions and scholarly trajectory. Find out if your institution runs a mentoring programme and consider getting involved in it. You need not find mentors from your own discipline area. Indeed, in some instances, someone from outside your field can offer a very helpful new perspective (see, for example, Crone, 2010, p. 64).

Over and above providing important emotional and psychological assistance, mentoring promises career and professional development support for mentees as well as role modelling focussed on achievement of skills and knowledge within specific organizational contexts. Mentoring may be enormously useful, but do be aware that it is not without problems. As Janette Long (1994) discusses in her work on its 'dark side', mentoring can bring problems like mismatched participants, personality and gender conflicts, role mismanagement and burdensome time commitments. Peer and peer group mentoring can also be problematic, sometimes spiralling downwards through shared despair, griping and negativity. As much as it is wicked fun to grumble along with like-minded colleagues, success is more likely to lie with uplifting peers and positivity.

BOX 4.1   BENEFITS OF MENTORSHIP

For the protégé or mentee

- Developing and refining professional skills and knowledge.
- Building professional and collaborative networks.
- Deepening insights to academic and professional communities.
- Distinguishing exciting research ideas from pedestrian ones.
- Increased confidence and motivation.
- Exploring potential career options and strategies (e.g., do you need to seek a different job?).
- Identifying beneficial areas of growth and learning (e.g., how you can better 'balance' work and life).

For the mentor

- Reviewing their own career path and reflecting on accumulated knowledge and insights.
- Leaving a legacy through guiding and supporting talented new academics.
- Developing new skills and insights through mutual discussion and enquiry.
- Learning of new fields of knowledge and issues that inform their own work and reflections.
- Identifying potential talent that might be recruited into their own research group or projects.
- Developing potential research partnerships and collaborations.
- Developing joint publishing/projects.

Arguably, informally arranged, 'organic', or participant-driven mentoring offers all of mentoring's advantages with fewer of the disadvantages of its more formally organized counterparts. You may find in the course of your everyday study and work that there are more senior colleagues whose counsel you welcome and from whom you receive emotional sustenance.[1] Which of your more senior and accomplished colleagues do you respect? Whose opinion do you value? Mentoring relationships may flourish simply and spontaneously or you may wish to be a little more proactive, approaching colleagues to ask if they will be a mentor and setting out the kind of assistance you seek from them – recognizing that not every mentor will be able or even willing to discuss every aspect of your career development with you. But leaving this caveat to one side, many will be honoured and flattered and are likely to take the invitation very seriously. Such mentors – who are likely to come and go across your career depending on the stage and place – can be tremendously valuable allies, providing short-term as well as more strategic support. They may listen attentively to your concerns, offering sage advice when called for, and reducing your apprehensions about the pathway you are following through academia. They may extend stronger guidance, directing you to calls for papers, conferences, career openings, counselling, professional development opportunities and scholarships that you were not aware of or might never have dreamed of. And they may even come to be an advocate for you as you negotiate your academic setting.

If your own university does not offer the kind of mentoring and support services you would like and you cannot find a coach from amongst your own circle of colleagues you may find help from one of the swelling group of private academic coaching services offered on a fee-for-service basis by a distinguished senior or retired academics. Some of these services may be on a face-to-face basis but emerging communications technologies mean that you now have access to a larger and more diverse group of mentors than ever before. However you find a coach do remember though that while it can be helpful to listen to colleagues and mentors, it is your career. You are the one who must exercise control over your professional destiny.

If you do find yourself with a mentor – or several, offering different qualities, expertise and experience to the relationship (Crone, 2010, pp. 64–5; Debowski, 2012, pp. 38–41) – do keep them apprised of your activities and remember to thank them for their support and insights. While most mentors value the opportunity to assist colleagues, most receive little short-term reward for their contributions. They will welcome some measure of gratitude and acknowledgment for their guiding role in your brilliant career!

Even though you may have a mentor or two, it is helpful to seek out advice from a few other people. Develop a good open relationship with your PhD adviser, supportive senior colleagues and with peers – maybe through a peer mentoring group. These are people who know you personally, know your work and have the background and capability to listen to your concerns and offer guidance or insights as required. A good diverse network of people you can talk to about your career and its different facets is a great asset. Sometimes just voicing out loud perplexing or troublesome matters can help clarify them, but for this you need a trusted listening ear. Of course, there is a difference between listening to every voice with something to say about your situation and listening to wise counsel. Be careful to mind the difference.

NOTE

1. For women and scholars from minority groups, any lack of suitable senior role models and mentors can be a problem. One strategy proposed by Tower et al. (2015, p. 528) to overcome this kind of difficulty is to seek out or implement peer mentoring. They cite Jabour (2012, p. 25) who contends that female circles of friendship, same-sex partnerships and single-sex political networks have been shown to facilitate women's political effectiveness, professional causes and personal fulfilment.

5.   Prepare a good CV

Across your career you will do a great deal: write papers, give presentations at professional conferences, perform significant and not-so-significant service roles and so on. It is vitally important that you keep a comprehensive and detailed record of these activities (see Box 5.1). This record, your CV (curriculum vitae, vitae, or résumé), can serve as the basis for evidence claims when you respond to criteria associated with promotion, grants and job applications.[1] While your master CV may include details extending to all the professional development classes you have attended or led, and seminars you have presented as well as the more significant items that appear in most forms of your résumé (e.g., books written, journal editorial boards), for many purposes such an inclusive document may shroud some of the most relevant matters you wish a grant reviewer or prospective employer to know about you. So, use your master CV as the resource from which you extract details to produce shorter tailor-made résumés for specific purposes such as applying for a grant or award or to accompany a book proposal to a publisher. Shape your résumé to meet the precise objectives of what is required.

Aside from serving as a record of activity, your master CV can also function as a helpful diagnostic tool for professional development, revealing those areas where you have particular strengths or where some improvement is required. For example, a master CV documenting your achievements against the kind of structure set out in Box 5.1 makes it easy to identify areas where you have an abundance or shortage of evidence of professional performance. Creating a profile in LinkedIn can also reveal areas to which you might give attention in your CV as well as insights to the kinds of evidence of achievement used by other scholars and people in different areas of activity (see Chapter 9 for additional discussion). If appropriate, take remedial action to build on strengths and to fill the gaps. You may also wish to speak to peers and advisers about the structure and content of your CV as a document recording your professional activity. And have look on the web for examples of CVs uploaded by scholars you hold in high regard.

BOX 5.1   SETTING OUT AN EFFECTIVE ACADEMIC CV

Below are some preliminary guidelines on useful and common headings to include in one's CV. (More specific formatting guidance is offered in Box 5.2.) The list is based on many examples plus detailed and helpful advice set out in 'Dr. Karen's rules of the academic CV' (Dr. Karen, 2016) as well as that provided by Elsevier (2023). You may find that some entries relevant to your own specific academic career or the job you are applying for are missing (e.g., journal editorship, country of citizenship). Add these where you think they sit best. In doing this, it may be helpful to consider Dr. Karen's advice that the organizing principle of a CV is peer review and competitiveness. So the categories below may be used to arrange your CV but they need not be presented in exactly the same order as they are set out below. Those roles and activities that are most competitive (e.g., professional appointments) take priority and so, for instance, invited talks take priority over a volunteered conference paper. Notwithstanding this remark, it is customary for the first three sections below to be presented initially and in the order set out here.

Personal details
Begin your CV, of course, with your name, followed by your best postal, electronic and phone contact details. If it is appropriate, add your visa or citizenship status. Then set out content under the following headings:

Education
As with most entries, list your educational qualifications in reverse chronological order (most recent first), specifying the institution and year of completion. There is no need to include the starting date for each degree. If you are a recent graduate, it is useful to include the title of any theses or dissertations. This is less important as the years pass.

Professional appointments/employment
Include any postdoctoral, contract or 'tenured' roles so that any reader can 'place' you institutionally. Give institution, department, title and dates (year only) of employment. Roles as a teaching assistant, research assistant or tutor should not be listed here. These come later in the CV.

Awards, honours and fellowships
List by year, giving the name of the honour and the awarding organization.

Publications
This is a key part of any academic CV but after some years it is possible that

the list of publications grows so large as to make the subsequent parts of the CV difficult to locate. If you find yourself in this position, consider alternative presentation strategies such as listing key publications in the CV and adding a comprehensive list of publications as an appendix or supplementary file. Increasingly, measures of publication 'impact' are being woven into this section of CVs. For instance, some people preface their full publications list with details of their h-index, i10-index, total citations, or other such metrics. And some include with each publication details such as total sales (for books) or the publishing journal's impact factor or Q-ranking. Publications are most commonly listed under subheadings in the following order:

1. books;
2. edited volumes;
3. refereed journal articles;
4. book chapters;
5. conference proceedings;
6. book reviews;
7. manuscripts in submission (include journal title);
8. manuscripts in preparation;
9. web-based publications;
10. other publications and output (e.g., patents, newspaper commentaries).

Grants
Listed by year in reverse chronological order. Include the name of the funder and grant name. Whether the amount of the grant is included depends on one's discipline but it seems increasingly common and important to state the amount received.

Invited talks
This refers only to talks at places other than your own university. These should include, in order, the talk's title, the event (if appropriate), the location and the date (including day and month).

Conference activity/participation
These are most commonly listed under subheadings in the following order:
1. conferences organized;
2. panels organized;
3. papers presented;
4. discussant.

Entries include year, name of the paper, name of the conference and date range of the conference (e.g., 20–23 May).

Campus and departmental talks
List these as you would for invited talks, being sure not to include guest lectures in courses. That is generally regarded to be padding out your CV.

Teaching experience
If you have taught at more than one institution, set out details of your teaching experience under subheadings for each institution. Unlike other entries, list courses by title, not year. However, to the right of the course name, include the years taught. This allows you to show how often you have taught a course without having to state the course name repeatedly. It may be appropriate to include some brief statement as to whether you were the course designer or convenor, especially if you are an early-career academic. There is no need to list course codes/numbers as these typically mean little outside your home institution.

Research experience
Here you can include experience as a research assistant or laboratory assistant. Unlike most other entries in your CV, there is some scope for single-sentence elaboration of the project you were involved in.

Service to the profession
List roles serving professional organizations. Depending on how significant it is as an element of your work, add a subheading under which you record journal manuscript review work. List the names of the journals for which you have served as a referee.

University service
Include work on committees, departmental reviews, appointments to university senate and so on.

Extracurricular service (optional)
This might include contributions to service and sports clubs, for example, where appropriate.

Community involvement or outreach (optional)
Include matters such as work with boards, local councils or public lectures.

Media coverage (optional)
Include television and radio interviews or press stories based on your work.

Related professional skills (optional)
Here you might refer, for example, to specific technical skills or expertise in discipline-specific software.

Languages (optional)
List these with some indication of proficiency. For example:

- English: native language.
- French: intermediate (speaking, reading); basic (writing).
- Spanish: fluent (speaking, reading, writing).

Professional memberships/affiliations
This should include all organizations you belong to, including the year of joining as a marker of your commitment to the field.

References (optional)
Provide, without elaboration, the postal, email, web and phone addresses for your referees. This will usually be about three people, each of whom should have consented to be a referee. In the early stages of your career it is usual to include your PhD adviser in this list. Later it may be useful or important to include someone with employment-related supervisory responsibilities over you (e.g., your dean or vice-chancellor). Consider other referees carefully, thinking about those aspects of your professional life (e.g., teaching, research) that they can comment on as well as the balance of referees. It can be helpful to have referees from different institutions. Keep referees informed about any positions you are applying for and give them a copy of your CV.

There are many useful examples of academic CVs available on the web. But when looking for these, be aware that academic CVs differ in style and content from those in many other fields.

Be sure that your CV is accurate and error-free. Do not misrepresent your achievements. Egregious misrepresentations will almost inevitably catch up with you. For instance, a dean of admissions at Massachusetts Institute of Technology (MIT), was forced to resign her post after it was discovered she had lied about having a number of academic degrees 28 years earlier: 'Ms. Jones had on various occasions represented herself as having degrees from three upstate New York institutions. In fact, she had no degrees from any of those places, or anywhere else' (Lewin, 2007). In Texas, a Houston Catholic business school dean was forced to resign in disgrace from his University of St Thomas position after allegedly lying about several degrees. He had asserted that he earned a doctorate from a university in his native Italy that does not offer PhDs and the college from which he claimed he received a Bachelor's degree was a high school (Guzman, 2022). And while misrepresentations in your CV may not get you sacked, they are likely to upset or anger colleagues whose support you need.

Your CV must also be free of obscure language, abbreviations and course codes that may mean little to readers (e.g., tripos, Michaelmas, DoS, FHASS, HIST1002). It should, of course, be well presented, though not lurid and garish. First impressions count, and the first impression that some colleagues and most potential employers will have of you is going to be based on your CV. Represent yourself as someone who is well qualified, well organized and capable of 'sorting the wood from the trees'. Your CV needs to set out your relevant credentials in a clear and legible fashion (Box 5.2). To overdo things through excessive detail or design extravagance may suggest to a reader that you either have way too much time on your hands or a narcissistic personality disorder!

BOX 5.2   FORMATTING A CV – SOME HELPFUL GUIDELINES

- 2.5 cm (1 inch) margin on all four sides.
- 12-point font throughout.
- Single spaced.
- No switching of font sizes for any part of the CV, except perhaps your name at the top of the first page. This might be in 14 or 16 point.
- Headings in bold and all capital letters.
- Subheadings in bold only.
- No italics of any kind except for journal and book titles.
- One or two blank lines before each new heading.
- One blank line between each heading and its first entry.
- Left justify all elements of the CV. Do not fully or right justify any part.
- Do not use bullet points.
- No 'box' or column formatting. This obstructs the frequent adjustments and additions you will need to make to a dynamic CV.
- The year of every entry should be left justified with a tab or indent separating the year from the substance of the entry.
- There is no need for any narrative to describe components of your CV. This includes, for example, duties or responsibilities or paragraphs describing books, other projects or personal experiences.
- Put your name at the top of the CV, centred, in 14- or 16-point font. This will be one of the very few elements of your CV that is not in 12 point or left justified.
- Include the date of your CV immediately below your name.

- Then follows your best postal, phone and electronic contact details.

Source: Adapted from 'Dr. Karen's rules of the academic CV' (Dr. Karen, 2016).

Give thought to putting your CV, or appropriate parts of it, online – taking care, of course, to remove any elements you would prefer not to disclose to the rest of the world (e.g., a mobile phone number). While the web has become a 'hunting ground' for shadowy millionaires asserting their ambition to deposit large sums of money into your bank account, it is also a place where book editors seek out chapter contributors; journal editors look for referees and editorial board members; students hunt for advisers; and grant-awarding organizations search for reviewers. If you have no useful web presence, you reduce your chances of being approached to participate in such activities (see also Chapter 9). To conclude, it is important not to regard your CV as a bothersome record of activity. It is instead a vital tool for promoting yourself and advising relevant others of your abilities as well as an important instrument for diagnosing your own professional strengths and weaknesses. Structure your CV wisely, review it critically and update it regularly.

NOTE

1. New forms of CV are emerging (e.g., video CV) but for most academic jobs in the humanities, arts and social sciences (HASS), the traditional 'paper' version as described here remains current. It is worth noting too that academic CVs are typically quite different and much longer than their counterparts used in the corporate sector. Where necessary, however, the detail captured in a full academic CV can usually be pared down and shaped into the one- to two-page documents sought by some employers and organizations. There is voluminous online advice available on how to write a corporate CV, often associated with employment companies and professional networking sites (e.g. Indeed; LinkedIn; Monster; Prospects; Seek).

PART II

REFINING YOUR ACADEMIC SUPERHERO CREDENTIALS

6.   Focus your powers

While you may have diverse interests, reflecting your brilliance and capacity to connect and see wonder in everything around you, your academic career will probably be more objectively successful if you specialize, develop *and* get known for your particular capabilities (Feibelman, 2011, pp. 2–4; Gray and Drew, 2012, p. 10; Kim, 2022). One social demographer colleague of mine took this advice to heart early in his career, focusing his attentions on well-being and development issues in India, Papua New Guinea and Timor-Leste. He quickly became one of the key 'go to' people on these matters for international agencies, research students, colleagues and media. People contact *known* experts for advice, to participate in events, to write papers, to contribute chapters, to be reviewers, and to deliver keynote addresses at conferences. Not surprisingly, many objective measures of academic success follow from being known for your specific expertise. The two key elements in this sentence are both of importance: having an area of expertise and being known for it.

So, as early as you can, work out who you are (as a scholar), what you are doing, what you do well, and where you are going in your career. It may be trite to say but to sustain a successful long-term academic career it is critical that you not only have a publicly discernible research theme but that you also work on matters you regard as important or significant. Follow your heart and your desire. Little could be more dispiriting and stultifying for a scholar than going to work each day to face trivial intellectual problems. Although your own interests and passions are vital, do not discount the need for the challenges you identify to be important to others. High-quality work of personal significance may be satisfying and valuable to the overall development of knowledge, but it may not be as helpful to the development of your career. Stake out your claim on an area that is noteworthy to you *and* to others – whether they be scholars or members of the community and relevant professional groups.

In some disciplines (e.g., archaeology, physical geography, psychology) you may find that as part of their own research programme your adviser presents you with noteworthy research problems to deal with in your early research as an honours, masters, doctoral, or postdoctoral scholar. As you work through these problems and develop expertise in the field, you may come to love the challenges offered and begin to see new, related matters to study. With luck this will indeed occur, because at some early stage of your career you need to step beyond the projects other people assign you, moving on to determine the underpinning themes, rationale and significance of your own work. An adviser-led approach to your embryonic research can help ease the sometimes paralysing introspective quest for relevance that troubles early-career academics (ECAs) in some branches of the humanities and social sciences. Students in those areas are typically expected to uncover and initiate their own research agenda from the outset of their scholarly career.

Finding a personally and professionally satisfying focus on meaningful work may not come directly from a dedicated search. Locking yourself in an office for a long spell of contemplation might not be the most successful focussing strategy. Instead, significant opportunities may surface serendipitously (see, for example, Simon Blackburn, in Reisz, 2013) as the result of an off-hand remark by a friend, a headline in a newspaper, or an encounter in a café. It may also be helpful to speak with your (prospective) adviser to get a sense of what is happening in your general field and what is on the horizon over the next few years. Look too at the research areas major funding agencies are emphasizing. This will provide some indication of significant areas of disciplinary interest and public good, although be aware that, rather like fashion, research trends do wax and wane (Johnson, 2011, pp. 14–15).

Behind each of these possibilities for identifying research problems and establishing a research theme, however, is the groundwork you do in your field. Read widely, speak to colleagues and friends, ponder which areas you find especially interesting and why. Prepare the metaphorical intellectual soil for the right seed of an idea, for as Louis Pasteur observed over 150 years ago: 'Dans les champs de l'observation le hasard ne favorise que les esprits préparés' ('In the fields of observation chance favours only the prepared mind'; Louis Pasteur's University of Lille lecture on 7 December 1854).

In my own career I failed to do this properly, struggling half-heartedly, independently and frustratingly for well over a decade to uncover the central ambitions of my work. Perhaps avoiding some of the hard choices required to isolate research themes, I laboured without clear direction, following my heart and seizing, more or less ad hoc, attractive scholarly opportunities as they presented themselves. Fortunately this ended with a Eureka moment one summer while I was assessing a PhD thesis. A single reference in that thesis to the work of a distinguished political scientist provided a key piece in the jigsaw puzzle of my research career. It allowed me to make sense of all of the work I had done earlier and provided a vital framework for work that followed. But those early years, without a clear trajectory, were troubling and disabling. They may have contributed less to my career development than they could have otherwise, but I was lucky in that I had already found a secure job where I maintained a good level of 'productivity'. I also maintained faith in the probable interconnections of my interests and passions, which allowed me to carry on regardless. Not everyone is so lucky or so stubborn and I do not advocate the 'carry on regardless' approach as best practice! A better strategy perhaps is to seek critical counsel and guidance from advisers and mentors. Seek their input as you make challenging decisions about how to identify and shape your scholarly identity.

7. Make an early impact

The early years of one's academic career can be critical to the trajectory and shape of the years to follow, with your PhD and first five to seven postdoctoral years being especially important in getting established and focussed (see, for example, Laurance et al., 2013). It is in this early phase that you will establish many fundamental professional associations with colleagues, and, importantly, it is a time when you will be signalling to existing and future colleagues your diligence, productivity and collegiality.[1] Do this through your work and your personal engagements. Make yourself known to your peers as well as to more senior colleagues (see related material in Chapters 9 and 28). This in turn may lead to valuable invitations to give conference papers, review manuscripts, supervise theses and join research teams.[2] Do be careful to send the right signals. Think about your longer-term career plan (see Chapter 16) and take on jobs and opportunities judiciously, allowing time for other important parts of your personal and professional life, and making sure you do them well. For example, do try to get papers published but be sure they are in good journals, or produce a monograph with a respectable publisher if you can (see Chapters 18 and 19). Take advantage of the expanding array of early career opportunities to attend conferences and secure research grants. Many organizations and funding agencies make a point of specifically offering research grants, travel awards, and other forms of support to ECAs (e.g. Australia Research Council Discovery Early Career Research Awards [DECRA]; Open Philanthropy; Wellcome Early-Career Awards). Though understandings of 'early career' vary, the term often takes in scholars up to and including the five to seven years (sometimes ten) after a PhD. Securing support during this critical time not only provides helpful resources and opportunities but it also lays important foundations for continued success as a mid-career scholar when the criteria for awards typically become less generous.

If the chance to, say, contribute a chapter to a book, deliver a keynote lecture, assume a professional service role (e.g. with your main disciplinary body), or work within a professionally relevant community group (e.g. history trust, anthropology society) presents itself, give serious thought to how it will fit within your everyday life as well as your career plan. If you have doubts or questions, consult your partner or significant others, adviser, mentor, or a senior colleague. It can certainly be flattering to be offered some opportunities but make sure you accept those prospects that will also serve all of your interests most effectively. And do avoid the temptation to seize every opportunity that presents itself. To use a questionable metaphor: imagine you are preparing a photo show of your most recent holiday. A wise photographer will use only the very best images, leaving aside the poor ones. This way, not only will your audience be hankering for more but they will also come to believe that all of your photos are of high quality. To use poor images will weaken your show and devalue your skills as a photographer. So, make your career choices carefully, selecting those roles that offer the greatest promise. Having said this, there may be some career opportunities that present themselves to you that do not really seem to fit with your intentions and yet you have a strong positive 'gut feeling' about them. Do not discard those options. Do not be too rigid in your ambitions. If the opportunity is something you really want to do, seize it and make the most of it. You never know where it might lead.

NOTES

1. As discussed in Chapter 35, it is also a time that often coincides challengingly with pregnancies and childrearing.
2. Be aware that there is a growing incidence of 'invitations' to deliver keynote addresses, contribute journal articles and so on from questionable sources (for useful discussions, see Makvandi et al. 2021, Pecorari 2021, and Sidaway, 2016). Scrutinize all offers and solicitations carefully as ill-considered decisions here can drain energy on activities which may not only be of little value but which may actually be detrimental to your career. Seek advice from senior colleagues if you have any concerns.

8.   Get informed and stay current

If you are to be an academic superhero, it is imperative to keep abreast of scholarly work and current events in and around your field. What is going on? Who is doing what? Why? Where? You will probably find yourself doing this out of natural curiosity, but it is also rewarding to be comprehensive and systematic in your quest.

First, find out about the key professional and scholarly societies in your field and, if your budget allows,[1] join those that seem most important to you and your work. Read their newsletters and journals as these are often useful sources of information about 'who is working on what', grants, job openings and forthcoming conferences. Many societies offer substantially discounted student memberships as well as funding opportunities for ECAs to attend key conferences in the field. A single conference attendance subsidy or grant may not only cover more than the annual costs of society membership, but it may also offer useful leverage from other agencies or your university to secure additional funding.

Second, make a point of reading the latest issues of key journals or at least signing up for their email alerts. Many scholarly publishers will provide you with electronic alerts outlining new contents of journals you have specified. Alternatively, some university library systems have options that allow you to set up email notifications advising of new publications based on your research preferences. (Check with a librarian to see what options exist and how they work.) Information from these alerts and your reading will allow you to see connections between your work and that of others. It may also help support your professional development by keeping you up to date with new techniques and ideas.

Third, you can receive personally tailored email or news feed updates on new publications from sites such as Academia.edu, Google Scholar, Mendeley, and ResearchGate. In many, but not all, cases these require you to 'follow' individual scholars' work. The specific means of creating these alerts are available at each site or other through easily accessible online resources. Though it can be very useful, one problem with this strategy is that you may receive too much information at the wrong time in the form of extra emails for instance. Try using email filters to divert notifications to an appropriate folder until you are ready to consult them.

Fourth, consider taking advantage of social media to stay informed, connected and current. Though its star has dimmed significantly, Twitter (now X) has been a useful information network for academics, with colleagues 'tweeting' advice of new publications, conferences, webcasts and so on. Facebook is used by some individuals and organizations as a business medium. For instance, many scholars in India maintain their professional networks through Facebook. And, of course, sites like LinkedIn, Academia.edu and ResearchGate specialize in professional networking, highlighting research, and career development. There is a helpful emerging literature on social media for academics for those who which to explore this further (e.g. Allen et al., 2023; Carrigan, 2019).

Fifth, find and join relevant listservs or discussion groups, even as a lurker (i.e., a member who does not participate actively) (Box 8.1). Generally, scholarly listservs are free to join, so you can easily expand your disciplinary networks beyond the societies discussed above. At first, scholars' names on publications, in professional society newsletters and on listservs may have little significance to you but over time you will probably begin to see some repeated often. If you were not already aware of these people, they are likely to be (but not guaranteed to be) amongst the 'movers and shakers' in your field. This background information may be helpful as you seek to become better known and connected.

BOX 8.1   HOW TO FIND A USEFUL LISTSERV?

1. Search scholarly society websites: Many scholarly societies host listservs dedicated to researchers at particular points in their career (e.g. student, ECA) or to specific sub-disciplines. Browse the websites of scholarly societies in your discipline to see if they host listservs. You don't necessarily have to be a paid-up member of a society to join though in some cases you do. Scholarly society listservs tend to be the most widely used.

2. Ask a colleague: Colleagues, mentors and supervisors should be able to offer recommendations on useful listservs to follow. They may be able to advise you on best listservs to follow for job announcements, where to find the best new publications, and what listserv audiences are especially kind and engaged when answering questions.

3. Search the web: Of course, another way to find relevant listservs is with search engines. Brainstorm keywords related to your discipline and also your specific area of study, a particular type of analysis, and so on. Then

search for the term in conjunction with the words 'listserv', 'google group', or 'email list').

Once you have found a listserv, or perhaps several, evaluate its worth. Review the listserv's archive and consider the following questions before deciding to sign on:

1. How active is the listserv? If no one's posting to it regularly, the listserv is unlikely to be of much value.
2. Who is posting? Have you heard the names of those who are contributing or are the listserv participants people you have never heard of? And are all of the posts from only a small number of people or is it more broadly active?
3. What content is being shared? For instance, is it only 'calls for papers', job alerts, or perhaps it is dysfunctional and spoiled by flaming (i.e. exchanges involving intense conflict)? Or are contributors discussing and sharing diverse content regularly and courteously?

Of course, if you sign on only to find that the listserv does not satisfy your needs, unsubscribe!

Source: Adapted from University of Oklahoma (2023).

Sixth, read relevant parts of newspapers, online media and other sources. Although their bleak accounts of research funding and university politics can sometimes make specialist higher education newsletters (e.g., *Campus Morning Mail*), newspapers (e.g., *Campus Review*, *The Chronicle of Higher Education*) and higher education supplements or sections of major newspapers such as *The Australian*, *The Guardian*, *The Times*, or *The New York Times* disheartening, they do remain key vehicles for maintaining a good overview of scholarly activity, key policy issue changes and other matters that may have a bearing on your work. As you advance through your career, these matters may become more and more significant, as will your need to be attuned to them.

Seventh, you employ the work of students to help keep you informed and current. For example, if appropriate, assign students assessable work relevant to their own learning as well as to research areas of interest to you. This offers mutually rewarding benefits. The students' own work may reveal new sources and ideas relevant to your work, and, as discussed elsewhere in this book, the students are likely to be enthused by the passion and energy you bring to the subject.

Eighth, there is value in looking beyond your own discipline to see what scholars in other fields are doing on your research subject – the same challenges may be taken up elsewhere in insightful ways. This is a matter some academics seem to overlook not only at their individual professional expense but also to the detriment of productive scholarly inquiry into issues that honour few disciplinary boundaries (see, for an example, Carlson's 2014 intriguing insights to economists' lack of awareness of the significant work of geographer David Harvey).

Getting informed also applies to understandings you develop about activities and opportunities in your own university (see Chapter 10):

> Although many useful support and training opportunities may exist, it is very hard to find out anything unless you are already familiar with the procedures and who to contact. Most of this information trickles through eventually, but sometimes this is too late. For example, I have just discovered that I should have applied for sabbatical more than a year ago, so now my sabbatical is only possible more than a year later than it should have been. (Lecturer, female, 35–39 years, cited in Sutherland et al., 2013, p. 53)

As this lecturer makes clear, it is important to make yourself aware of opportunities close to home. Many institutions do publicize these through websites and emails but in the flurry of electronic activity that confronts many of us each day these can be lost or ignored. A challenge then is how best to sift through these. Planning can be vital. Each day a great deal of information may appear in our inboxes. Arguably, this makes us 'informed' but sadly much of that information will not register in our consciousness unless we have some specific need that makes it relevant. So, if you have a clear scholarly focus and a strategic plan for your career (see Chapter 16), you may be better attuned to relevant opportunities that present themselves.

Finally, many universities, research agencies and professional societies run – if not mandate – research and professional development programmes for their staff. Take advantage of these so you can apply new knowledge and skills to maintain and improve your professional performance. In the initial stages of your scholarly career, the programmes of most use to you may deal with new software, data coding, effective small group and large group teaching practice, questionnaire construction, quantitative analysis, or negotiating ethical issues. As you scale academia's lofty heights, your needs will change. You might actually find yourself running some of the courses for early-career staff while at the same time taking advantage of other offerings on financial management, media engagement, leadership and managing difficult people. Aside from their intrinsic value, your active participation in such courses makes a useful CV inclusion, providing tangible evidence of your commitment to life-long learning and continuous professional development.

NOTE

1.   Seek assistance from your department on either an ad hoc basis or as part of any employment package to cover the costs of professional society membership. If such support is not available, professional fees qualify in some jurisdictions as tax deductions. Check with an accountant or reputable tax agent.

9.   Get known and networked

Crone (2010, p. 63) observes astutely that academic 'relationships partly control and shape your place within your profession and field. You can negotiate your way through such a system by establishing a variety of connections and relationships on multiple levels'. In Chapter 4 I discussed the development of worthwhile relationships with mentors. In this chapter I focus more on the promotion of other valuable relationships, critical to objective – as well as subjective – constructions of career success.

Irrespective of the importance of your scholarly work or its intrinsic merits, you will almost definitely need to promote its existence to colleagues and community. This is not a matter of 'big-noting' oneself – of being egotistical. It is, instead, a vital part of the whole research development and dissemination process. There is little point in doing scholarly work unless others have an opportunity to know about it and benefit from it. Promotion of your own work is also a valuable part of the career development process. Scholars are producing and publishing so much that it can be difficult for colleagues to keep abreast of all developments in their field. Indeed, there are so many scholars, books, journals, classes, workshops, seminars and conferences that it can be easy to be lost in the maelstrom of information and activity. So, avoid having your contributions disappear into the mass of work by bringing it judiciously to colleagues' attention. This is especially important in the early stages of your career as you struggle to gain peer recognition. In the later stages of your career, once you have achieved some acknowledgement, self-promotion may be less important. Instead, you may be rewarded by disproportionate professional recognition, in what distinguished sociologist Robert K. Merton (1968, p. 58) described as the 'Matthew Effect'.[1] This 'consists in the accruing of greater increments of recognition for particular scientific contributions to scientists of considerable repute and the withholding of such recognition from scientists who have not yet made their mark'.

It may be self-evident that the primary strategy of gaining peer (and broader) acknowledgement is to do good work, undertaking high-quality research; getting good grants; publishing good papers in carefully selected high-impact journals; teaching well; and engaging with professional and broader communities. These vital foundations provide raw materials you can 'advertise' to help secure peer recognition, though it is worth noting that publicizing your work needs to be conducted as an integral part of that work rather than as something that is undertaken after it is completed. So, how do you get known and networked?

CONNECT WITH GOOD COLLEAGUES; BE A GOOD COLLEAGUE

In recent large-scale research reviewing over 40,000 job advertisements for European academic positions Mantai and Marrone (2023) found that having international connections is a clearly evident and very important requirement for academic career progression. But the degree of connectivity is presumably more than quantitative. The qualitative dimensions of those connections are also important. To be blunt, it pays to identify (with) the 'eagles' in your field (i.e., those who are soaring intellectually) and flock with them, not the turkeys. Gray and Drew (2012, p. 9) assert that most academic fields are dominated and shaped by fewer than 100 powerful people. In some areas, the number may actually be much fewer. Gray and Drew (2012) recommend that you work out who (many of) these people are, and ensure they know who you are – for the right reasons! But just how do you position yourself as the bright new star that those in the existing constellation want to be associated with?

Not surprisingly, a good place to start is by establishing and securing personal bonds with scholars in your specific field. This is probably most easily and naturally achieved with peers you meet as part of doctoral training, postdoctoral appointments, and at the formal and more informal (e.g., social events, dinners, field trips) components of conferences. Without even being aware of it you will probably find that you develop a group of like-minded colleagues whose work and interests you understand, and they yours. Personal relationships with colleagues can be enormously helpful in making sometimes harsh and competitive academic environments friendlier and much more conducive to a satisfying long-term career (see, for example, Crone, 2010, p. 67).

After your PhD or postdoctoral experience you may move from one city, country, state, or province to another. If you find yourself in this position you may have to work hard initially to establish new connections. But do not forego the networks you established earlier. Keep in touch with your existing colleagues socially as well as professionally, letting them know about local conferences and employment opportunities and keeping them posted on your own work. Aside from their great personal value, these foundations can be very helpful in long-term career development (see Chapter 35).

Through your reading and conversations with colleagues, determine who the key local, national and global figures are. Who is writing the key, current books in your area? Who are the prolific journal authors?[2] And who is active in relevant professional societies? Become familiar with these people's works. Then – without making a nuisance of yourself – make yourself known to them by, for example, sending copies of your recently published or presented papers and news about your work, inviting them to join reference groups for projects you are leading, or advising them of workshops, special sessions or conferences you are organizing. While you may consider putting together a mailing list of colleagues you can send this information to, do be sure to personalize your correspondence to the luminaries you seek to impress. If you send details of a recent paper, be sure that it is presented in a format that makes it easy for recipients to read. Although there is a chance your audience will encounter the article in the course of their work, there is also the possibility they will have missed it, especially if your name or work is unknown to them. An offprint, link or a PDF with a short personal note will help heighten your profile.

Connect with eminent colleagues through professional social media, such as LinkedIn, or invite them to examine theses you have supervised. In any communications with these scholars, make it clear how your work is related to theirs or the role their work has played in stimulating your academic interests. They will probably be grateful to see that their efforts have inspired others – that they have left a legacy – and, knowing of your interest, be more inclined to invite you to contribute to special journal collections, to submit chapters for books and so on. More than this, active senior scholars are often very keen to know who are the up-and-comers in their field and so your approach is likely to be welcomed.

You might also ask relevant high flyers to be advisers for grant proposals or for input on manuscripts you are preparing for publication. There is some risk, however, that the person you send the manuscript or idea to will plagiarize it (see, for example, Markin, 2012). Take care with that, engaging only with people you trust. And even then, do keep a detailed record of any communications.

Having made contact from a distance with illustrious colleagues, build on this work at conferences and other professional gatherings by (re)introducing yourself to them. It always helps to put faces to names. Do not feel shy about letting senior scholars know about you and your work. Many will welcome such advice and will probably be keen to know exactly what you are doing. For them, this is one way of keeping current and of maintaining their overview of new developments in the field. Because of their expertise in a particular area, senior scholars are occasionally approached for recommendations on new appointees, prospective contributors to journals, referees and so on. At such moments they especially value the depth and currency of their own networks.

If there are particular scholars you are developing good professional relationships with, find out about funding arrangements at your university or more broadly for supporting them as visiting researchers or speakers. The relationships that flow from these visits can be enduring and productive for you and colleagues. For example, when I arrived at one of my first Australian jobs, my department included no female academic staff or other senior women. There were no female role models for women students who comprised about 50 per cent of the student body. And in my field at the time gender issues were of growing conceptual and practical significance. To help fill these lacunae I organized a lecture series on gender and geography, featuring guest lectures from key women who were scholars in the area. Not only did this make a strong statement to staff and students within the department about the disciplinary significance of gender issues, it also helped raise my profile and that of the department around the university and more broadly. As a new arrival to Australia it also allowed me to develop closer working relationships with key scholars in my field.

Do take some care with your efforts to cultivate good relationships with colleagues. Appropriate arrangements need to be handled well. I recall one experience where I had been invited very kindly by a junior colleague overseas to visit his department for several months. The visa arrangements to be made on my behalf were not completed. I was to be met at the airport – that person was nearly two hours late. Furnished accommodation had been organized – it was poorly equipped and filthy. Meetings with senior academic staff kept being rescheduled at short notice. After three days I returned home, feeling deeply let down. In other words, if you commit to supporting a colleague, honour that obligation.

Few people wish to be associated with objectionable, inconsiderate others. And news of poor behaviour can circulate quickly. So, if you wish to be known in scholarly circles for the right reasons, be a good colleague and role model (see also Chapter 32). Treat your colleagues as you would like to be treated. Value their time as highly as you value your own. Where you can, reciprocate professional favours and courtesies that are extended to you. If you cannot do this (e.g., reciprocating an adviser's letter of support for a grant), 'pay it forward'. That is, extend some act of goodwill to others instead of to the original benefactor.

Mutually respectful behaviour is important but you do need to exercise a little caution to ensure that your collegiality is not exploited by others who impose inconsiderately on your time, effort and good nature to advance their own interests. Be attentive to your work and personal schedules and commitments and do not be afraid to say 'no' where you consider it necessary to do so (see Chapter 17). Having said this, part of being a good colleague is contributing service as a manuscript reviewer, book review editor, thesis examiner, or even editorial board member to key journals in your field. Despite incentives such as examiner payments and review recognition through the Web of Science, it is increasingly difficult to coax or cajole colleagues to undertake these key academic tasks (see, for example, Hay, 2016b). The excuses 'too busy' or 'not in my area' are all too common. Not only might you endear yourself to an editor or thesis adviser by accepting these occasional assignments, but also such tasks can provide useful insights to other departments, recent research in your field, and editorial processes.

ESTABLISH AND RAISE YOUR PROFILE

Aside from developing good relationships with great colleagues, a key to getting known and networked is being able to describe your work interests succinctly at professional and social occasions. People will almost always seek to characterize or pigeonhole you in some way, so build your own roost, rather than letting someone else do it for you. One way to do this is to develop a concise professional self-description, sometimes known as an 'elevator pitch' (see for example Morgan and Wright (2021) – so called because it is about as long as the time you might spend on a ride in an operational elevator with someone! Imagine your elevator pitch to be a bit like an oral business card (Box 9.1). Present yourself as you want to be understood by whoever is your audience. Extend that self-identification to more public arenas such as professional networking sites like ResearchGate, Academia.edu or LinkedIn (though see Chapter 33 for some words of caution).

BOX 9.1   DEVELOPING YOUR ORAL BUSINESS CARD

Imagine you are at a cocktail party with a mix of people from local professional and community groups. Someone in your circle of conversation asks you what your work and research is about. Exactly how do you answer them? Think about who you are; what is the major problem or challenge you work on and how are you addressing it; why is this this work valuable and what do you want to achieve; and at what stage of your career are you? Keep the answer short (30–60 seconds), comprehensible and engaging.

If you have multiple scholarly interests and cannot identify a deep theme that runs through your work, do not despair (see Chapter 6). Perhaps take on some general label that embraces most of your work (e.g., historian of nineteenth-century Europe; critical sociologist with interests in crime and justice) while you continue to isolate a more precise theme that better encapsulates your research.

Develop a good web presence, using your own institution's facilities as well as others available to you (e.g. LinkedIn). This is a key part of the vital public face you present to colleagues – as well as to the broader community. Box

9.2 sets out the uses to which difference academic social media are put and provides a quick outline of the work involved in maintaining them.

BOX 9.2   FUNCTIONS OF SELECTED ACADEMIC SOCIAL NETWORKING SITES AND WORK REQUIRED FOR PROFILE MAINTENANCE

Academic social networking site	Use	Work involved
Google Scholar	Scholarly web search engine, bibliometric ranking program for scholars, a listing of co-authors, publication profile of scholars with visual of scholar, journals, and institutions, and list of document access links.	Set up a profile and make sure it is updated.
ORCID	Provides global digital IDs for researchers, includes publications, jobs, and grants.	Set up a profile and make sure it is updated.
ResearchGate (RG)	Research document depository, job lists, who you work with in a 'lab', research Q&A features, research profile of scholar with visual, and RG score of scholars.	Load up abstracts and details of publications, tag them. Update profile.
Academia.edu	Promotion of research, generation of citations and development of networks. Shows the extent of research impact and network	Load up abstracts and details of publications, tag them. Update profile. Download and analyse basic statistics on reach and readership.
LinkedIn	Promotion of your career and research. Useful for media contacts can be linked with Twitter account.	Update profile regularly. Load up research article links, presentations (Slideshare), events and media stories.
Blogs	Detailed views and expertise on scholarly issues and comments on related areas.	Blogs need to be updated at least once a week with considerable and interesting detail.

Source: D'Alessandro et al. (2020).

Because the Internet is one of the primary means by which colleagues and community members track down research partners, reviewers, consultants and chapter contributors it is important to make your presence accessible, clear, comprehensive and informative. Box 9.3 sets out some advice on steps to heighten your online visibility. To help with this process, reflect on how you find details of colleagues or prospective collaborators on the Internet. If you were looking for yourself on the web, would you find you and how? Look at the online presence of colleagues you respect. How are they represented? What can you learn and apply from this?

BOX 9.3   HEIGHTENING YOUR ONLINE VISIBILITY

1. *Appraise your current online presence.* How do you look online? Search for yourself online with a range of search engines (including DuckDuckGo – 'the search engine that doesn't track you'; Google Scholar; Scopus; Altmetric; Web of Science). Check text, images, videos, news and so on. What materials exist about you or have been posted by other people, institutions or automated systems?[a]
2. *Decide on the online profile you want and improve your presence.* What kind of presence do you want and how much time are you prepared to spend updating it? It is better to have a smaller, current and well-maintained profile than one that is sprawling and outdated. Be sure to create your ORCID profile. Work out which of the sites such as university websites, Academia.edu, LinkedIn, Google Scholar and ResearchGate you and relevant colleagues consult and focus your attentions on those. Do you also wish to extend your professional online presence into social networks like Facebook and Twitter? Again, focus on those media you are most likely to want to use and that relevant others use. Social networks can be a great way to get details of your work out to on-academic audiences.
3. *Heighten the availability of your work.* Make it easy for others to see what you have done. Include references to your work in your online profile. Put online as many of your works as legally permitted. Your copyright agreements with publishers will affect the extent to which you can independently post your works online. If in doubt about copyright, consult a site like SHERPA/RoMEO to check which version of your work you can share online. Give serious consideration to publishing with open access journals.
4. *Communicate and interact online.* Engage and network with colleagues through social media, listservs and the discussion component of other sites mentioned above (e.g., ResearchGate).

Note: [a]See material in Chapter 33 on preserving your online reputation later for guidance on dealing with problems that may emerge such as online doppelgangers.
Source: Adapted from Goodier and Czerniewicz (2014). See also Konkiel (2015) for excellent advice and 'how to' guidance.

Ensure that your online presence includes keywords describing your teaching and research interests, links to publications, your professional contact details, and even all or part of your CV (though not with sensitive information such as your residential address, phone details, or date of birth). If you feel that requirements about content and 'look and feel' of your university web page are too restrictive, you may choose to develop you own website. Other websites such as Academia.edu, LinkedIn, Expert Guide and ResearchGate may also offer more, with greater flexibility.[3] You may even be able to link between them or. Together with your own institutional web presence, such online services offer journalists and representatives from government, business and the community means to connect with academic and professional experts. They will make it easier for members of the community to find you, to draw from your work, or to offer you research or consultancy opportunities.

As noted above, you may also wish to set up your own independent website that includes, for example, personal details, publication, and a blog. If you do this, be careful in your choice of domain name as well as the content you post. Avoid questionable names like hotkitten.com or speedofart.com. And remember, things you post on the web, be they your own website or on major social media platforms, can come back to haunt you. For example, one associate professor was suspended from Marquette University in the US state of Wisconsin for writing allegedly offensive blog posts (Friedersdorf, 2015). A celebrated University of Tasmania Earth Science professor found himself under investigation for criticizing his institution's planned campus move on Facebook (Baker 2022). And an associate professor at Mount Allison University in Canada was suspended following complaints that her blog posts were discriminatory and offensive (Sutherland, 2021). Consult credible online resources and relevant experts in your institution to create a useful and 'safe' online presence that maximizes the kind of hits you want.

Another way of getting known in your specific field is to organize a symposium or conference (session) in your area of current or desired expertise. And if you can link the activity to a special issue of a journal or an edited book, so much the better. This not only makes the event more attractive to prospective participants but it also can heighten the profile of the work produced as a result of the meeting. For example, the *Journal of Asia Entrepreneurship and Sustainability* welcomes papers drawn from conferences. According to their website (2022),[4] their policy on such collections is that:

> [w]e consider conferences that have a global audience/interest, focus on a robust academic discourse of topics related to the Journal's mission and are open to the wider academic community for participation.

Usually the 8–10 best conference submissions are selected to create a Special Edition, and either online versions or hard copy printed editions are possible. Special Editions for conferences can be created to be available during/before the conference, many times also offering conference sponsors an opportunity or commercial exposure, or they can be created after the conference has been concluded.

Approach your professional body to underwrite or publish the proceedings of any such conference. Contact the editor of a relevant journal to ask about including papers as part of a special edition. Look at past issues of the journal to see if this has been done and how.

Less onerous than organizing a conference session, but also important, is speaking to new colleagues at conferences, in hallways, and at university functions (see Hay et al., 2005 and Konkiel, 2015 for detailed advice). Speak also with people in the broader community. Let them know what you do. Find out what they do. Offer to speak to schools, the University of the Third Age (U3A), lifelong learning institutes and other community organizations on your scholarly activities (see Chapter 20). Aside from advancing the profile of your discipline, this may lead to collaborations, guest lecturers in classes you teach and new links in your local and broader community. Depending on your specific scholarly area, community organizations like U3A can be treasure troves of expertise and contacts, with membership that includes people from a diverse array of professional and personal backgrounds.

Get active in relevant professional organizations (see Chapter 26). Do not just be a member. Consider doing a little more. Many professional organizations and scholarly societies welcome to their councils or executive boards bright, enthusiastic colleagues brimming with good ideas. Such service roles open up remarkable and often very interesting opportunities to shape the activities of your own professional body, as well as to develop strong relationships with key – often very senior or ambitious – figures in that discipline. And if you are a more senior scholar, mixing with innovative new colleagues can be invigorating. Having said this, because you need to balance the other demands of your scholarly career and personal life carefully with the demands of doing good service, do find out exactly how much time and work will be involved. This can be a particular issue for scholars from underrepresented groups who may be sought to address imbalances in organizational leadership profiles. As an active academic, consider leaving 'time sink' (Crone, 2010, p. 69) roles such as secretary or treasurer to others such as retirees. It is all very well to take on a service or leadership role in a professional body but you must honour its responsibilities and expectations. You can do yourself reputational damage by taking on a challenge and then failing to deliver. So, if you do take on such a role be prepared to commit yourself to it.

You can also heighten your profile effectively by participating in relevant speciality or study groups within your professional associations. These groups typically engage in a range of activities like running special sessions at conferences or indeed convening entire conferences and developing theme issues of journals, edited books, or shared teaching resources. And because they comprise disciplinary colleagues with refined and related interests, they can be enormously valuable for developing links to colleagues working in areas closely related to your own.

Consider becoming a 'media tart' (see Baron, 2010; Hay and Bass, 2002; and Konkiel 2015). Make it known to your university's public relations unit and to local media representatives that you are available and willing to speak about issues linked to your scholarship. If you have conducted research that you believe may have broad public appeal (e.g., causal factors behind anorexia nervosa; why a local collapse in house prices is inevitable) let appropriate public relations or media staff know about that work. But do take care in dealing with the media. While outlets such as radio, television and (online) newspapers can certainly bring your work to the attention of many people, you will have little control over the ways in which 'your' story is handled and interpreted (Hay and Israel, 2001). Also, avoid devaluing your own credibility as well as that of your institution by commenting on matters outside your area of expertise.

An alternative but increasingly popular and highly effective approach to engaging with the media is to write for The Conversation, whose tagline is: 'Academic rigour, journalistic flair'. The Conversation Australia and New Zealand was founded in Melbourne in 2011 and now operates as a global network with dedicated teams working in Africa, Canada, France, Indonesia, Spain, UK and USA. According to their website (The Conversation, 2023):

> Everything you read here is created by academics and journalists working together, supported by a team of digital technology experts. Our professional editors turn knowledge and insights from academics into easy-to-read articles, and make them accessible to readers like you.
>
> All our work is free to read and free to republish under Creative Commons. We do this as a not-for-profit company guided by a clear purpose: to provide access to quality explanatory journalism essential for healthy democracy.
>
> We place a high value on trust. All authors and editors sign up to our Editorial Charter. Contributors must abide by our Community Standards. We only allow authors to write on subjects on which they have expertise. Potential conflicts of interest must be disclosed.

The Conversation offers an excellent way for scholars around the world to reach and influence broad audiences without some of the complications of dealing with other forms of mass media. Its website offers detailed advice and access to courses on how to write for the media, industry, policy makers and the public.

In addition to presenting a public face to the broader world, remember to develop and sustain your profile at your own institution. Let your department, faculty and university public relations units know of your work. Tell your associates what you are up to, through discussions over a cup of coffee or by giving talks as part of regular research seminars. Aside from supporting your own local research culture, this will have the important effect of allowing your colleagues to better represent you in their discussions with their own colleagues and acquaintances. It will also make it simpler for your advisers to support your career by passing on news of relevant opportunities and writing strong letters of support for promotion and funding.

Attend departmental seminars and guest lectures in your own and cognate fields. While some of these may be out of your immediate area of scholarship, they can offer fascinating and productive insights into the ways in which research is conceived, conducted and communicated in other fields. They can spark new ideas and help you to identify fresh connections in your own work. Attendance will also help get you known in fields allied to your own.

Your faculty, college or university research offices will also appreciate knowing of your work and will welcome a good professional relationship with you. This is of mutual advantage. For instance, while broadcast mechanisms exist to alert staff to grant and award opportunities, on some occasions advice of such prospects may come at short notice. Research office staff may be at a loss to know where best to direct them. It can be helpful to be one of the people who come to mind at such times. An active research profile and links to your research office may also see you asked to become involved in matters of research review and oversight. While these roles take you away from the day-to-day conduct of your own research and teaching, they do also offer opportunities to become better acquainted with, and therefore successful in, research activity.

Not only is it important to make clear your professional research identity to colleagues but you should also make it evident to students. Many students will come to know you best through your teaching and will assume that the areas in which you teach are the areas in which your research interests lie. This may be the case but, if not, find some ways to let students know about your research activity and that you welcome Honours, Masters or PhD students in those areas. You can do this in class for local students and you can also make it evident from your personal or professional websites or through your research presentations on campus or at conferences. Through their diverse and extensive networks, students can be very effective public voices for the value of your work.

NOTES

1.   So called because of the biblical verse (Matthew 13:12), 'For the one who has, more will be given' (Sutherland, 2015, p. 9).
2.   Web resources such as Google Scholar can be useful tools in trying to identify key figures in your specific field (e.g., providing details of citation numbers by scholars in certain areas).
3.   There is abundant advice online setting out great ways to 'turbocharge' your online profile (see, for example, Konkiel, 2014; Stanton, 2014).
4.   Accessed 16 June 2022 at http://www.asiaentrepreneurshipjournal.com/createspecialeditions.html.

10. Learn about local cultures and use 'the system'

Human activity is enabled and constrained by the context within which it occurs. Most departments, faculties and universities have cultural norms that guide and shape the behaviour of members. These may have been produced and reproduced by academics over many years and can be very important in setting the local tone for behaviour and 'productivity' standards. For instance, some departments may have a long tradition of serving relevant professional societies. Others may value research productivity at all costs. And still others may emphasize collegiality, cooperation and the individual contributions diverse staff can make to the collective whole. As in other fields of endeavour, these cultures can affect hiring and tenure decisions, sometimes in ways that are discriminatory or inequitable (see, for example, Leighton 2020). Moreover, academic staff for whom there is a good cultural fit are more likely to be able to thrive whereas those who fail to understand or 'fit in' to the local cultures are likely to find themselves at a significant disadvantage. For example, in the context of a department characterized by ruthless self-interest, an individual's collegiality may be exploited mercilessly by others. Or, by contrast, a self-absorbed scholar may find themself ostracized by colleagues in a department that understands itself to be a 'community'. It really is vital to recognize, learn about and work with these local cultures. Though important for all academic staff, this can be especially important for academic leaders who may, for instance, come into an institution from outside and find that their particular leadership style sits uneasily and unproductively with local ways of acting and thinking. Not surprisingly, for example, an autocratic leader is likely to be poorly received in an institution with a long tradition of effective consultation and democratic decision-making. So, in the institution you find yourself in, work to understand local systems and cultures and uncover ways to work with them – perhaps trying to gradually transform the less desirable aspects of some as you go – that will allow you to achieve the kind of success you seek. Of course, there is always the risk that the culture will ultimately prevail, seeking to claim you in ways you find undesirable, unwelcome or unacceptable. If you find yourself in such a situation you may find it necessary to look for employment elsewhere – if you are in a position to do so and if you can find a 'better fit' – or to seek counsel on ways of negotiating the context in ways that are not emotionally damaging.

Over and above their local cultures, universities and allied institutions are complex systems within systems. They are increasingly regulated organizations, subject to external control as well as to rules devised internally. Fortunately, because many universities remain staffed by advocates of procedural transparency well accustomed to documenting their practices, their policies and procedures may be recorded in detail and placed on school, faculty, or university websites. It is a very good idea to familiarize yourself with such practices – as well as with locally specific 'cultural characteristics' – not necessarily all at once, but certainly as and when specific issues manifest themselves in your professional development or working routine. While they may not offer perfect advice, these documents usually spell out a valuable and carefully considered approximation of good or required practice. (They may also serve as a starting point for the development of your own better ways of working in alignment with the institution's rules.) For instance, amongst its student-related policies and procedures, my own university developed clear and helpful ways of dealing with incidents of plagiarism and academic dishonesty. Promulgated online these discuss a step-by-step process that moves from gentle counselling of misguided students to increasingly serious consequences, depending on the nature of the offence. Aside from providing unequivocal direction for action, such documents can dispel time-consuming and emotion-sapping confusion by making clear to all parties involved how things should work.

An appreciation of the various 'systems' you operate within (e.g., external grant-funding organizations, institutional promotion procedures) can allow you to better comprehend good ways of working. It can also afford opportunities to exploit those systems or use them to your advantage. It really does help, for example, if you know the criteria for promotion, what conference travel funds are available and to whom, when you are eligible for sabbatical, or even how to get a reserved parking space. But do maintain a light and friendly touch in your use of the system. 'Bush lawyers'[1] are widely disliked and poorly regarded.

Beyond exploiting systems to your advantage, an appreciation of institutional and other system policies provides valuable insights to ways of forestalling or confronting odious and problematic matters such as workplace harassment, unlawful discrimination, corruption and maladministration that you might have the misfortune to encounter. That should go a long way to ensure you have a successful career.

NOTE

1. 'Bush lawyer' is an Australian slang term for someone who professes to know the rules and yet does not. Commonly too a 'bush lawyer' will often and vigorously seek to better their own position through actions, assertions and arguments based on their misguided understanding of rules.

PART III

APPLYING YOUR ACADEMIC SUPERPOWERS WHERE THEY ARE NEEDED

11. Cultivate high-quality referee reports

Getting a good postdoctoral fellowship or academic job[1] will depend not only on matters such as your scholarly credentials and publications and preparedness to relocate but also on the quality of your referees' reports. Referees are the people you nominate for a prospective employer or funder to consult in order to gain a confidential assessment of your professional capabilities. At the outset of an academic career you may require about three referees and as you climb through academic ranks you can expect to have to provide a longer list, with it not being uncommon for five or six to be required for appointment to (full) professor. It is crucial that you try to get good references from well-regarded scholars who know you and your work. If possible, include amongst your referees scholars from institutions other than your own and from abroad. This is especially important the higher up the academic scale you proceed, as it may help demonstrate that you have a national or international reputation. Give careful attention too to gender balance in your list of referees.

Before you approach them, you ought to have already developed a professional relationship with referees through your undergraduate and graduate education, scholarly work, conferences, or some kind of discipline service. Occasionally, senior academics get reference requests from people they barely know. This places them in an uncomfortable position. They can refuse the request and so appear rude or callous or they can accept and prepare what is likely to be, at best, a lukewarm, poorly informed testimonial that does the applicant few favours in any competition for employment or promotion.

While senior academics frequently write letters of support and so may be well-practised in the task, they be will very grateful if you make their job as easy as possible – without writing the reference itself! So, be sure referees know what kind of position you are seeking (although they may actually have told you of the vacancy) and provide them with a copy of the job description or duty statement for any positions you are applying for, together with your CV and letter of application. And if you have any capacity to do so, be sure to give your referee sufficient time to prepare their testimonial. Except in the most extreme of situations, an urgent, last minute plea for a reference will scarcely endear you to someone you are hoping to write kindly on your behalf.

Although some referees will actually copy their letter to you, it can be difficult to know how supportive a reference someone will write. There are some malicious people who will agree to write a reference on your behalf, only to prepare something that is weak, damaging, or otherwise harmful. So, if you apply for a position, make a point of soliciting feedback from the hiring organization about the quality of your references, checking to see if there are any damaging reports or other problems. When you seek such feedback, also ask for detailed, constructive comments on your application and performance in any interview or seminar associated with your application. Whether or not your bid for employment was successful it can be helpful to get guidance that you can take into account for future applications.

It is fairly well known that there are two main styles of reference writing, sometimes characterized as the US and the British varieties. Although the pattern may be changing, the former has traditionally seen effusive praise bestowed upon the candidate; the latter has tended to be rather more subdued and circumspect (see for example Stearns, 2018). Arguably, a job candidate with several referees who write in the British style will be placed at a disadvantage relative to a candidate with American referees, especially where the readers are more familiar with the US model. However, as new privacy and legal changes occur, it is becoming increasingly likely that candidates will be able to read references written on their behalf (e.g., under Freedom of Information provisions) and referees may become less inclined to write anything that could be regarded as critical. So, as Wolff (2013) has observed, 'reference inflation has set in, and everyone is simply wonderful'.

NOTE

1. While this book is about academic careers it is worth heeding Wilbur's (2007, p. 123) advice that '[n]ot all graduate students are larval professors ... There is life outside the university – in industry, in government, and in private foundations for students in all fields.'

12. Find the right job

Not all universities are made equal. And just as the institution you receive your doctorate from can make a difference to the early stages of your academic career (Chapter 2), so your first or second job can make a profound difference to your career's ongoing trajectory.[1] If you work first in a role or at a university with significant teaching responsibilities there is a very good chance you will have less time and fewer opportunities to advance your research than you would at a larger, research-intensive university where high levels of high-quality research activity are typically expected and encouraged. And even if you do beat those odds (see Box 12.1 for a British example) some prestigious universities appear to discriminate against prospective faculty members on the basis of their past/current associations, irrespective of the candidate's demonstrated performance (Oprisko, 2012). Indeed, as Clauset et al. (2015, p. 1) revealed in their vast US study: 'Faculty hiring follows a common and steeply hierarchical structure that reflects profound social inequality among institutions'. There is a certain irony in this, for those who have excelled at more poorly regarded institutions may have some unique talents and characteristics that have allowed such exceptional performance. Nonetheless, institutional conceit may well underpin the circulation of academic staff amongst particular groups of universities (e.g., the UK's Russell Group, Australia's Group of Eight, China's C9 League, the USA's Ivy League and Tier 1 universities) with little movement between groups – except 'downwards' from more prestigious institutions to those of lesser standing (see Oprisko, 2012). In other words, a few years at the wrong institution can mean many years at the wrong institution. If you have the opportunity to do so, choose your workplace well and perform well there.

BOX 12.1 FROM TEACHING ON A TEMPORARY CONTRACT TO A TEACHING–RESEARCH POSITION

I took on a role as a 60 per cent part-time teaching fellow at the end of my PhD, starting the day after I submitted my thesis. It was my intention to run a 40 per cent part-time research postdoc alongside the teaching, which I saw as an opportunity to create a sort of 'lectureship' role. I found that keeping the teaching within the contracted time was impossible. Field trips, marking, spending too long preparing for lectures all took up more than full-time hours. I was even told that research wasn't part of my job description and was distracting from the teaching role. I was able to deliver on the analysis required for the research, but neither the papers from my PhD or the postdoc [*sic*]. This was something I was embarrassed by, particularly in job interviews for teaching and research lecture-ships. It was a glaring hole in my CV and something I was told made me not ready to hold a lectureship role. I thought I'd be trapped in fixed-term teaching roles forever. Eventually, as yet another short-term teaching contract was up for renewal, I was advised at a workshop for teaching-focussed academics to turn the role around, and make it a selling point. I worked towards a Higher Education Academy (HEA) fellowship, I gathered evidence of my teaching abilities and sold that equally alongside my research abilities. This led me to securing a per-manent teaching and research position at an institution that recognized my time as a teaching fellow was a challenging, but ultimately positive experience that meant I was ready to take on full teaching responsibilities and leadership roles. (Participant at a workshop to support academics on teaching contracts, cited in Dyer et al., 2016, p. 312)

It helps to be in a department where you like the people and where there is scope for collaboration in research and teaching with colleagues (Richards, 2012, p. 9). This makes for a good, productive workplace – somewhere you want to be and where you can flourish. But you should also give informed consideration to department and university rankings such as those produced by QS World University Rankings; Times Higher Education (THE) World University Ranking; Academic Ranking of World Universities (ARWU – regularly referred to as the 'Shanghai Ranking' because it is produced at China's Shanghai Jiao Tong University); the CWTS Leiden Ranking; and the Webometrics Ranking Web of Universities. Although it is very difficult to define and identify world-class universities meaningfully (Altbach, 2004a; Hazelkorn, 2019), rankings serve increasingly and importantly as basic measures by which colleagues, prospective students, funding agencies, philan-thropists and others estimate the quality of universities. Rankings reflect and sustain prestige, though not necessarily academic substance. They are an arte-fact of the criteria used and those criteria may bear little or no relationship to your own or others' understandings and expectations of a good academic posi-tion or a good university. For instance, according to its website, ARWU uses six indicators, including: number of alumni and staff winning Nobel Prizes and Fields Medals; number of highly cited researchers selected by Clarivate Analytics; number of articles published in the journals *Nature* and *Science*; and the number of articles indexed in Science Citation Index – Expanded and Social Sciences Citation Index, and per capita performance of a university. There appears to be a clear slant in the direction of the physical sciences in these criteria. The CWTS Leiden Rankings do not include book publications! And Webometrics rankings are based on web presence and impact, rather than measures of scholarly productivity. So while ranks are important to include when thinking about where to work, find out about their methodologies (typically set out on their websites) and use the results advisedly and with caution.

Try also to find out about the broader politics and economic/cultural context of any academic job you are contemplating. At the 'local' level, what are the prospects for growth in the department? What is its financial position? Are there any retirements on the horizon? What is the likelihood of promotion or of a shift from a precarious employment contract to something more permanent? Will the expectations of the job afford you opportunity to advance your career? How well do staff get on with one another and so on? And stepping up from the department to the institutional or even national level, what does the future hold? For instance, I was approached once about a senior role at a university in New Zealand. And while many aspects of the position were attractive, I had recently been made intensely aware of government funding priorities for that country's universities and those did not augur well for either the demands of the role or for that institution as a whole.

But the right job is not only about the workplace; it is also about finding employment where you want to live – if you are fortunate enough to have some control over this. In your search think carefully about the kind of place where you, and any family you may have, would want to stay for several years if not for the best part of a lifetime. Consider factors like connections to extended family, the price and availability of real estate, educational opportunities for children, job prospects for your spouse/partner, weather, cultural openness and diversity, political context, proximity to key transport services, such as international airports, and recreational attractions. Think through options carefully. Do not dismiss prospects out of hand and, if possible, spend time checking out possible destinations. Some places can be pleasant surprises and others unlikable wonders.

Although academic jobs are advertised throughout the year, there is a discernible seasonality to them. Many are advertised about six months before the commencement of the following academic year (e.g., September in the southern hemisphere for a February start; March in the northern hemisphere for a September start). This has at least two implications. First, if you are looking for a position out of these cycles, you should not fall into too deep a despair if there appears to be a dearth of prospective roles. There are probably jobs on the horizon. Second, if you are finishing a PhD aim, if you can, to complete your work so it most usefully matches the relevant recruitment cycle, even though this means you need to write job applications and attend interviews at about the same time as you are wrapping up your degree. While you must be prepared for that, it may enable a seamless transition from your degree to your first academic job.

If you find that your post-PhD CV is not sufficiently strong to capture a job at the kind of institution you aspire to, there may be value in seeking out a post-doctoral fellowship as a bridge to that future (see Box 12.2). More common in science, technology, engineering and mathematics (STEM) than humanities, arts and social sciences (HASS), a 'postdoc' offers scholars who have recently completed a doctorate about one to three years of salaried, supervised and advanced training intended to enhance their research and professional skills and credentials. Post-doctoral fellowships are often attached to specific research grants and require the recipient to focus their work on the funded project. A good 'postdoc' may be easier to find than a lecturing position and if you perform well in that role, racking up a good number of high-quality publications, making yourself known and useful, gaining the respect of three or four staff members, and otherwise expanding and strengthening your background, you may be better positioned in a few years to secure the kind of academic job you seek (Feibelman, 2011, pp. 35–7).

BOX 12.2 HOW TO FIND DETAILS OF POSTDOCTORAL FELLOWSHIPS AND ACADEMIC JOBS

Personal networks
Use your personal and professional contacts to find out about positions that you are qualified for. Let everyone know you are looking for a job. Professional networking sites such as LinkedIn offer options for you to do this, discreetly if you wish. Tell your adviser what you are looking for, let your friends and colleagues know, speak to faculty and staff at conferences, meetings and social gatherings, and phone colleagues in other universities to see what they know. Get the word out and let your networks work for you.

University websites
Most universities carry listings of their own vacancies on their website. If there are specific institutions you wish to work at, check their websites frequently and sign up for job alerts if that service is offered.

Internet/newspapers
Some universities and research and scholarly organizations continue to publish advertisements in local and national newspapers but this has been displaced almost entirely by online advertising. The following list sets out in alphabetical order several, but by no means all, online job resources:

AcademicCareers.com	A global academic job site for jobs in education and academia more broadly.
Academic Jobs Wiki	A somewhat clunky but helpful resource setting out many scholarly positions in the social sciences, arts and humanities.
AcademicJobsEU.com	Provides details of jobs in a number of European academic institutions on a somewhat unwieldy website.
AcademicKeys.com	A US-focussed site that provides details of available jobs as well as resources for job-seekers to post their details for prospective employers.
Akadeus.com	International site for academic, research and managerial careers in leading business schools and universities worldwide
EURAXESS – Researchers in Motion	A pan-European initiative providing information about research careers in Europe.
FindAPostDoc.com	UK based but embracing Europe, this site is dedicated to listing jobs for new and recently qualified PhDs. Tends to be dominated by advertisements for science postdocs.
HigherEd360	Offers details of academic vacancies at North American universities plus information about disciplinary associations, conferences, and various career resources.
HigherEdJobs.com	A large, high-quality US-focussed website offering searchable access to thousands of jobs in higher education.
H-Net Job Guide	Produced by an international organization of humanities and social sciences scholars this site provides access to a growing list of position announcements, mainly in the USA but also more broadly.
Jobs.ac.uk	Widely used UK site providing details of academic, science, research and administrative jobs available globally. Includes extensive career advice.
The Chronicle of Higher Education	Linked to the newspaper of the same title, this is a large, high-quality US-focussed website offering searchable access to thousands of jobs at all levels in higher education, plus other job-seeking resources.
THEunijobs	Established in 1997, UniJobs describes itself as higher education's global job board.

Professional societies and conferences
Through their newsletters, websites and conferences many discipline-specific and professional societies advertise position announcements, run job placement services, or offer job-seeking advice in their field. For example, the American Association of Geographers (AAG) offers a very useful online job-finding resource (https://jobs.aag.org/jobs/). This advertises discipline-specific roles in universities and provides a range of career resources. The AAG also convenes career information and search sessions at each of its vast annual conferences. The American Political Science Association (APSA) offers eJobs (http://www.apsanet.org/eJobs), a members'-only database.

WORK WITH SOURCERS AND HEADHUNTERS

As noted in Box 12.2, although they generally recruit for senior positions, 'headhunters' are in the general business of matching prospective candidates to attractive roles. So, if you are looking for a new job, consider developing a relationship with appropriate sourcing and recruiting staff at such an agency. There are many such firms, ranging from the local (Hender Consulting in Adelaide), national (India's CETMATRIX), regional (e.g. UniRecruit in Australia and New Zealand) and international (e.g. Odgers Berndtson). Assuming you have a suitable background, your approach is likely to be welcomed. David Schueneman, senior partner at CPS Inc., an Illinois-based recruiting company remarks: 'I love a phone call, because it shows that a candidate is truly motivated … We can't want it more for them than they want it for themselves' (in Fertig, 2015). More than this, a direct approach may actually help the recruiter because sourcers spend much of their time identifying passive candidates (people not actively searching for new jobs) by using social media platforms such as Academia.edu, Facebook, LinkedIn, and various application-tracking systems (ATSs), for example Naturejobs, Monster.com and CareerBuilder.com (there are others that specialize in specific research fields). If the sourcer thinks your profile is attractive, they will store your CV and other details in their database. Then when a recruiter or company is looking for someone to fill a position, they may be able to pass those details on to the responsible hiring manager.

You may find yourself contacted by a sourcer about a specific role. Very often, they will not ask you outright if you are interested in the position but may instead ask if you know of any likely applicants. If you are not interested, you can treat such an approach at face value and point to some prospective candidates you may know. However, if the role is one that appeals, or is the kind of position aspire to, do say so and see where the conversation takes you.

Maintain a good relationship with sourcers and recruiters but always bear in mind that ultimately they are working for the employer, not you. They are after their commission. While they may offer you some assistance – usually on a fee-for-service basis (including interview skills) – they are not there to offer career guidance or to help you develop a more compelling case for employment. That really is in your hands.

NOTE

1. For some academic labour markets the title of this chapter might better have been 'Find a job, any job' for as Chapter 1 made clear, university employment in many jurisdictions is fickle and uncertain. I acknowledge these conditions and their implications for the forms and duration of work scholars are able to secure. However, the scope of this book is also limited by its own circumstances so the focus is necessarily constrained. I trust the counsel provided may have broader applicability.

13. Write a compelling job application

It is all very well to ready yourself for an academic role by conducting research, developing teaching skills and engaging in relevant service activities (discussed in Part IV of this book), but one absolutely critical step in securing a position at a university is preparing an application that successfully conveys to a selection panel the extent of your preparation and your readiness for work. While the characteristics of a good job application depend on geographical and institutional context as well as the academic level being sought (e.g., lecturer, professor, senior manager) there are some commonalities. Below is some advice focussed primarily on early- to mid-career applications in places like Australia, New Zealand, Singapore, South Africa and the United Kingdom. Also included are some tips on the different requirements and expectations in North America. Depending on your circumstances, you may find it helpful to draw from both to help develop a strong application.[1]

A typical job application comprises the following components: a one- to two-page cover letter, a statement addressing selection criteria and your CV. You may also be asked to provide copies of key publications and the names of prospective referees. In some contexts (e.g., North America) you may be required to include a short account of your teaching philosophy, including evidence of your teaching effectiveness, a research statement, and a diversity, equity and inclusion statement. The last of these is increasingly sought for more senior roles.

JOB APPLICATION COMPONENTS

Write a Compelling Cover Letter

Your cover letter is your first and most important chance to convince the selection committee of your suitability for the job. Indeed, your very carefully presented one- to two-page letter tailored to the job may be the only thing some members of the selection panel will read in their initial assessments of candidates. So keep the letter brief and make sure it will have great impact. You will find many examples of, or templates for, good cover letters online, particularly through university career counselling services.

In terms of its relationship to your responses to the selection criteria (discussed below), treat your cover letter like the abstract of a scholarly paper.

Set out your key strengths against the essential criteria very early where their influence will be greatest. Why are you the best person for this job? What can you offer? To answer these two questions you will need to spend some time discussing relationships between your activities and interests (what do you plan to accomplish early?) and those of the department you hope to join. Make sure you do your homework on this. In your cover letter, do not admit weaknesses (e.g., 'While I do not have any university teaching experience …'). Focus instead on those strengths you can bring to the post and in response to the selection criteria. Write positively. Avoid passive language. And never, ever lie.[2]

Respond to the Selection Criteria

As noted in Chapter 1, the requirements for some academic posts have reached extraordinary, superhero levels, demanding satisfaction of over 20 selection criteria. In many cases, however, an application for a typical academic job will require thoughtful, evidence-based responses to eight to 12 selection criteria that generally seek to clarify your educational background; teaching and research strengths; ability to communicate and work effectively with students, colleagues and other institutional stakeholders; contributions to professional and disciplinary service (e.g., committees, community engagement); and management and leadership skills. Some examples of specific criteria are:

- extensive experience and track record of scholarly activities, including publications in national/international peer reviewed journals;
- excellent competitive grant-capture track record and leadership of significant research projects;
- demonstrated ability and enthusiasm for engaging in high-quality teaching at undergraduate and postgraduate levels;
- demonstrated ability in course coordination;
- outstanding interpersonal skills, including the ability to develop and promote effective relationships with colleagues and the ability to relate confidently and credibly to a wide range of external agencies including research, government, industry and communities.

Be sure to respond to every criterion clearly, taking care to provide evidence of your claims against them. For example, do not just say that you are an enthusiastic teacher who thinks teaching is important. Provide evidence in the form of teaching strategies and student evaluations. Make sure your response to each criterion is easily discernible. Different positions will, of course, give different emphasis to each of these areas. If there are no specific selection criteria, prepare an application that covers the areas noted against the bullet points above together with any others you believe to be relevant. In the absence of stated criteria it may be helpful to use the selection measures for similar roles at similar universities as a framework for your responses.

Responses to some criteria can be dealt with swiftly (e.g., requirement for a 'PhD qualification') whereas others take more space to answer adequately (e.g., 'Extensive experience and track record of scholarly activities, including publications in national/international peer reviewed journals'). Leaving aside a response to a PhD requirement, you might expect to write 500–1200 words per criterion. Be aware that together with other components of your application your responses will serve as an indication of your writing skills (Wilbur, 2007, p. 128).

On the subject of writing clarity, some advertisements are written poorly, if not appallingly, with many overlapping or duplicated criteria (e.g., 'High-level leadership skills in academic governance, teaching and research' together with 'Demonstrated leadership skills in planning and people management, including the ability to implement change'). In such cases, consider amalgamating the criteria and preparing a single response. If you do, be sure that the selection committee know you have done this deliberately and that it is not the result of some oversight or error on your part. This is important because in some institutions or jurisdictions only those applicants who satisfy all selection criteria can be appointed and where there are many applicants for a single role, an 'incomplete' application is quickly expelled from the selection process.

Provide a Comprehensive and Carefully Presented CV

There is detailed advice in Chapter 5 on developing a good CV and tailoring it to suit specific purposes. Be sure the CV you submit is up to date. I am amazed at the number of applicants who submit a CV that has clearly not been properly updated for months if not years! Confirm that your CV is free of typographical and formatting errors. These will reflect badly on you.

NORTH AMERICAN MODIFICATIONS

North American academic roles may require some additional documents within a job application, such as a research statement and a statement of teaching philosophy. Though once confined largely to the United States and Canada these extra materials appear to be increasingly popular in institutions elsewhere except where online job application systems permitting submission of a limited number of documents (commonly one!) are employed.

Research Statement

This two- to three-page document sets out a coherent tale of your research programme, linking details of your past research and accomplishments, current work and plans for the future. If possible, connect your plans explicitly to the role for which you are applying. Illustrate how your research will be successful in the new context, taking care to acknowledge the needs and facilities of the employer (Cornell University, 2023; Wells et al., 2013, p. 41). Avoid being over-ambitious in your claims for future work. Avoid being too finely grained in your statement: focus on the metaphorical forest as well as the trees. And be sure to present a clear sense of research direction and continuity.

Statement of Teaching Philosophy

North American universities typically expect even new PhD graduates to have done some teaching (e.g., as a teaching assistant). The statement of teaching philosophy requires some reflection on that experience. Typically about two to three pages, this document should set out the why and how of your teaching. Why do you teach? From what principles do you draw when designing courses and how are the specific learning and teaching practices you employ aligned with those principles? In writing your statement it is wise to bear in mind the advice of Wells et al. (2013, p. 41):

> Assume that everyone who is applying for this position (a) loves teaching, (b) thinks teaching is important, and (c) uses multimedia to illustrate difficult concepts. [Your] statement should convey enthusiasm for teaching, mention the classes you have taught, and list the classes you would be excited to teach ... Set your statement apart by conveying enthusiasm with concrete examples of creative teaching strategies rather than flowery language.

You may also be asked to or wish to include a teaching portfolio with your application. This is a carefully curated collection of materials that attest to your teaching prowess. It typically includes copies of peer and student evaluations of your teaching (together with appropriate benchmarks such as school or faculty mean scores), any teaching-related publications you have written, or resources you have created. It is also useful to include any syllabi you have developed. Syllabi point to the extent and currency of your expertise in your field. If you wish or need to include them, digital components of a teaching portfolio might add an online lesson, blog, vlog, website, or social media components that demonstrate your experience. Overall however, remember that the selection committee will be seeking assurance that you can construct and deliver a coherent and interesting course.

Diversity, Equity, and Inclusion Statement

A diversity, equity, and inclusion statement explains your experiences with, and commitments to, diverse populations of students and staff. The selection committee will be trying to ensure that you are familiar with its university's student – and faculty – populations and that you are willing to support them. A successful diversity statement may refer to your own background/positionality (if you wish to include that) but it should certainly draw from your past experience to illustrate how you will continue to contribute to equitable and inclusive learning and work environments. For example, how do you ensure that your 'classrooms' and syllabi are inclusive? What have you done in research and service to support equity and diversity? What might you do in your new role to support diversity, equity and inclusion (e.g. groups or committees whose work you can support) (Henville, 2022; University of Carolina at Chapel Hill, 2023).

Letters of Recommendation

True to label, these are solicited letters from advisers and colleagues extolling your virtues. I stand suspicious of the value of recommendation letters submitted by a candidate with their application, wondering who would include a less than supportive document but, with others (e.g., Sheehan et al., 1998; University of California – Berkeley Career Center, 2022), acknowledge that confidential letters from credible, distinguished scholars and advisers well informed about your work can carry great weight. Choose carefully three to five people to write letters on your behalf. And unless there is very good reason not to – and that you can explain to the selection committee – your letters should include one from your immediate supervisor or someone senior in your institutional reporting line ('chain of command') who is well acquainted with your work. Where appropriate and possible, include some international representation amongst your referees, to help illustrate your work's wider significance. This becomes more important as you move through the academic ranks. And be sure to give consideration to gender balance in your letters. It is increasingly likely, for instance, that a set of four or five letters from men or women alone will attract some questions. For more information on letters of recommendation, consult sites such as the University of California – Berkeley Career Center (2022) on approaching appropriate referees and letter content.

SOME OTHER POINTS

Sing your own praises – astutely. Your application must highlight your strengths and major achievements – especially very early in your cover letter –

but it is important that you do not hide or dilute the impact of your significant career milestones in a litany of minor achievements and efforts. And do state the obvious: just because your friends and immediate colleagues know who you are, what your professional interests are, and what you have done, does not mean anyone on a selection committee does. Tell the committee, but try not to sound conceited as you do. Acknowledging that some scholars find it difficult to write such self-promotional material, Wells et al. (2013, pp. 40–41) recommend being achievement focussed. For example, 'In recognition of my independent research I was awarded the X Award for Research Excellence and the results have been published in well-regarded journals such as *Journal Y* and *Journal Z*'. Such a statement provides clear evidence of excellence unalloyed by hyperbole.

Check spelling, grammar and other details – and then do it again. A good application can be spoiled completely by silly errors that signal to a reader laziness, ignorance or incompetence. Check the details. And if you are writing to a specific individual, make sure you spell their name correctly.[3]

And finally, before you hit 'send' do make absolutely sure that the content in your application tallies with information about you on your professional and personal media profiles!

NOTES

1. Qu (2021) provides a very helpful, engaging and comprehensive discussion of the academic job search process in the USA. Though based on personal experience in electrical engineering and computer science, much of the content is applicable to other fields.
2. If any 'special circumstances' surround your application, such as having an academic partner who may also seek a job, being pregnant, or having small children for whom you are the sole carer, Wells et al. (2013, p. 44) recommend not disclosing these circumstances during the initial application phase. You may raise them yourself or they may become apparent during the interview.
3. For more information on academic job searching, see resources such as Debowski (2012, Chapter 3); University of California, San Diego (undated); Vick et al. (2016); and Wilbur (2007).

14. Perform well at job interviews

There is a good chance your comprehensive and beautifully written job application will advance you to the next stage of the selection process – the interview. While these are increasingly conducted electronically (e.g., phone conference, Teams, Tencent/VooV, Zoom), most continue to be run as face-to-face meetings over a period of one to three days. Depending on the level of the position, they typically involve a spoken presentation to relevant staff; meetings with students, colleagues and other stakeholders; a tour of the campus; dinner with prospective colleagues; and, of course, a formal interview with a selection panel, the specific composition of which will vary from institution to institution and the seniority/purpose of the role.[1] The job interview experience can be exhausting, as well as informative, providing fascinating insights into the detailed workings of another institution and to the characters of some of your colleagues.

DO YOUR HOMEWORK

Before your interview and campus visit, find out about the department and university. Who are the academic staff? What do they do? What is taught? What kind of research is pursued? As Wilbur (2007, pp. 129–30) observes:

> [a] bit of recognition will flatter your hosts, reveal your awareness of the profession at large, and demonstrate that you are serious about the position. A review of the department's course listings tells about the interests of the faculty and gives you a preview of the character and balance of the department. Such a preview may provide you with questions that you need to ask in order to evaluate the department as a potential home. Prior knowledge demonstrates your sincerity and depth of interest.

IT IS A TWO-WAY STREET

One thing academic departments, and, more particularly, university human resource departments, sometimes forget is that the interview and appointment process is a 'two-way street'. While they are scrutinizing you carefully and in a fairly well-prescribed fashion, you should also be analysing the people you hope to work with and the place itself. If they treat you poorly as a potential colleague and employee, what does that tell you about the institution, its people and its culture? Most universities are welcoming and friendly, keen to make a good impression, even if they do forget to do things like offer you an orientation to the campus and its surrounds. Others, however, show unfortunate traits that do not reflect well on them. For instance, over many years I have been involved in job searches that have quite literally dragged on for a year as one committee after another evaluated the recommendation of its predecessor; that have been held at venues other than where the position was based; where designated contact people could never be reached; that have failed to allow applicant questions of the interview panel; and have shamelessly asked racist or ageist questions at interview. So, no matter how much you want a particular job, be as dispassionate as you can and check to see what you are letting yourself in for. Will it be a university wrapped up in stultifying red tape? Is it a department with antiquated and uncomfortable facilities? Is it an institution where no one is present, instead 'working at home'? Is it a place characterized by autocratic leadership? Or is it a work environment where you will be made to feel uncomfortable by virtue of matters like your gender identity, age, or ethnicity?

Before you go to an interview and site visit, think about what you expect from, or hope for, in a good work environment and set those out explicitly to yourself. Discuss your expectations with a few close friends and your partner or spouse and perhaps your family. And then when you are on site, seek answers to your questions and record your observations and impressions for subsequent reflection.

HOW TO ACT; WHAT TO SAY; WHAT TO WEAR

Irrespective of what you may be told, people *will* be judging you at all times for the duration of your visit – watching, listening and evaluating you as a prospective colleague. Be yourself and show your enthusiasm for your work and the job at shared meals, over coffee, or in cross-campus walks that are all part of the 'selection process'. It is worth heeding Malcolm Gladwell's advice (2000): '[Y]ou have to come across as being confident in what you are doing and in who you are. How do you do that? Speak clearly and smile.' You must also be prepared to be evaluated so do take care to moderate any extremes of behaviour. Sexist, racist, or ageist remarks, off-colour jokes, or derogatory comments about colleagues or your current employer are unlikely to endear you to most employers and prospective colleagues.

There are some scholars with overinflated egos who treat postgraduate students, junior colleagues, administrative staff and others with indifference or condescension. Even if members of the selection panel do not observe such behaviour directly, word of it can get back to them through formal or informal mechanisms (e.g., a casual chat between committee chair and departmental secretary) and colour the committee's assessment. While respect for others should be a matter of common everyday courtesy, do take extra care to treat everyone you meet politely.

During your visit to the university you can expect to be introduced to many potential colleagues, some of whom will have a direct say in whether or not you are appointed. Most of these meetings will be brief and impromptu, hallway or café queue encounters, allowing you opportunity to utter only details of where you are from, what your area of expertise is and what you are working on now (You might find use for the 'elevator pitch' discussed in Chapter 9 on 'getting known and networked'). Be sure to have prepared answers to these questions as well as to others you expect to encounter frequently. Listen carefully to these people's own responses to your queries – that information may be useful in the interview where you can point, for instance, to prospective collaborations, or if you take up an appointment at the university. Observe the interactions between existing staff members to gauge levels of collegiality and congeniality. Other meetings will be of longer duration. You might get to meet many departmental staff and university managers. Let them interview you but take these opportunities to ask questions of your own (e.g., working conditions and workload; key 'cultural' characteristics of the workplace; professional development opportunities; any dark clouds on the horizon such as budget cuts).

And as for what to wear for the duration of the job selection process: a useful rule of thumb is to be slightly better dressed than those you are meeting as part of the selection process. Look neat and professional. This applies to the interview, your talk, or an informal dinner with students. And you should be comfortable with what you are wearing. If, for example, you will be donning a suit or a frock for the first time in many years, be sure that it still fits, that you feel relaxed in it, and that you avoid making reference to how infrequently you wear it!

THE 'TALK'

Academic job interviews generally demand that you deliver a talk of one kind or another to an audience comprising academic staff, the selection committee and graduate students. This presentation will typically require you to speak for 30–60 minutes (with additional time for questions), introducing yourself, discussing your research trajectory and giving particular attention to your most recent work and your plans for the next three to four years. You might also be asked to discuss your philosophical and practical approach to teaching and how you see your interests (teaching and research) complementing and supplementing those of the department. Of course, if the prospective appointment is for a research- or teaching-only role the balance of content in your talk will necessarily change. As you move up the career ladder, the sort of matters you might be asked to discuss in an appointment talk are also likely to change. The emphasis will generally shift from your own work to one that seeks insights to the ways you lead research, teaching and people, and the vision you have for the department or other organizational unit (e.g., faculty, university). And at the same time, the breadth of the audience is likely to expand, with members drawn from the broader bailiwick you will fit into.

For some senior roles (e.g. Dean), you may be asked to speak only to the selection panel, setting out your vision for the future of the role, unit or institution. In some cases you may be given opportunity to speak for some time (e.g. 20 minutes, with notes or even visual aids) but much more commonly these presentations are very brief (as brief as two carefully timed minutes) and demand that you engage with and inspire the selection panel. In such cases do not read from notes. Do not use a handout. Keep the panel's attention on you and your great ideas.

Irrespective of whether it is for an early-career or more senior-career post, be sure that your talk is of high-quality, well-rehearsed,[2] of the required duration, illustrated effectively with examples and anecdotes, and that it addresses the issues you were asked to discuss. Your presentation is as much about how you represent yourself (and how you will represent your potential employer and colleagues) as it is about the brilliance of content. Emphasize both style and substance. As well as providing insights to your research, the talk will also serve as an indicator of your capacities to teach in 'traditional' lecture mode and to be an effective and compelling public speaker.

The audience that greets your talk may be kind or ruthless, depending on all sorts of factors such as departmental or institutional culture, internal factions and power struggles, and your position as a favoured candidate (or not). A rigorous question-and-answer session can signify that your talk has been stimulating and provocative; that no one agreed with a word you said; or, more rarely, that some folks are out to get you excluded from further consideration. On the other hand, a benign session may be the outcome of a talk the audience regarded as bland and uninspiring or it may be because the audience is itself bland and uninspiring or because there is a favoured candidate and the selection process is a sham.

Based on decades of attendance at research and job interview presentations, Box 14.1 sets out some of the kinds of general questions you could be expected to answer as part of an early-career talk after you have set out details of your research. You are most unlikely to face all of these but you can be more or less assured that you will encounter some.

BOX 14.1 CHALLENGES COMMONLY THROWN DOWN AT RESEARCH PRESENTATIONS

- What is your central question?
- What is the theory? What are you seeking to explain? What's the point?
- Why are you interested in this sort of question?
- What are the components of the theoretical base? How do they fit together?
- On what basis have the basic (concept-level) definitions been selected?
- Can you put your research into the context of contemporary literature in the field?
- Do you know what all of the terms mean? (e.g. 'Can you clarify what you mean by...?')
- Who has done pioneering work in the field? Can you compare and/or contrast your work to theirs?
- Have you covered the literature thoroughly?
- Describe and explain your research methodology.
- Have you used the same scale of analysis throughout (scale shifts, context shifts)?
- How are the examples/cases/participants selected for the study appropriate?
- Can the results of this study be put into another context?
- How can the results of this study be applied?
- Who can (will) use the results of the study? And what are the limits of application?
- What broad significance does this study have?

MEETING GRADUATE STUDENTS OR ALL STAFF

Many academic interviews will include an opportunity for you to meet a group of postgraduate students and/or academic staff from the department, perhaps over morning coffee or afternoon tea. A representative from this group may be on the selection panel or the group as a whole might be asked by the appointment committee for their opinion of each of the candidates. Such groups can be very good to meet, not only because they comprise the people with whom you may work for some years to come but also because they may be very happy to disclose many of the secrets of the institution, its strengths and weaknesses. If you are able, try to speak with everyone present. Listen to them carefully and, if necessary or appropriate, verify some of their observations. Often, the postgraduate students – who may themselves be looking at following the same steps as you in a few years – are deeply interested in hearing from you and about you to gauge their own place in the academic career 'market'. In these meetings with staff and students be prepared for an open and potentially revealing conversation. Take the lead. Introduce yourself. Find out who each person is and what they are working on. Ask them questions. But also give them some scope to quiz you.

INTERVIEWING SUCCESSFULLY

A 30–60-minute interview with a small selection committee is usually the most important and nerve-wracking part of any job selection process. Selection committees typically comprise five to nine people, including your potential direct supervisor, prospective colleagues, external panel members drawn from other parts of the university or from other universities, and commonly a representative from human resources to ensure that proceedings are conducted in accordance with the law and university policy and to answer any questions about appointment procedures.

Interviews can be organized in ways that make them either cordial conversations between colleagues around a small table or intimidating interrogations in an imposing meeting room. Irrespective of the context, hold your nerve. Be yourself and try neither to be lulled into a false sense of security in which you 'overdisclose', revealing to the committee some of your weaknesses and worries, nor so intimidated that you are rendered senseless and speechless. You may find it helpful to have practice interviews with colleagues and friends.

For most academic jobs, the selection committee is trying to answer two central questions. From the pool of candidates are you the person who can do the job most effectively? And how well will you 'fit' in terms of both the existing culture and enhancing the skills and abilities of the current staff? To assess these they will seek to evaluate your skills, knowledge, experience, character, credibility and continuing potential to do this job well. Questions posed at interview are often structured around the selection criteria you have already responded to in writing. For example, you may have already set out your 'significant undergraduate teaching and assessment experience' but the committee could ask you to elaborate, exploring the ways you teach, aspects of your philosophy, your willingness to try innovative teaching methods, your experience with online education and so on. So, before an interview, review the selection criteria associated with the position and think about answers to the kinds of questions a committee could foreseeably ask about each of them. Over and above these, contemplate some of the more general questions you may be asked. Some of those are set out in Boxes 14.2 and 14.3. There are many more questions that may be asked in interviews and a quick web search will present you with many more than you might ever wish to know.

BOX 14.2 SOME (COMMON) ACADEMIC JOB INTERVIEW QUESTIONS

In developing responses to some of these questions, use carefully selected examples. This will bring your answer to life and will make it more memorable to the selection committee:

- Tell us a little about yourself.
- Why do you want this job? What has attracted you to apply for this position?
- What particular talents and skills can you bring to the post?
- Where do you see yourself in five to ten years?
- What are your strengths?
- What are your weaknesses? (What do you regard as your gaps in ability to perform this job?)
- Tell us about your research. (You are expected to discuss its origins, character, significance and the plans you have for future work.)
- Why are you working on [your field of expertise]?
- What are your plans for research over the next two to five years?
- What is your experience with interdisciplinary research?
- What is your philosophy of teaching?
- What makes you a good teacher?
- Tell us about your experience in online teaching?
- What are the relationships between your research and teaching?
- What courses would you most like to teach and how would you teach them?
- Tell us about your experience improving the quality of teaching.
- Do you have any questions for us?

Rehearsing interview performance and responses to questions is a good idea but too-focussed rehearsal to a long list of potential questions can make you seem flustered and underprepared at interview as you struggle to match the wording of a question asked with the answers you have prepared (Marr, 2014). So, at all times, keep in mind the key question and any other matters you believe will be fundamental to the particular selection committee's decision-making.

In some jurisdictions certain kinds of question are illegal. These might include queries about your marital status, age, health status, current salary, plans for children or sexual identity. Before any interview, think about checking with colleagues, your union, or human resources staff, to see what the local rules are. If you are asked a question or questions that you believe to be illegal or in some other way inappropriate (that is, it does not have anything to do with your skills or experience for the job), you can end the interview; or decline to answer and, if necessary, later weigh up how to handle the situation. Of course, declining to answer can be difficult but strategies include trying to avoid the question gracefully, perhaps steering the conversation elsewhere; redirecting the question to your interviewer; or asking the interviewer how the question is relevant to the role. If there is a human resources person on the interview panel they may step in to resolve the situation or you might seek their guidance afterwards.

BOX 14.3 SOME ADDITIONAL INTERVIEW QUESTIONS COMMONLY ASKED AT ACADEMIC MANAGEMENT JOB INTERVIEWS

- What makes you a good leader?
- Describe some leadership or management difficulties/challenges you have encountered and how you overcame them? Why did things reach the point where they became a problem?
- Give an example of a conflict situation with a colleague or student that you were involved in and describe how you managed it.
- Have there been any situations at work that have made you angry? How did you handle them?
- How would you develop a research partnership with an agency external to the university?
- Tell us a little about your experience managing budgets/managing change?
- Describe a situation in which you were able to positively influence the actions of others to achieve a desired direction or outcome.
- How would you set about implementing new policies and procedures? In your experience, what makes for good change management?
- What did you enjoy about your former role as XXX? What did you like least?
- In what areas do you think you need or would like more professional development?
- What would be your priorities in this post in the first year?

Almost always an academic interview will conclude with a statement by the committee chair setting out the process from here (i.e., how quickly the committee will make its decision) and asking if you have any questions. Your response may be taken as a measure of your tact and emotional intelligence as well as a sign of your level of interest in the role. There are at least two appropriate ways of responding. First, if you believe the interview has gone very well and you have also had adequate opportunity to speak to staff and students and to see the department, it can be tactically sound to say something like: 'Thank you for the opportunity. I have already had many of my questions answered during my visit but if I am offered the position I am sure I will have a few more specific questions.' This saves the committee some time; it closes proceedings on the high of your earlier good responses; and suggests to the committee that you have been doing your 'homework' throughout the site visit. Do not say: 'No, I don't have any questions right now' as this sounds as if you have little interest in the role and even less natural curiosity. Second, you may have some genuine and important questions whose answers have not been available through relevant websites, conversations with prospective colleagues, or other means. But in most cases do not ask questions about salary and conditions. Those matters can be taken up if you are offered the job. And do not ask questions simply because you feel you should.

NOTES

1.   If the details of the process and the make-up of the selection panel are not made explicit when you are advised of the interview, ask.
2.   Wells et al. (2013, p. 43) wisely recommend 'overpractising' the first five minutes of your talk, as this is likely to help overcome the high levels of anxiety you may experience at that stage of the process.

15. Manage job interview failure and success

DEALING WITH REJECTION

Unless you are exceptionally talented or enormously lucky, it is more or less inevitable that some – if not many – of your applications for jobs will be unsuccessful. Of the tens or hundreds of people who apply for any single position, only three or four will usually be interviewed and only one of them will be successful. So, the odds of rejection are, for most people, high. But rejection is not necessarily about any failings you may have. It may simply be the elusive matter of 'fit'.[1] Some people's research interests or intentions or aspects of their character make them better for some departments. Many appointment committees find themselves faced with having to 'sort diamonds', choosing one jewel over another. Take consolation from this.

If you are not selected for appointment, do contact the recruiter or selection committee chair afterwards, thanking them for the opportunity and for any assistance they provided – particularly if you were interviewed for the role. You might also send personalized notes to those colleagues you met but who were not on the selection committee to express your pleasure at meeting them and perhaps exploring possibilities of future collaboration. Not only will this kind of messaging help enhance your reputation as a courteous colleague it may also consolidate the foundations for future opportunities. If you are thoughtful enough to thank these colleagues, they may be more inclined to support your future professional efforts.

Do also ask for some critical feedback. Remarkably, very few job applicants do this. What were the reasons for the outcome? What can you do differently in future to help increase your chance of success? But be sure you do not turn a feedback conversation into an argument. The appointment decision has already been made. No matter how unjust that decision may seem to you, do not make things worse by quarrelling about the way you and your application have been interpreted or by lamenting what could have been 'If only ...'. That simply will not help your cause. Instead, take note of critical observations and consider carefully whether they require you to change something about the ways you approach your job search. Disappointingly, while a small number of interview selection committee chairs are unwilling to engage in post-decision conversation and some can be circumspect in their remarks, the fact remains that critically constructive feedback can be tremendously helpful and is certainly worth seeking.

DEALING WITH SUCCESS: NEGOTIATING THE OFFER

So you got offered the job! News of this is likely to have come first in the form of a telephone call from the chair of the selection committee, advising that you are the recommended candidate and that you will soon be receiving a formal letter of offer. Feel free to express your enthusiasm at this point but do not commit yourself to anything. And take care to avoid making irreversible decisions and life-changes based on a phone offer. There are instances when unforeseen challenges such as institutional financial crises or the COVID pandemic of the early 2020s mean that offers may be suspended or withdrawn (Qu, 2021). Wait until your formal letter of offer has arrived and you have evaluated the alignment of the offer with your expectations and explored the details. You will probably have about two weeks to accept the formal offer and you should use this time wisely, finding out as much as you can about the position and negotiating conditions.

Try to arrange a (follow-up) visit for you (and your partner or spouse) to check out the department and local area a little more informally than was possible during your interview. You may be able to get some financial support for this from the university. This trip will allow you to consider matters such as lifestyle, access to an airport, the cost of living, spousal employment opportunities, the availability of schools and other amenities or services you value and that you could not appraise fully on your earlier visit – if such a visit was part of the selection process.

In a very tight employment market it may be tempting to seize the offer, accepting whatever salary and other benefits are set out initially. Do realize, however, that in the period between job offer and acceptance, you are unlikely to ever be in a better or stronger position to negotiate your future working conditions. And gains such as academic rank/level, salary, and start-up grants you may achieve in this period of negotiation could take years to achieve after you have accepted and commenced work in the role. But do not overestimate your clout! In many cases, a selection committee will have wrestled long and hard trying to determine who amongst a strong field of candidates it should appoint. So while you should not undersell yourself, if you play the negotiating game a little too hard, the offer may be withdrawn or you risk alienating your supervisor and new colleagues even before you have started work. It pays to consult with friends, colleagues, human resource contacts and your union and look across the Internet to see what you can fairly and reasonably expect or hope for. Some of the matters you might give attention to in negotiating your deal are set out in Box 15.1. In your negotiations, be well informed; be fair; be firm.

BOX 15.1 EMPLOYMENT CONDITIONS AND BENEFITS FOR CONSIDERATION AND NEGOTIATION

Salary

While salary itself may not appear to affect your scholarly career, it is important. First, if you are being paid well, relative to colleagues, you may spend less time looking for alternative employment and more time focussing on your work. Second, the salary is likely to serve as a base against which future pay increases may be made. Many institutions are bound by their own regulations about annual increases after an initial appointment. Others have salary 'steps' or 'bands' through which one progresses from the initial appointment or there may be regular percentage salary increases. It is worth noting too that should you ever seek to move from one institution to another, there is a good chance that your current salary will serve as a benchmark for any new salary offer. So, get your initial offer as high as possible. It can have long-term flow-on effects.

Some universities and research organizations make their salary levels explicit; others state that salary will be 'commensurate with experience', putting the burden on you to investigate an appropriate level of compensation. Fortunately, a good deal of salary information is now fairly easy to acquire. Many institutions make their salary ranges public, typically online. News media (e.g., The Chronicle of Higher Education), and some websites (e.g., Glassdoor.com) offer comparative information within jurisdictions. Occasionally, large accounting firms or professional bodies prepare national and international salary comparisons (e.g., American Association of University Professors; European University Institute). Ask people in your current institution's human resources/personnel department about ways of uncovering relevant data and handling negotiations. Do not be afraid to ask an appropriate representative of the employing institution outright about internal salary equity. You do not want to arrive at your new university to find that all of your colleagues are earning more than you! Aside from destroying your goodwill, it may see you back on the job market, a move neither you nor your new employer wish for.

In most countries the annual salary quoted will be for 12 months but if you are applying for a position in the United States it may be for only nine or ten months, with payments annualized, leaving you 'free' to take up other pursuits over the summer (e.g., travelling, resting in a hammock, writing papers or a book). Check the details. Think carefully about the pay relative to the cost of living in the place you are thinking of moving to.

If you find yourself in the fortunate position of having two offers available to you, do not hesitate to make this known to your prospective employers. It may spark a little competition. And compare the offers to see if there are elements of one you might like to see in the other.

Tenure and promotion arrangements

Is there any probationary period associated with the position? If so, what are the conditions and how long does probation last? How does one move from a probationary appointment to a 'permanent' one? What are the pathways and requirements for promotion to more senior levels and how successful have past applicants been? Find out if account of absences due to significant life events (e.g., maternity/paternity leave) is taken in promotion decisions (see Chapter 35).

For instance, some compassionate institutions consider 'performance relative to opportunity' at promotion time.

Underpinning position (known in the United States as 'retreat rights')

Some appointments (e.g., department head) are for a fixed term, typically five years, sometimes with the possibility of renewal subject to performance and institutional circumstance. If you are offered a limited tenure role of this type – and if you have not already established this when conducting your 'due diligence' prior to applying – see if you can negotiate an arrangement that allows you to move/return to a permanent academic role in the appropriate department at contract's end.

Teaching expectations

Find out exactly what teaching you will be expected to do and how much of it. What classes and in what capacity? Will you be expected to spend countless hours supervising repetitive computer lab work or student workshops? Will you have any assistance (e.g., tutors; teaching assistants)? Will you be delivering lectures in topics quite unrelated to your research? Are you eligible for a reduced teaching load in the early stages of your appointment to allow you to develop new classes and consolidate your research profile? If you find your prospective employer is reluctant to provide much detail about such matters, perhaps citing the uncertainties of student numbers with the consequences that has for teaching demand, tread carefully. While there may be some legitimacy to such claims, they may also signal a poorly run department or mask burdensome teaching loads.

Service roles
What committee and other departmental, faculty or university service are you expected to perform?

Rules on outside work
Are you permitted to do 'outside' consulting and what are the institutional rules surrounding such work?

Clerical and other administrative support
You may not have a personal assistant, but is there sufficient support to allow you to focus on your primary work rather than the so-called 'administrivia' that takes increasing parts of scholars' days? What kinds of secretarial and related support do you have access to?

Computing facilities and access to office services
Do not assume you will be provided with a good computer and printer – or any other computing facilities vital to your role. The printer may be a shared one, located in another building – for which you have to pay for each page. If there is a computer it may be someone else's outdated hand-me-down. And who pays for photocopying, phone calls and scanning? Ask too about the frequency with which computers and other technology are replaced. While you might be getting a new computer on appointment, will it ever be updated? If so, how often?

Adequate journal and other research holdings
Check to see that library holdings include all of the resources you will need for your work and that there are good interlibrary loan or other reciprocal facilities.

Appropriate office and laboratory space
Be sure that you are getting access to space that will allow you to work productively. Will it be shared with other people? Under what terms? Does your office have a window? Is the size and location of the office consistent with those of your colleagues? Some of these matters may seem petty but minor annoyances and perceived injustices can cause tensions later.

Study/leave/sabbatical entitlements
This could include some extra time off in the early years of an appointment to facilitate research development.

Support to attend conferences
Establish how often any such support is available, under what conditions

and its extent. Many universities will make an annual allowance available to permit you to present conference papers. Having the opportunity to attend several conferences a year in the early stages of your career can be valuable.

Start-up research funding
Because it can often take several years to secure a good external research grant, try to get some start-up or seed funding to help your research along, particularly if you are taking up your first appointment or moving from one funding jurisdiction to another (e.g., internationally) and cannot carry prior funding with you. Check for any time limits on start-up packages.

Funding for research/teaching assistance and/or postdoctoral support
Some wealthy institutions are in the fortunate position of being able to provide new staff with funds to support the appointment of research or teaching assistants, typically drawn from the local postgraduate community. This provides the dual benefit of supporting postgraduate students through relevant work and enhancing the 'productivity' of academic staff.

Professional subscriptions (e.g., journals, professional societies)
The costs of maintaining professional subscriptions can be high, especially as your career develops and expands to embrace a wider array of activities. Not only might you find yourself paying full rates for membership of one or two discipline bodies, you may also need to cover the subscription costs of academies, management organizations and so on. Seek help to contribute to these costs.

Opportunities for ongoing professional development
Does the institution have meaningful and well-regarded professional development programmes you can participate in and that will support your vocational ambitions? Are there funds available to allow you to enrol in relevant courses elsewhere (e.g., those offered by professional societies). And for more senior roles, will you have access to leadership development opportunities?

Key personal benefits and requirements
Are benefits such as annual leave, maternity leave, carer's leave, long-service leave, sabbatical, superannuation/pension scheme, health insurance, life insurance, children's university fees, childcare subsidies or facilities available to you? Is there any job placement assistance for your partner/spouse? Are you eligible to have the costs of your relocation paid for or reimbursed? Is there temporary accommodation available while you settle in or does the university offer a housing subsidy or per-

manent accommodation? This can be important in very expensive locations (e.g., Auckland, Hong Kong, London, New York, Sydney). If you will need to drive to campus, what parking arrangements exist – and how much does it cost? What public transport options are there? As excited as you may be about your prospective new role, try to think as dispassionately as you can about how you and your family would live your life in the foreseeable future in your new location.

And what about my (academic) partner?
If a university really wants to appoint you, they may be able to make some employment arrangements for your partner, although those arrangements may not be all that he or she might desire. The job may be at the university, or the institution may be able to assist with securing external work. If you think it may be helpful, ask for support for your partner. While Wells et al. (2013, p. 45) suggest wording like: 'I am very excited about this offer but for me to accept the job I need to have plans for my partner', something a little less 'all or nothing' may be more suitable.

Many of the matters set out in Box 15.1 might be clarified conversationally with the selection committee chair or human resources staff who can point you to the relevant policies or outline local practices. But for any matters that are critical, make sure you have *explicit* and *authenticated* assurances about any conditions you are promised. If the conditions you have discussed are not provided in a formal letter of offer or in institutional policies, get the details in writing. Leaving aside the possibility that the person you are negotiating with may themselves move to another role, some people do lie or forget about assurances they have made. So, how do you get conditions in writing without calling into question your new employer's trustworthiness? Box 15.2 sets out an example of a letter intended to achieve that end.

BOX 15.2 EXAMPLE OF A LETTER INTENDED TO CLARIFY NEGOTIATED EMPLOYMENT CONDITIONS

Dear Dr Honcho,

I appreciate the time you spent discussing my professional opportunities at [location]. As I understand it the position you are offering will include the following: [Specify the important terms here …]

Please let me know whether this list reflects our conversation accurately so that we may proceed accordingly.

Yours sincerely,

Dr Ima Mover

Source: Adapted from Feibelman (2011, p. 103).

If you find yourself in the rare but delightful position of having multiple simultaneous offers, you then have a difficult decision to make. Though that decision may ultimately come down to your 'gut feeling' about which place is better for you (and your family), there are other factors that may affect your thinking (Qu 2021):

- How enthusiastic do academic staff (and postgraduate students) seem about your appointment?
- How do you get on with the staff?
- Is there potential for productive collaborations?
- Are their prospective mentors in the department and will senior staff support and champion you?

In my own experience I have found it helpful to create a 'pros and cons' list for key alternative pathways when they have presented themselves. But frankly, while these can be informative and helpful, it has eventually been instinct or intuition that has driven the final decision.

Do not be greedy or unrealistic in your negotiations and do be cognizant of the general conditions that prevail in the institution and more broadly, but do bear in mind that it is in the institution's best interest for you to be successful. You may have to remind them of that and of your desire to have the resources required to live up to your promise.

As soon as possible after you have commenced your new role, demonstrate your 'go-getting' capacities by seeking out any other opportunities for departmental, university and external support (e.g., early career grants, teaching assistance, matching funds for successful grants). In some cases, details of resources available may be less than transparent or support will go on an ad hoc basis to those who ask for it. So, ask and you may receive. Your chances of success are likely to increase if you can demonstrate some significant achievements in your work. Success begets success.

If, after careful deliberation, you determine that the job you have been offered is just not for you, decline promptly so the selection committee can make alternative arrangements to fill the position. In general but positive terms outline your reasons for declining (e.g., 'I received another offer that I felt was a better fit for me'). Avoid burning any bridges. Always bear in mind that scholarly communities are small and people have long memories.

NOTE

1. Of course, there are also some positions advertised for which there is already a favoured candidate and the selection process may be a frustrating charade conducted to satisfy legal or other requirements.

PART IV

PERFORMING AS AN ACADEMIC
SUPERHERO

16. Manage your career

There is a great deal to do if you are to be an academic superhero. In fact, the activities and work required could stretch on almost infinitely, filling every hour of every day. Quite simply, there is always more that can be done. There is always scope to improve teaching or to better engage with students. There is always an extra paper to write. There is always additional committee work. And then, on top of that, there are the extra administrative tasks being moved by universities to academic staff. There is always more, more, more ...

There are at least three ways of responding. First, you can simply do less, less, less ... putting your 'head in the sand', and probably farewelling a successful academic career. Second, you can try to do everything at once, working yourself into a frenzy of publication, reading, consulting, committee meetings, community service, very quickly foregoing other parts of your life such as exercise, family and fun. The result *may* be some form of objective career 'success' (see Table 1.1 in Chapter 1) in the short run, but the long-term outlook is likely to be an unsustainable career. A third option is to acknowledge Angela Thody's counsel set out below and develop workable plans that acknowledge the variability of life and academic work and that will allow you to satisfy long-term and short-term career, as well as personal, ambitions.

> Throw yourself into your priorities, and don't try, or expect, to achieve on all fronts at once. At each life stage, prioritise teaching or research or family or unpaid employment or publications. Don't aim to balance them all each day, week or even year, but be assured that each can be adequately covered over the course of a lifetime. (Angela Thody, in Reisz, 2013)

Planning your academic career at several different time scales – decade, year and week – is helpful if you wish to develop a superhero academic career while maintaining your health, sanity and social relations. Having asserted the need for planning I have a great deal of sympathy with Crone's personal remarks:

> I am frequently asked to give talks to graduate students and new faculty about career planning. I find this difficult to do. Although I think I am one of those people who is a planner, I rarely do it in a systematic way. Often, I make lists of my projects and future proposals, write down goals for long-term projects, and draw maps of different paths I might take. However, I rarely save these things and seldom look back at old versions. I think that is because I realize that my plans are constantly changing, and I don't want to be pinned down by what I thought I might do a year

ago. Nonetheless, I think the exercise is an important thing for me to go through occasionally. It helps me focus on the immediate goals and plan my next move with a long-term plan in mind. (Crone, 2010, p. 93)

A telling part of Crone's position is having a long-term plan *in mind*. So, even if her (or my own for that matter) planning may not result in the development of explicit, written objectives with associated waypoints and key performance indicators, it does help to clarify broad ambitions (e.g., find a full-time academic role; be a full professor by age 40; complete a monograph within three years of graduating with a PhD; secure a senior management role at a leading university), which may be an entirely appropriate and flexible way of proceeding given the caprices of academic environments and personal lives. So, whether you opt for a carefully structured plan or something a little more fluid, give serious thought to career planning.[1]

To begin, it may be useful to consider what you want to be doing in five, ten or 15 years. Research, teaching, or university management? Where? At what kind of institution: will it be Ivy League, provincial powerhouse, suburban redbrick, or funky urban? These matters require a good deal of introspection. Dream large. Do not underestimate or undersell yourself. While you should be optimistic and seek out challenging goals, be sure those goals are realistic too. If, in your heart of hearts, you do not believe that your plans can come to pass, it is unlikely they will. However, if you are going through this process, there is a good chance you have the ambition and capabilities to bring to life most of what you want. What you need now are the right circumstances and chances. Your plan is not meant to be limiting or constraining. For example, during your career you may be presented with opportunities you have never considered before or even envisaged and that seem really attractive. Simply because they were not in your plan does not mean they should be dismissed out of hand (see Kindsiko and Baruch, 2019 for a discussion of chance events and how to manage them).

Once you have established your ambitions or targets, give some thought to the ways you will achieve them. Again bearing in mind Thody's advice that not everything must be tackled simultaneously, exactly what do you need to do to work towards these goals? Other than the advice of any mentors you have or the ways you see successful negotiating their career, you may find so-called university academic profiles helpful. These are explicit statements of the research, teaching and other expectations universities have of staff at different academic levels. More and more universities are developing these and other means of building clarity around what successful academics do and to guide appointment and promotions decisions (Debowski, 2012). They are a very helpful career development tool. A comprehensive example is set out in Box 16.1. Use academic profiles strategically. Have a look at the performance expectations at different academic levels. These may be clear on areas you need to do well in but they may 'not be clear about how much, how often, for whom and when' (Sutherland, 2015, p. 14), so discuss with mentors exactly what you need to achieve and how to go about it all, and then plan ways to achieve those objectives as you move towards your academic career ambitions.

BOX 16.1 JUST WHAT IS EXPECTED OF A (FULL) PROFESSOR?

The following is an explicit but slightly abridged statement of the kinds of expectations of a (full) professor. Although the statement is drawn from promotion policy documents at Flinders University, South Australia, its contents provide a useful template for common expectations of a (full) professor and signal the directions ECAs can work towards. The statement sets out quite detailed expectations under the headings: qualifications, teaching, research, and university, professional and community service.

Skill Base and Qualifications

Appointment or promotion to a Professorial position normally requires a PhD or EdD or equivalent qualification AND recognition of academic standing as an eminent authority in the discipline area AND distinction at the national (and where appropriate) international level.

Teaching

- Provides leadership and fosters excellence in teaching / scholarship of teaching.
- Makes original, innovative and distinguished contributions to scholarship and teaching.
- Provides sustained leadership to the discipline.

Relevant activities may include:

- playing an active role in maintenance of academic standards and in the development of educational policy and curriculum within the discipline;
- making a distinguished personal contribution to teaching at all levels;
- undertaking a leadership role in international delivery and/or collaboration;

- responsibility for curriculum development and teaching methodology for topics and programs of study/courses; and
- reflection on practice.

Research and/or Creative Activity

- Provides leadership at the national and/or international level in their discipline and fosters excellence through original, innovative and distinguished contributions to research and/or creative activity.
- Makes a contribution to the University's research agenda commensurate with their standing in the profession and as a Professor of the University.

Relevant activities may include:

- making a distinguished contribution to research and/or creative activity in the discipline;
- a sustained track record of obtaining competitive research grants/ support from sources outside of the University;
- providing leadership and expertise to foster the research and/or creative activity within the discipline, school and/or related disciplines, including leadership of a large team;
- development of research policy; and
- providing leadership and expertise to foster collaborative links across the University, with industry and with other institutions as appropriate.

University, Professional and Community Service

- Provides leadership and fosters excellence in administration and management within School, Faculty and University.
- Makes a significant contribution to the discipline and/or profession within a relevant external professional domain and within a wider community context at local, national and international level, which draws upon the staff member's University-related professional profile and which enhance the reputation, strategic engagement and/or income of the University.

Relevant activities may include:

- undertaking managerial and senior-level administrative responsibilities at School, Faculty and University level;
- leadership in School/Faculty/University-wide external quality assurance/regulatory/accreditation processes.
- contributing to University policy development;

- leading the development and maintenance of effective industry/community/government relationships and partnerships (local or international);
- development of beneficial professional relationships, consultancy work, responsibilities on professional/community bodies/committees/associations and appointments to significant external bodies; and
- leadership role in relevant professional association and/ or peer leadership in the profession at state/national/international level.

Source: Adapted from Flinders University (2015).

If this or other similar profiles do not match your own situation and your own institution has no relevant profiles, another way to map out a career development path is to examine the qualifications and experience sought in academic 'situations vacant'. If, for instance, you wish to become a research professor at a major international university or a teaching-focused academic at a well-regarded regional university, look to see what such universities expect of those people they appoint at that level. Some examples of the expectations of full professors at a number of universities are set out in Box 16.2. You will see that there is a relatively small group of common themes, such as outstanding research publication record and research leadership; record of successful competitive grants; and the capacity to develop productive alliances with internal parties and external agencies. Recent work by Mantai and Marrone (2023) analysing job advertisements in Europe provides some valuable insights. Armed with this knowledge, and with some years to achieve those targets, you can work realistically towards achieving your ambition.

BOX 16.2 EXAMPLES OF WORK EXPECTATIONS OF PROFESSORS AS EXPRESSED THROUGH EMPLOYMENT ADVERTISEMENTS

Chair in Egyptology, Uppsala University
'Overarching responsibility for research and post-graduate education within the field of Egyptology, as well as for developing said subject area. Teaching and supervision at all levels. Carrying out research in the subject. Upon demand providing information about the research and development work within the subject. Planning, heading and participating in research projects, including applying for research grants. Collaborating with … other … disciplines both as regards education and research projects. The incumbent should also be prepared to assume managerial duties, including positions of leadership within the department and at other levels of the

university administration.'

Professor of Human Geography, University of Auckland, New Zealand
'Applicants will possess an outstanding research record in Human
Geography as demonstrated through publications in top-ranked journals
and/or books and success in attracting research funding. The successful
candidate will be expected to develop a strong research program in Human
Geography, establish research collaborations within the university and with
external agencies and attract external research income. The candidate will
also be expected to take a leadership role in the refinement of research-led
undergraduate and postgraduate teaching in Human Geography, and build
a cohort of postgraduate research students.'

Professor of Language Literature and Communication, University of Fiji
'Candidates: must hold a PhD in Language/Linguistics, Literature, Arts,
Education or any combination of these related fields from a recognised
University with at least 10 years of tertiary teaching experience; must
have a record of demonstrated scholarly and professional achievement in
the relevant disciplines with demonstrated ability to teach undergraduate
programmes as well as postgraduate programmes through in-person, online
and HyFlex or hybrid modes; are expected to have experience in course,
programme, and research development as well as curriculum design and
should have peer-reviewed journal publications; must be able to demonstrate ability to supervise students at Masters and PhD levels; must possess deep appreciation of the multiplex diversity of the University of Fiji's
staff and students including in gender, culture and expression; must have
the ability to organize high-level exhibitions and Film Society events; and
must possess a keen understanding of the human values foundation of the
University.'

Professor of Law, Griffith University, Australia
'The University seeks a Professor in Law to provide leadership in research,
teaching and professional engagement in an area relevant to the strengths
of the Griffith Law School. Applicants will have a strong research track
record, be able to advance research performance, including attracting external grant income, and establish collaborative partnerships that support the
learning and teaching, research and service of the School and the broader
community. Applicants with a strong interest in the legal profession or interests in international legal issues are especially encouraged to apply.'

Professor of Modern Jewish History, Harvard University, USA
'The successful candidate must have a distinguished record of publication and instruction; she/he will teach and advise at both the undergraduate and graduate levels. Candidates for this appointment should also demonstrate intellectual leadership in the field, as well as potential for significant contributions to the Department, the University and the wider scholarly community. An earned doctorate is required.'

Sources: Examples drawn from AcademicPositions.eu, akadeus.com, Harvard University, Times Higher

It may also be useful to review the websites and social/professional media sites (especially LinkedIn) of contemporaries and high-performing colleagues – in your own field and beyond. These public records may include copies of their CV or clear and informative indicators of the pathways they are following in their career journey. This review might highlight for you some opportunities such as grants, fellowships, and service roles that could help make a difference to your own trajectory. But do recall in any such review that these autobiographical records generally focus on the good, the great and the grand of people's careers and do not reflect the circumstances, struggle and despair that may lie behind them. Take care not to be overwhelmed by or obsessed with the achievements of your colleagues. There is a growing literature suggesting that comparisons with others is associated with unhappiness and impostor syndrome (Arad et al., 2017; Gaillard et al., 2022; Jaremka et al. 2020). It can be helpful to accompany comparison of others' successes with comparisons of their failures! Consider talking to colleagues close to you about your setbacks and failures and they may open up to you about their own. There is also an emerging movement among some scholars to publish records of failure in the form of CVs of failure (Cheplygina, 2021; Gaillard et al. 2022; Haushofer, 2016; Stefan, 2010) and blogs like Veronika Cheplygina's 'How I Fail' (Cheplygina, 2021) which comprises interviews with researchers about their thoughts on failure. These may provide a helpful counterbalance when all of those success stories get to be a little too much!

In making your long-term plan, seek the assistance of trustworthy, supportive and ambitious mentors (see Chapter 4). Get a small number of mentors, but not too many, and consider some representation from outside your own discipline. As Sternberg (2013) observes: 'No one person or committee can be relied on to give you definitive career advice. In the end, you need to seek out multiple sources of advice, sort the good from the bad, and take responsibility for your own career development.' The next time period to consider in your planning is of shorter duration, say two to three years. Plan beyond your next goal: what steps will you take after you PhD, your postdoc, or after associate professor and how will you make that progression happen?

Then plan the next year. What conferences will you attend, and why? Do you have any publication targets, in terms of number or outlet? What grants can you apply for? As you explore the options, keep a file of interesting possibilities you encounter. While some of these (like sabbatical grants, visiting scholar schemes, biannual research grants) may not be relevant immediately, they may find a place in your longer-term plans.

All of this medium- to long-term planning can be much more difficult than you might think. By its very nature an academic career is typically a voyage of not just 'scientific' but also personal discovery, often disrupted by chance events (Kindsiko and Baruch, 2019). As a result, even the best thought-out plans can sometimes come apart or at least require substantial revision (e.g., as the result of an unplanned pregnancy, a pandemic, a partner's illness, international economic events, redundancy, or an unexpected job offer). Nonetheless, with a plan you will have some sense of direction and purpose. You will have taken the opportunity to think about your ambitions and how your labours can best be organized to satisfy them in ways that are rewarding and sustainable.

NOTE

1. But do take some advice from Burkeman (2016) on the degree to which you *focus* on your career goals. He counsels against concentrating too much on long-term goals, observing that: 'the more you do that, the more of your daily life you spend feeling vaguely despondent that you have not yet achieved them. Should you manage to achieve one, the satisfaction is surprisingly brief – then it's time to set a new long-term goal. The supposed cure just makes the problem worse.'

17. Manage your time

Having done your best to plan the overall direction of the coming years, the next critical step in ensuring your enduring performance as a successful academic is to plan your week and days. The relative autonomy of most academics working in the humanities, arts and social sciences (HASS) disciplines means we are, for the time being, still able to organize how, when and where we work. To paraphrase Wolf-Wendel and Ward (2015, p. 30), as long as we write the book, get the grant, submit the article, teach the class, or do the marking where and how we get this work done is up to us. For many of us, time management is vital to satisfying work-related productivity demands as well as to maintaining any semblance of work–life balance given that '[p]art of the greedy nature of academic work is that no one tells professors when they are done or what is too much' (Wolf-Wendel and Ward, 2015, p. 26). And at the same time institutional workload demands on academics have been intensifying at a furious pace (e.g. NTEU Australia 2020; University and College Union, 2022). What this means is we must know when to work and, just as importantly, we must know when to rest.[1] Each of us needs to confront the fact that we can never do everything. We can never fully bring order to all aspects of our lives (Burkeman, 2016). And if we don't endeavour to pace ourselves we will stop – one way or another.

Over and above the limitless demands we face, academics also work in environments that offer many opportunities for procrastination and where our various teaching, service and research responsibilities make us prone to distractions. As Duncan et al. (2015, p. 7) observe, interruptions disrupt and slow work, harming 'productivity of ongoing tasks due to cognitive issues associated with context switching, recollection time and an increased potential for errors, and, for highly intellectual tasks, the costs of interruptions are higher'. On the basis of their research in Australia, Duncan et al. (2015, p. 7) found that:

> for a teaching and research academic, the ideal day is a long day spent entirely on research activities without the interruptions of administrative or teaching tasks. Academics can individually act to create these types of days for themselves, or can carve up smaller portions of a week to be devoted regularly to research, and the literature from the work fragmentation of technology workers suggests there are large personal gains to be made from this.

Unfortunately, in most academic roles, you will face an incessant and limitless barrage of everyday interruptions to your research and teaching activity: email, student counselling, Zoom, email, teaching, email, marking, Teams, email, meetings, email … Paradoxically, 'the more efficient you get at ploughing through your tasks, the faster new work tasks seem to arrive' (Burkeman, 2016). It can be very easy to let these responsibilities overtake your working schedule, squeezing out any time for research and teaching development. And for women and identified minority groups, the demands to be involved in many service roles, for example, may be greater as institutional ambitions to ensure gender equity and diversity in all activities are pursued[2] (Perkel, 2015, p. 518; Wolf-Wendel and Ward, 2015). Interruptions can diminish your scholarly productivity and waylay your ambitions as well as making you frustrated and angry as you see weeks pass and little tangible output to show for the time. A fundamental way of dealing with this is to pursue carefully considered time management strategies, some of which are set out in Table 17.1.

Table 17.1   Time management strategies

Strategy	Implementing Time Management Strategy
Set realistic and attainable goals	Develop long-term scholarship goals. Develop intermediate and immediate activities to achieve long-term goals. Identify goals/objectives that are measurable and attainable within a structured time limit. Periodically review goals for: – achievement/lack of achievement; – factors that facilitate or act as barriers to achievement.
Optimize realistic planning	Create daily 'to do' lists and check off as tasks are done Break complex tasks, such as manuscripts, into manageable components with defined deadlines. Create detailed timeline of activities. When you end your work session, make an agenda of 'to do' items for next sessions while it is fresh in your mind. When you have finished a writing session, jot down notes of what to write in the next paragraphs. Automate some processes (e.g., sign up for automated notices of funding opportunities and research papers). Identify and seek needed assistance early in the process.

Strategy	Implementing Time Management Strategy
Prioritize	Acknowledge the primacy of your work, perhaps scheduling – and keeping – appointments with yourself.
	Arrange your objectives/goals in order of priority. Work on the highest priority goal first and consistently until you have achieved the goal or have temporarily exhausted available resources.
	Write down priorities – if request or opportunity is not in line with priority, say 'no'.
	Learn how and why to say 'no'.
Effective scheduling	Schedule blocks of writing time (and blocks for other important tasks such as class preparation). Schedule far in advance of deadlines.
	Create a recurring calendar with scholarship blocks.
	Use an electronic calendar and make it available to others so they can see your availability (outside those times blocked for scholarly productivity).
	When meeting with others, schedule time-limited appointments.
	Consider scheduling a 'research sabbatical' (formal or informal) aimed at completing selected tasks.
	Set aside time to deal with email; where possible, handle correspondence only once.
Maintain focus on research programme	Select opportunities that advance your research programme (e.g., student work, service commitments).
	Link your teaching and service with your research. Monitor any drifting to other 'interesting topics'.
	Develop ways to work with multiple students on one project that also contributes to your programme of research.
Involve a team	Delegate work to divide labour among team members.
	Seek early peer review for potential revisions to publications.
	Actively enlist support to facilitate research productivity at the school level.
Reward yourself for achievement	Plan rewards for achieving 'to dos' (e.g., replying to non-urgent emails for ten minutes; going for a short walk).
	Reward completion of parts of large projects instead of waiting until the entire work is finished.
Manage potential distractions	Create a work environment that is free from external distractions.
	Schedule work in a 'secure' or cloistered setting.
	Create a physical space where you keep your materials 'set up' and ready.
	Turn off visual and auditory interruptions (e.g., email/text alerts, phone).
	Determine potential internal distractions and create a separate list so when these distractions develop, they can be briefly recorded and dismissed from thought to focus on the work at hand.
	Avoid multitasking as this leads to unnecessary distractions and does not increase productivity.
	Learn how to say 'no' (see Table 17.3).

Strategy	Implementing Time Management Strategy
Solve problems and manage barriers	Appraise barriers and discuss solutions with mentors and peers. Test barriers' management strategies and assess for effectiveness.
Balance life	Plan and set time aside for adequate rest, sleep, family commitments, social engagements and regular physical activity.
Analyse progress and time management strategies periodically	Reassess productivity levels after applying time management solutions and implement changes where necessary. Reassess major goals at least quarterly. Consider using 'productivity' or 'project management' software.

Source: Adapted from Chase et al. (2013, pp. 157–8).

Critical to this is a work plan – which may sound really boring and look really 'old school' but can be a life-saver. At the beginning of each semester or study break, make a *realistic* weekly work plan – and stick to it! Table 17.2 is an example of a plan structured around an 8am–5pm, Monday to Friday work week and incorporating work-related activities only. Let me stress that this is an example. The scheduling illustrated is very clearly not going to work for everyone! For instance, as one woman academic has observed: 'If I don't stay up and grade after my kids go to bed, I just can't keep up' (Wolf-Wendel and Ward, 2015, p. 26). *Your* plan needs to accommodate *your* specific personal and institutional circumstances and it must allow sufficient time for you to actually accomplish the activities you have forecast. Allow time for all of your commitments, including not only those required to move you towards your scholarly ambitions, but also those needed to maintain your physical and mental health and sustain your personal relationships.[3] If you believe there is just not enough time in the week to do all that you need or seek to do, weigh up your priorities and, if possible, jettison those tasks that seem least likely to contribute to success and sustainability. Bear in mind too that there is no point in devising a plan if you know in your heart that it will not allow you to achieve all that you really need to do.

Table 17.2   *Example of a weekly work plan*

Time/Day	Monday	Tuesday	Wednesday	Thursday	Friday
0800	Email and admin	Email and admin	Email and admin	Flexible for overflow from unanticipated matters.	Email and admin
0900		PhD student meetings	Class preparation		Class preparation
1000	Class preparation		Teaching		
1100	Teaching	Staff meeting or school research seminar	Journal and community service activities	School morning tea	
1200				Research and writing	Teaching
1300	Lunch	Lunch	Lunch		Lunch
1330	Class preparation	Office hours, email and marking	Office hours, email and marking		Research and writing
1400	Teaching	PhD student meetings	Research and writing		
1500					
1600	Email and marketing	Class preparation			
1700					

As suggested above, the schedule shown in Table 17.2 does not incorporate time for exercise, time with partner, any other jobs you may have, pets and family and so on. Instead, it apportions to work-related activities a 'typical' 8–5 working week and assumes that weekends and the hours before 8am and after 5pm can be dedicated to commitments to family and friends, religious devotion, and other rest and recreation activities, however you plan those. Just do not forget to take those hours 'off'! As one academic observed in a study by Wolf-Wendel and Ward (2015, p. 26), 'I love my work. I love what I do. No one tells me when to stop.' And if there is no one to tell you when to stop, to insist that you spend time with family, to encourage you to exercise, or even to eat, you must to do that for yourself. I know from my own experience and from those of colleagues that if you do not choose to slow down, to take a break or to stop, your body and mind may find interesting ways of insisting on some respite.

You might look at a work plan such as that shown in Table 17.2 and think that an 8–5, Monday to Friday work schedule (plus allowances for breaks) does not allow enough time to do all that you feel you need to do. But in a fascinating blog, Meghan Duffy (2015) dismantles the myth that to succeed in academia you need to work 80 hours a week. Not only does Duffy make clear the physical impossibility of that duration of labour but she also makes a strong case for the need to work more efficiently for fewer hours. To put this into practice she advocates logging work hours, as a lawyer records billable hours, to see exactly how much time you devote to research, teaching and service activities and how much is 'wasted' in breaks between projects or tasks. On the basis of her own analyses she found that as an early-career academic working as hard as possible, she could toil about 60 hours each week. More typically, however, she worked 40–50 hours, a commitment her historical evidence indicates is sustainable. And if those hours are used efficiently, they can be very productive. 'Efficiencies' can be achieved by a range of means including cutting preparation time for teaching (e.g., some more senior colleagues may be prepared to provide guidance on amount, depth and pace of material to be covered in classes and ways of ensuring classes are taught effectively as well as efficiently); offering clearly specified office hours for student consultation; and seeking out/accepting only those institutional service roles linked to your research programme (Perkel, 2015, pp. 517–18). Because having children is quite remarkably said to help some scholars be more productive, you may find it helpful to speak to a colleague with children to see how they manage their professional and personal time. On this matter, one academic interviewed by Wolf-Wendel and Ward (2015, p. 26) remarks: 'I used to waste a lot of time, but now that I have a baby and I need to drop her off and pick up, I need to be more focused with my research and writing. I piddle about a lot less than I used to.' In short then, it is not the number of hours you claim to work that is important; it is what you do with those hours that matters.

But there are some other key matters you may wish to consider in establishing your everyday work hours – just how much work will you be doing for 'free'? How much of your labour are you prepared to give away for no payment? And what do your individual 'donations' of free work imply for your colleagues and for others trying to secure diminishing numbers of academic jobs? Let me explain. While 'permanent' academic staff may not be paid an hourly rate, most have salary and entitlements based on a notional work week – typically between 36 and 40 hours. For example, at England's University of Oxford (2022) academic-related staff work such hours as are reasonably required to carry out their duties but for the purposes of calculating pro-rata salary and holiday entitlements, a figure of 37.5 hours per week is applied. The Faculty of Arts at Aarhus University (2018) in Sweden expects academic staff to work 1643 hours per year, which equates to 35.7 hours per week (allowing for the prescribed six weeks of annual holiday). And across Australia, the maximum number of ordinary working hours across the economy is 38 hours per week (Trounson, 2015). However, research by Australia's National Tertiary Education Union (NTEU Australia, 2015), involving almost 7000 university staff, suggested that through labours in excess of that for which they are paid, academic staff donate in the order of 20 million hours of in-kind labour to the nation's universities, which translates into almost 12 000 full-time equivalent jobs. In financial terms, and at the time of the research, university employees were effectively 'donating' A$1.7 billion each year to the sector through unpaid overtime, making them the largest philanthropic contributors to the country's public universities! And according to the United Kingdom's University and College Union (2022), staff at universities and colleges across the UK are doing the equivalent of at least two days of unpaid work every week! So, while you as an individual may feel the need to work long hours to achieve some elements of academic success, do give some consideration to their financial cost, in terms of the reduced hourly pay you are attracting; to the burdens you are applying to colleagues struggling to find work; and to the time you are spending away from family, recreation and hobbies and other activities that are part of a healthy, successful life.

Taking into account such matters, draw up an hour-by-hour weekly plan setting out all of the tasks that you must do at specific times (see Table 17.2), giving heed to Boice's (2000) wise counsel to always be moderate in your activities. In your timetable, try to set aside dedicated times to stop for lunch, to exercise, or to catch up with friends and colleagues over coffee. Aside from being personally reinvigorating, such meetings are critical to the intellectual life and well-being of a university. It may be helpful to have large blocks of time, such as a day each week, for research, writing or professional reflection. Some people work differently, isolating a few hours every working day to maintain their research and writing momentum. A good deal depends on your personality, the kind of work you are doing and so on. Nonetheless, however you do it, make the time to write and participate in research projects or to make useful inroads to your teaching. And work out how much time you realistically need to dedicate each week to tasks such as responding to emails, community service activities, postgraduate student supervision, class preparation, marking and research (Box 17.1). Make space in the timetable for all that you must do, bearing in mind that you are more or less preparing an employment contract with yourself whereby you will not be able to work on teaching, for instance, when you have assigned yourself time to manage correspondence. Demarcate the time you spend on these tasks. Block out interruptions such as phone calls, email and knocks on the door. Apply yourself diligently and consistently to the tasks you have assigned yourself. This kind of planned, solid work should allow you to achieve all you can reasonably expect – and maybe more – within a well-balanced work week. Importantly it should also offer the opportunity to be productive, committed, connected and enthusiastic. But do be aware that it can take some self-discipline to honour your 'contract':

> I have chosen to prioritise work–life balance and organise my work day to take advantage of when I am most productive. I feel I work hard at work, but relax after hours, although in reality I do spend quite a lot of time worrying and thinking about work when I am not there. It takes considerable discipline to leave work at work. (Lecturer, female, 35–39 years, cited in Sutherland et al., 2013, p. 23)

BOX 17.1 POSSIBLE FIELDS TO INCLUDE IN A WEEKLY TIME MANAGEMENT PLAN

- Email, other correspondence and routine administration.
- Complex administration.
- Marking.
- Postgraduate student supervision.
- Research/writing.
- Community service activities.
- Journal editing
- Manuscript reviewing.
- Class preparation.
- Office hours/student contact hours.
- Meals.
- Physical exercise, meditation and other self-care activities.
- Family time.
- Domestic duties.
- Personal commitments (e.g., time for medical or dental appointments).

Over and above self-discipline, another vital affiliate to a planned work week is building up your capacity to say 'no' (see, for example, Richards, 2012, p. 7 and Table 17.3). 'The motivation for saying no is that you can say yes to projects you really care about' (De Cruz, 2016). While we all arguably have a duty to our colleagues to do our share of refereeing and guest lectures and so on, you should feel entitled to say no once you have done some amount that seems to be a reasonable share. De Cruz (2016) suggests, for example, refereeing at least three times as many papers as you submit in a year. If you believe you have honoured fair levels of supplementary collegial work you can feel free to dedicate yourself to your personal scholarly pursuits.

Table 17.3   *How to say 'no': tactful ways of declining requests that might reduce your capacities for a successful career*

Strategy	Sample Wording
Do not make an immediate decision: the time delay offers opportunity to consider whether the activity fits your priorities[a]	Let me think about it and get back to you. I will review my other commitments and let you know. I need to talk with my mentor/supervisor before making any commitments. That is an interesting opportunity. I will need to carefully consider my other obligations and get back to you. I need to examine my other commitments to make sure I would have adequate time to do high-quality work. I will let you know by …
Delay additional time commitments	I am unable to assume any new responsibilities until ___ happens (e.g., my grant application is submitted next year). I am sorry, I can't help you now. Please ask again after ___ happens.
Declare that you are not the right person for the job	I wish I could help you but that is outside my area of expertise. I am sorry: I don't have the knowledge to help with this problem. I think ___ would be much better qualified to work on this.
Acknowledge an excellent opportunity: this allows you to recognize the importance of the work without becoming personally involved	This is a great opportunity. Unfortunately, I am unable to participate at this time. I appreciate the offer to be involved in this important work and am sorry I cannot participate. Thanks for letting me know about this excellent opportunity. I am sorry I am not in a position to accept this offer.
Blame your mentor/supervisor (but only if they have agreed to be blamed!)	My mentor told me not to take on any additional service responsibilities at this time. My chair asked me to discuss all time commitments with her/him before making a decision. My mentor is insistent I do not join any other committees until my grant application is submitted later this year.

Strategy	Sample Wording
Compliment the requestor before declining	I would love to work with you because I know you are an expert in this area. Unfortunately I am unable to join the project. I admire your dedication to this topic and am sorry that I am not able to work with you at this time. I would really enjoy working with you because you are an expert and regret that I have to decline this wonderful opportunity. There are few people I would rather work with and am sorry I am unable to participate.
Express gratitude at being asked, then decline	I am flattered that you think I could help with ___. Unfortunately I am unable to be involved.
Avoid specific excuses, unless the excuse is incontrovertible, especially if the inviter is likely to argue about the excuse	I appreciate this opportunity but I'm afraid it just will not work for me. I am sorry but I am not able to help you. You are doing important work. Unfortunately I cannot help you. That is not something I do.
Acknowledge that this is an important problem to the requestor without becoming personally involved	I know you care deeply about ___. I am sorry I cannot help at this time. I agree this is a very important problem. Unfortunately I am not able to help. I see this is an important challenge. I am sure you will find a good solution. Sorry I can't help you develop the solution.
Suggest a smaller role than the one offered	I am unable to be a task force member, but perhaps I could offer ideas related to my area of expertise at one of its meetings? I cannot join as a co-investigator, but I would be glad to participate in occasional meetings to discuss ___. I am unable to take on a co-author role, but I am willing to comment on a draft of the paper.
Negotiate trade-offs to meet the requestor's needs	I could help you with ___ committee if I were released from ___ committee. Are you able to arrange that? I am unable to join the task force this year. Could I become a member next year?

Note: [a]In my own experience, any need I feel for a long period of consideration signals a fundamental reluctance to accept the request.
Source: Adapted from Chase et al. (2013, pp. 174–5).

To conclude, managing your time effectively – if not ruthlessly – is critical to developing and sustaining a successful academic career. Indeed, it is probably the single most useful strategy you can pursue to ensure a rewarding work life, balanced productively with time for rest, recreation and a satisfying social life.

For your own sake and for the well-being of those around you, give it serious attention.

NOTES

1. One respondent to the Times Higher Education 2016 University Workplace Survey observed: 'I thought this was my dream job and would stay until I retire, but [the] workload is unmanageable.' She went on to point out that all of her colleagues are also working unspeakably long hours (Grove, 2016).
2. Perkel (2015, p. 518) suggests that a department chair can be a helpful ally to women scholars (and presumably members of identified minority groups) deciding which service requests to accept.
3. Over half (51 per cent) of academics who completed the 2016 Times Higher Education University Workplace Survey in the UK said their job has a negative impact on their health (Grove, 2016).

18. Publish papers

> Get started on publishing as soon as you can. It is the key determinant of progression.

> Focus on research and international publications; do as little teaching and service as possible.

> (Anonymous university managers, New Zealand, cited in Sutherland et al., 2013, p. 26)

As these quotations from a major study of academic success in New Zealand proclaim, publishing is regarded by some as the key activity expected of an objectively successful academic in contemporary universities. For universities, funding agencies and other organizations, publishing offers a fairly straightforward, high-quality empirical marker by which the 'performance' of individual academics from almost every discipline may be assessed. Although the quality of the marker is becoming increasingly questionable as dubious new journals and predatory publishers emerge (see, for example, Beall and Anonymous, 2021) and as academics and universities learn to 'game' output-based evaluation systems (e.g., Bonnell, 2016; Delgado López-Cózar et al., 2014; Gans, 2011; Lin, 2013), publication productivity remains a central consideration in individual and institutional assessments of worth and excellence (e.g., Center for World University Rankings; Times Higher Education World University Rankings). The combination of simplicity of measurement, arguable cross-disciplinary comparability, and the growing public relations significance of academic ranking systems (discussed in Chapter 12) mean that publication output, and, to a lesser degree, quality, have been stressed increasingly by universities since the late 1980s.

And as institutional emphasis on publications has grown, so too has the volume of advice on how to get published. There are now very many good books, articles, webinars and blogs on all aspects of academic publishing (e.g., Brunn, 1988; Day, 2007; EURAXESS et al., 2022; Fargotstein, 2014; Klingner et al., 2005; Leyshon, 2013; Obeng-Odoom, 2014) whose detailed guidance I will not replicate in detail here. Major journal publishers like Sage and Wiley-Blackwell provide valuable assistance on writing in ways that will help make your article accessible and successful (e.g., Wiley-Blackwell's 2022 advice on writing to maximize the chances of your article being found via search engines; Sage's 2022 excellent 'Help readers find your article'). Increasingly, universities are running helpful courses and workshops for postgraduate students, early-career academics and others on publication as a key element in developing a scholarly career. Especially given the pace at which changes in publishing are occurring (e.g., Conrad and Padula, 2022; Forgues and Liarte, 2013; McNaught, 2015), it is a good idea to take advantage of these and to read books, articles and posts on publishing. But, despite having promised not to duplicate advice on publishing provided in greater detail elsewhere, it is apposite in the context of this book to set out a small number of key summary points.

SOME KEY POINTS ON SUCCESSFUL ACADEMIC PUBLISHING

Familiarize Yourself with the Procedures of Publishing

Learn how the publishing process works and how you, as an author and maybe later referee, editorial board member, or editor fit in. What makes editors and referees tick? What annoys them? What are the current trends and developments in publishing? This background will help you better understand the place and significance of your work in the publishing process and make you a much more confident participant in it. Frequently updated guides to the mechanics of publishing are offered by many publishing houses (e.g., Elsevier's *How to Publish in Scholarly Journals*), academic libraries (e.g. University of Western Australia's *How to Publish and Disseminate Research*) and through countless blogs. Publishers run information sessions on developments in scholarly publishing. They provide reports to the regular conferences of the professional societies on whose behalf they publish. Take advantage of the insights these opportunities offer.

Learn About the Local Metrics and Cultures of Publishing

As implied in the introduction to this chapter, over and above disseminating research findings, scholarly publishing has other functions. These include providing metrics for the distribution of research funding; for the allocation of departmental resources; and in decision-making for promotions. But the ways in which these are conducted and the value given to different forms and types of publication vary from one place to another. In some institutions, joint authorships are regarded highly, with co-authored papers being assigned the same 'value' as sole-authored works. In other places the converse is true, with the 'value' attached to jointly authored works being divided equally by the number of authors. Likewise, the status of chapters relative to refereed journal articles may be contested. Edited books may be given little value or lots. A textbook, with a vast international student audience numbering in the thousands, may be regarded as a lesser form of publication than a scholarly book purchased by 300 academic libraries. Some disciplines give weight to forms of public output other than refereed works (e.g., art installations, documentaries). And in some departments, disciplines, institutions and jurisdictions, there are explicit hierarchies of journals and book publishers to which scholars are directed. Take steps to find out all you can about such idiosyncrasies, how they apply to you, and how you can use them to your advantage. If you move from one institution or jurisdiction to another, do not assume the 'rules' and culture will be the same. Consult your supervisor, your colleagues and your institution's research services office to find out exactly how things work. This all being said, through your investigations you are likely to find that at their heart, there do tend to be some consistent themes in many publishing evaluation systems and to satisfy these you need to focus on conducting good research and publishing as often as you can, in ways consistent with the maintenance of quality, and being sure that your work is disseminated through reputable journals/publishers communicating with audiences interested in your work.

Start Publishing Early in Your Career

Every time you write a paper for a class in which you are a student or each time you prepare a presentation for a conference, approach that work in a way that offers the prospect of a publication (Richards, 2012, p. 7). An early start to publishing can open up scholarship and fellowship opportunities and signal your research potential and credentials to prospective employers. That early start can even begin at the undergraduate level. There is an expanding array of opportunities to start publishing as an undergraduate student. In recent decades many online, peer-reviewed journals for undergraduate (and postgraduate) students have emerged. Some examples are set out in Box 18.1.

BOX 18.1 EXAMPLES OF ONLINE JOURNALS FOR DISSEMINATION OF WORK BY UNDERGRADUATE AND POSTGRADUATE STUDENTS

Berkeley Undergraduate Journal (established 1987) (humanities and social sciences)
Columbia Journal of History (established 2008)
Columbia Undergraduate Research Journal (established 2014)
Digital Literature Review (established 2014)
Graduate Journal of Asia Pacific Studies (established 2003)

Harvard Political Review (established 1969)
Metamorphosis (established 2009) (multidisciplinary)
Reinvention: An International Journal of Undergraduate Research (established 2007) (any discipline)
Afkar. The Undergraduate Journal of Middle East Studies (established 2019)
you are here: the journal of creative geography (established 1998)
Young Scholars in Writing (established 2003) (undergraduate research in writing and rhetoric)

Note: A more extensive list of undergraduate journals is published online by the US Council on Undergraduate Research and is available at https://www.cur.org/engage/undergraduate/journals/listing/

Besides providing an opportunity for nascent scholars to 'dip their toe' in publishing waters, journals such as those listed in Box 18.1 disseminate sometimes high-quality work that otherwise might not see the light of day, model excellent work to student-peers, provide tangible evidence of achievement that can be used to support scholarship and other funding applications, and provide budding academics with the chance to demonstrate the kind of ambition and talent essential to a successful academic career. Beyond the undergraduate level, work with your adviser or mentor to seek out ways of translating your Honours, Masters or doctoral work into meaningful publications. But remember this: your thesis is your intellectual property – a matter some advisers and supervisors would do well to remember.[1] As Richards (2012, p. 6) observes:

> Professors get paid to advise, so there is no obligation for you to list your adviser as a co-author on anything you publish out of your work. Once in a while a professor will try to make a student believe such a practice is the norm, but it is not. If the professor truly deserves credit on your dissertation, then it is not truly your dissertation, and you should not graduate.

Direct Your Work to the Most Appropriate Outlet

This is probably the single most important key to getting your paper published. Do your homework to find a journal whose aims are aligned with the content of your paper. Even the best-quality paper may not be published if it is submitted to a journal whose aims do not suit it. For example, irrespective of its merits, a paper on 'The impact of the Great Irish Famine on Ireland's economic history' is unlikely to be accepted by *Gender, Place & Culture*, a journal whose explicit aim is to provide a forum for debate in human geography and related disciplines on theoretically informed research concerned with gender issues. If you are new to publishing and given that the number of journals available globally is multiplying, further confusing a complex publishing landscape, it can be difficult to find the most promising outlets. Fortunately, however, there are several 'match-making' strategies that can help link your paper to the right journal:

1.	To begin, look at the reference list you have developed for your work to see which journals and publishers are recorded. There is a good chance that these are the channels you should be considering.
2.	Ask your adviser, supervisor, mentors, or experienced colleagues for their opinions and insights about the best journals or publishers for your work and career stage.
3.	Get involved in workshops convened by leaders in your field that will publish journal articles in special issues. This is a helpful way to align your work with influential others and to find a place in an appropriate journal.
4.	Get a useful sense of some of the most influential journals in your field by checking the Web of Science *Master Journal List* Manuscript Matcher or Clarivate Analytics' *Journal Citation Reports* (JCR). Amongst other things, JCR uses citation data to evaluate the significance of, and interrelationships between, the world's leading journals.
5.	Check major publishers' websites (Box 18.2) for journal ideas. These sites provide a wonderful overview of, and links to, the plethora of journals that are available. The outlet you select for your research needs to be aligned to the subject of your work and to your particular regional, temporal, methodological or topical approach.

## BOX 18.2	MAJOR SCHOLARLY PUBLISHERS AND THEIR WEBSITES

Hachette UK (formerly Hodder Headline)	https://www.hachette.co.uk/
RELX Group	https://www.relx.com/
Sage	http://www.sagepub.com/
Taylor & Francis	https://www.tandfonline.com/
Wiley (formerly with Blackwell)	wiley/com

6.	Use journal-finding software. While publishers' websites are very helpful, their 'stable' of journals can be so large as to be overwhelming. To help overcome this problem, several major publishers such as Elsevier and Springer as well as consortia of academics, publishers and software developers (e.g., JournalGuide) offer online facilities to help scholars find journals suited to their paper. Typically, these require you to enter details of your paper's abstract, title, keywords and general field of interest, and they use that information to match your paper to those of the publisher's journals that appear to offer a good fit.

7. Review potential journals' distinct explicit missions to assess the quality of the fit with your paper. Journals broadcast details of the kinds of work in they are interested in. A few examples are set out in Box 18.3. Likewise, most book publishers have particular markets and audiences that they announce on their websites. For example, Oxford University Press's offices focus on textbooks for their regions (e.g., Australia and New Zealand, Canada, United States), and British-based Edward Elgar Publishing specializes in law, business and management, economics and the social sciences for a global English-language market. Take account of these matters, as well as impact factors, when determining where to send your work. It will have much greater chance of a warm reception, acceptance and broad readership if you send it to the right journal or publisher.

BOX 18.3 EXAMPLES OF SCHOLARLY JOURNAL MISSIONS

American Journal of Sociology
'Established in 1895 as the first U.S. scholarly journal in its field, the *American Journal of Sociology* (AJS) remains a leading voice for analysis and research in the social sciences. The Sociology Department [at the University of Chicago] collectively publishes the journal, which presents pathbreaking work from all areas of sociology, with an emphasis on theory building and innovative methods. AJS strives to speak to the general sociological reader and is open to sociologically informed contributions from anthropologists, statisticians, economists, educators, historians, and political scientists. AJS prizes research that offers new ways of understanding the social; for example, a recent issue was organized around the topic of genetic influences on social interaction.'

British Journal of Political Science
'*British Journal of Political Science* (BJPo/S) is a broadly based journal aiming to cover developments across a wide range of countries and specialisms. Contributions are drawn from all fields of political science (including political theory, political behaviour, public policy and international relations), and articles from scholars in related disciplines (sociology, social psychology, economics and philosophy) appear frequently. With a reputa-

tion established over 50 years of publication, BJPolS is widely recognised as one of the premier journals in its field.'

The Journal of Modern History
'*The Journal of Modern History* is recognized as the leading journal worldwide for the study of all varieties of European history. The journal's broad geographical and temporal scope – the history of Europe since the Renaissance – makes it unique: JMH explores not only events and movements in single countries but also broader questions that span particular times and places.'

The New Zealand Journal of Educational Studies
'This journal presents original reports, critical reviews of educational theory and policy, discussions and commentaries on conceptual and methodological issues in educational research, reports on research in progress, and book reviews. Its multidisciplinary and interdisciplinary approach aims to nurture and promote educational research. The journal is an official publication of the New Zealand Association for Research in Education.'

The Professional Geographer
'Publishes short articles of academic or applied geography, emphasizing empirical studies and methodologies. These features may range in content and approach from rigorously analytic to broadly philosophical or prescriptive. The journal provides a forum for new ideas and alternative viewpoints. Contents include regular manuscripts, forums, commentaries on published PG articles, and research notes.'

A corollary of the advice set out above on finding the right journal is that you should also try to avoid publications regarded poorly in your field. These characteristically include unrefereed conference proceedings and technical and professional trade magazines which, for all their practical merits, are not usually regarded as prestigious or useful as good archival research journals for developing an academic career. Take particular care to avoid so-called predatory open access journals. There are helpful lists of some of these available online and it pays to consult them (e.g. Beall and Anonymous, 2021).[2] More positively DOAJ (Directory of Open Access Journals) publishes a credible and up-to-date list of reputable online open access journals at https://doaj.org/.

Different disciplines also have different hierarchies of publication type. For example, refereed conference proceedings may be very well regarded in some fields and not in others. As noted above, be sure you develop your understanding of your discipline's publication culture.

Aim for Quality, Not Quantity

Focus on the *best* journals (and book publishers). Distinguished American sociologist Robert K. Merton's 1968 (p. 61) observations on this are insightful:

> Outstanding scientists tend to develop an immunity to *insanabile scribendi cacoethes* (the itch to publish). Since they prefer their published work to be significant and fruitful rather than merely extensive, their contributions are apt to matter. This in turn reinforces the expectations of their fellow scientists that what these eminent scientists publish (at least during their most productive period) will be worth close attention.

He goes on:

> Fermi or Pauling or G.N. Lewis or Weisskopf sees fit to report this in print and so it is apt to be important (since, with some consistency, they have made important contributions in the past); since it is probably important, it should be read with special care; and the more attention one gives it, the more one is apt to get out of it. This becomes a self-confirming process, making for the greater evocative effect of publications by eminent men [*sic*] of science. (Merton, 1968, pp. 61–2)

In other words, hard work early in one's career to develop a reputation for high-quality, insightful contributions in good journals should pay dividends later. To some degree, assessments of quality and reputation are now being quantified, as evidenced by emerging global and discipline-focussed rankings of individual scholar impact using readily available Hirsch (h) index data such as that derived from Google Scholar. One such example is Webometrics' 'Highly Cited Researchers (h>100) according to their Google Scholar Citations public profiles'. It seems likely that just as university rankings have been used as proxies for quality these more individually-focussed assessments will find growing influence in, for example, decisions on academic and editorial board appointments and promotion decisions.

Publish Often

Publish often, taking the emphasis on quality as an important caveat. It is all very well for your reputation – and ultimately for your h-index – to publish a small number of high-quality papers that become cited widely, but at the same time you are almost assuredly going to be assessed at appointment and promotion time on the volume of your output too. So, you need to tread a fine line between publishing enough to satisfy institutional expectations and publishing work that is of sufficient quality to attract critical attention!

According to 'Drew's Law on publishing papers' (Gray and Drew, 2012, p. 10) 'every paper can be published somewhere'. This *may* be true, but whether there is value in getting everything published is quite a different question. Do your good research justice by publishing in high-quality outlets. One publication in a very good journal can do more for your career (e.g., promotions, job applications) than several in lower-ranked outlets.

Consider Publishing with Peers and Senior Colleagues

Publishing with peers and senior colleagues may enrich your skills in publishing (as well as those of your colleagues) and, depending on who you publish with, enhance your scholarly reputation. Choose your co-authors with care. If you do collaborate with others, be sure to have some explicit and shared understanding of the nature of your relationship. Perhaps develop a contract of sorts that makes clear what the author order will be;[3] who is responsible for what work, and when; and what journal you plan to send the paper to. Consider issues set out in the International Committee of Medical Journal Editors' *Recommendations for the Conduct, Reporting, Editing, and Publication of Scholarly Work in Medical Journals* (ICMJE, 2022a) when preparing for collaborative authorship. Specifically, the ICMJE (2022b) recommends that authorship be based on four criteria, set out in Box 18.4. Though written specifically for biomedical scientists, in the absence of many alternatives these guidelines provide exceedingly useful direction for researchers from other fields. COPE (Committee on Publication Ethics) is another useful source of guidance on authorship – as well as many other ethical matters. Their recent resource on 'How to recognise potential authorship problems' (COPE Council 2021) is helpful. Some universities, publishers and other scholarly organizations have guidelines that may be more useful and appropriate for your specific discipline. There are also national guidelines on publication, such as the Australian Code for the Responsible Conduct of Research.[4]

BOX 18.4   CRITERIA FOR AUTHORSHIP

To be included as an author a contributor should satisfy each of the following criteria:

* Substantial contributions to the conception or design of the work; or the acquisition, analysis, or interpretation of data for the work; AND
* Drafting the work or revising it critically for important intellectual content; AND
* Final approval of the version to be published; AND

• Agreement to be accountable for all aspects of the work in ensuring that questions related to the accuracy or integrity of any part of the work are appropriately investigated and resolved.

Source: ICMJE (2022b).

Develop a Pipeline of Papers

As a young scholar, one more senior colleague explained to me that to maintain a solid, steady level of publication output he always had one paper in press, one in review and one 'under construction'. (Some overachievers do this with books!) Because journal and book publishing is typically characterized by very long delays between submission and publication (Table 18.1) you cannot afford to sit around doing nothing awaiting referee comments or proofs of your latest paper. After you have submitted one paper or book for publication, take some time to celebrate that moment and then get moving on your next publication.

Table 18.1   Publishing process and timelines – journal articles

Step	By	Time Required
1. Prepare copy of article, write cover letter, submit through online manuscript management system or by email	You	1 day–1 week
2. Acknowledge manuscript's receipt	Editor's office	1–2 weeks
3. Decide who is to referee	Editor	1–4 weeks
4. Article details sent to prospective referees who may or may not agree to participate. Many prospective referees refuse and others accept, only never to produce the goods	Editor or editor's office	1–8 weeks
5. Manuscript review time and submission of referee comments to editor. Ironically, busy scholars are often the swiftest and most insightful referees!	Referees	1 day–16 weeks
6. Editorial accept/revise/reject/decision	Editor	1–3 weeks
7. Author revision period	Author	1 day–1 year
8. Editorial review (this may involve a return to step 4 if the revised paper needs to go back to referees)	Editor	1 day–4 weeks

Step	By	Time Required
9. Editorial accept/revise/reject/decision. Depending on the outcome, this could involve a return to step 7	Editor	1 day–3 weeks
10. Accepted manuscript put in queue for publication	Editor's office	1 day–1 week
11. Manuscript sent to production team	Editor's office	1 day–1 week
12. Manuscript is edited, typeset and subject to proofreading queries	Production editor	1–8 weeks
13. Manuscript (called 'galley proofs' or more commonly 'uncorrected proofs' if in digital form) sent to author for checking and response to proof-reading queries	Production editor	1 day
14. Galley proofs checked and returned to production editor	Author	1 week
15. Galley proofs and author responses checked	Editor	1 day–2 weeks
16. Manuscript prepared for final production and published as an online version of record (e.g., via Wiley's Early View; Sage's OnlineFirst). Process stops here for fully online journals	Production editor	1–2 weeks
17. Manuscript assigned to an issue	Editor	No time (completed while the manuscript is online)
18. Manuscript printed and issue bound	Production team	1 month–2 years depending on journal backlog
19. Journal issue is mailed to subscribers. Author may receive additional hard copy offprints or access to PDF of the published paper for distribution to family and colleagues	Production team	2–6 weeks

Avoid Perfectionism

Do not make the mistake of trying to edit and rewrite until your paper or book is flawless. That will just never happen. Moreover, as you labour to produce perfect sentences, your research may be dating quickly. And it is always easy to procrastinate, making the excuse to yourself and others that somewhere else someone else has just published something on the subject that really needs to be considered in your manuscript. So it is that you will never finish. So, pick a target date to stop writing and stick to that deadline. Get your work out swiftly. Remember too, few books or articles are accepted by referees or editors without suggestions for revision. No matter how perfect you think your work, there will almost always be someone who sees flaws in it. You will almost always have to make changes.

Revise Journal Papers Thoughtfully and Promptly

When you receive comments back on a manuscript you have submitted for publication do take care to revise promptly, but perhaps not so quickly that editors and referees have reason to believe you have given their recommendations faint regard and not so slowly that new problems are created. Most book, chapter or journal manuscripts received back from editors will require modification. It can certainly be frustrating to deal with these comments, especially when you disagree with them, but delaying things will not make things better. In the interim, editors or reviewers may change and the new ones your work encounters may emphasize different matters from their predecessors (Sternberg, 2013).

Persist

If at first your paper or book proposal is rejected, do not give up. Take heed of the referees' comments, revise, and resubmit or submit to another journal or publisher. If your work is good, you will find a publisher. And at all times in the sometimes frustrating publication process, treat editors with respect. Remember, many editors and referees are unpaid, doing the best they can with limited resources (see Hay, 2016b for a discussion). Be courteous. Be prompt. Be thorough.

Promote Your Work

It is all very well to publish in a scholarly journal, but with the vast growth in published output, it is easy for your work to become lost, even to colleagues actively seeking the kind of work you have prepared. Partly for this reason most large scholarly publishers (e.g., Routledge, Sage, Taylor & Francis) and individual journals now provide their authors with advice on how to bring published work to broader attention. That online advice is helpful – some of it is distilled and supplemented in Box 18.5. While advice such as that cited at the outset of this chapter to focus almost exclusively on publishing as a pathway to career success may be somewhat misguided, publishing high-quality papers in reputable journals is certainly a critical component of academic success. Take time to learn about publishing and put those lessons into practice. Neglect this dimension of your career at your peril.

BOX 18.5 SOME WAYS TO PROMOTE YOUR JOURNAL ARTICLE

- Add details of the article to your email signature block and to your personal and institutional web pages.
- Use social media such as Facebook, LinkedIn, and blogs to publicize your work.
- Send a note to key scholars you have cited and/or who are working in the field alerting them to the article's publication.
- Add your article to student reading lists.
- Deliver public lectures on the paper's material on campus, at other institutions, and to relevant community or professional groups.
- Engage with mass media (do radio interviews, newspaper articles, on-campus stories that may be picked up by broader media). Check with your institution's PR/media people to see how they can assist.
- Transform the scholarly publication into an article for a publication such as The Conversation (TheConversation.com) that has a broader public audience, some of whom may be persuaded to seek out the original work.

NOTES

1. Although the guidance comes from outside the Arts, Social Sciences and Humanities, the International Committee of Medical Journal Editors (ICJME, 2022a) offers very helpful and influential counsel about authorship. Their four key criteria are set out in Box 18.4 of this book.
2. The term 'predatory open access journal' was coined by American librarian Jeffrey Beall. From about 2008 he produced an influential list of such journals. On 15 January 2017 Beall's List, published originally on *Scholarly Open Access* at http://scholarlyoa.com/publishers/, was removed from the web for reasons that remain unclear. However, cached versions are still available. For example, Yale University Library offers a link of the cached version at https://archive.fo/6EByy. There is also a version at https://beallslist.net/ which is an updated rendering of Beall's original list (Beall and Anonymous, 2021).
3. Author order is significant in some fields and countries (Johnson, 2011, p. 32) and conventions on the placement of senior authors vary from one field to another. Seek counsel from a mentor or supervisor when you are working out author order on collaboratively written papers.
4. Accessed 20 June 2022 at https://www.nhmrc.gov.au/about-us/publications/australian-code-responsible-conduct-research-2018.

19. Publish a book (or two)

Publishing a book is a tremendous academic and personal achievement. A good book can very clearly launch or cement your role as a leader in your scholarly field. I have always been in awe of Paul Starr, who as a 34-year-old, wrote the magnificent *The Social Transformation of American Medicine*. This landmark 1982 volume traced, in exquisite, beautifully written detail, a 200-year history of the US health care system. The book won the 1983 Pulitzer Prize as well as a host of other notable awards, including the Bancroft Prize in American History, and helped to establish Starr's place as a leading contributor to sociology and public affairs. Aside from the career rewards book publishing can bring, 'Having the book physically in your hands, turning the pages and remembering the blood, sweat and tears that went into it, is a moment of euphoria' (Birkhead, in Murray, 2014).

Books generally offer more substantial and less ephemeral scholarly contributions than journal articles. As Paul Starr's magnum opus did, books can stand as major statements in a broader research and writing career as well as on your office bookshelves. A book allows you to explore and tease out complex ideas in more detail than is possible in shorter forms of publication. As your publication count grows, so you may find that your recollections and appreciation of the relative importance of most of your papers, commentaries and reviews diminishes. But even though more and more books are now published in electronic form, most are still issued as tangible artefacts and contribute to that sense that you are adding to the permanent record of scholarship in ways that journal paper writing may not.

In some academic contexts, publishing a book may be critical to your career. Indeed, there is enduring advice suggesting that in the United States securing tenure at most research universities requires publication of at least one book (Knox, 2023; Otis, 2008) and to secure a Fellowship of an organization such as the Royal Historical Society typically requires at least one book. For many early-career scholars, producing a book involves converting a dissertation – generally written for a particular purpose and for an audience who have to read it – into a book, which has readers who need to be convinced they want to read it. William Germano's (2013) book, *From Dissertation to Book*, provides careful counsel on this sometimes challenging task. Germano has also written another very successful book entitled *Getting it Published* (2016), which focuses on what publishers do and offers detailed advice on how to traverse publication successfully from contract to next book. If you wish to know more about the publishing process, you may find these volumes provide useful supplements to the material set out below, which moves quickly through book publishing practices for career success. There is also helpful advice available online and through organizations such as the US-based Textbook & Academic Authors Association.

FIND THE RIGHT PUBLISHER

There are at least four key matters to take into account when looking for the right publisher for your book. First, which publisher appears to be the best 'fit'? Be sure to match your topic with the publisher. Who published the books you have cited in the work you are proposing to the publisher? Who is publishing the best work in your field? As noted in Chapter 18 most book publishers have particular markets and audiences that they announce on their websites. As well as matching the topic and market to the publisher, give thought to the length of your book. Some publishers have now started to move towards producing short books of around 25 000 to 50 000 words and have special series for this purpose (e.g., Oxford University Press's hugely successful Very Short Introductions; Palgrave Pivot; Stanford Briefs). So, there is growing scope for shorter volumes as well as the 'traditional' 100 000–200 000-word productions. Look too for any book series that may be relevant. As Oxford University Press former Reference Acquisitions Editor Burke Gertenschlager (2016) suggests:

> [c]onsider submitting the manuscript for inclusion in a series. It will align you with an established list, raise your profile, and ensure purchase by academic libraries, which is more important than you think. Contact the series editor directly and ask if s/he would be interested in considering the work. With a series editor's imprimatur, you may get a better chance with an editor.

The second matter to take into account is whether the publisher is credible. Do they have a good reputation? Especially for your first book, aim for a prestigious university press (unless your book is one that you believe will be a significant commercial success). Publishing with a high-quality press will give you a great deal of career confidence and will also assure prospective employers of your abilities.

Do *not* make the mistake of sending your PhD to a dodgy publisher who has sent you an unsolicited email expressing their wish to publish your PhD without any revision. A number of 'publishing houses' (e.g., GRIN Verlag; Lambert Academic Publishing) appear to fish for prospective publications by monitoring institutional thesis repositories and other records of PhD graduation, and then sending emails to recent graduates indicating their interest in publishing the work with little or no editorial input and oversight. Aside from the fact that your thesis may already be available freely through institutional open access initiatives, publishing with such an organization will do little to advance your academic career. By contrast, it may actually harm it by damaging your reputation and constraining your copyright capacity to publish further from your work. If you receive any unsolicited approach from a publisher check their bona fides very, very carefully.

Indeed, in any quest for a good publisher, review online resources extensively and speak with staff in your university research services office and library to assess the quality of publishers. Look too for the ranked or annotated lists of publishing houses that a number of discipline bodies and universities now publish (e.g., American Political Science Rankings; American Philosophical Association's list of publishers; the SENSE rankings prepared by the Netherlands-based Research School for Socio-Economic and Natural Sciences of the Environment). Who do published colleagues recommend? Ask around. And do not be coy about making clear your ambitions to publish a book. While some less-than-charitable colleagues may mock your ambitions, most others will be supportive. And you will probably find that others who have gone down the book publishing path successfully will be only too happy to help.

Third, find out about the publisher's markets and marketing. Which publisher's books come to your attention on a day-to-day basis? Which publishers do you and colleagues pay attention to? Which publishers sell into markets relevant to your work? For example, if your book is about indigenous environmental management in Canada, is a UK-focussed publisher going to be in your best interests? Does the publisher distribute their books internationally? This can be difficult to assess accurately and is worth inquiring about. Some major 'global' publishing houses operate as a loosely interlinked collection of more or less independent regional entities and so while you may believe you will have access to international marketing opportunities, the reality may be different. Sales of your book may be confined to the much smaller local region of the publisher.

Finally, how long will it take to get your book published? Find out how many months or years will elapse between contract and hard copy and consider that timeframe against your personal and professional needs (e.g., time to next promotion or to a prospective job relocation). It can take several years for a book to see the light of day.

DEVELOP A PROPOSAL

Once you have found a prospective publisher, you will need to prepare a proposal for them to evaluate. Most reputable publishers provide proposal outlines online (e.g., Bloomsbury, Elsevier, Springer, Palgrave). You can also use one of those forms as a model if the publisher you wish to approach does not offer any such guidance. Alternatively, write to the publisher advising that you wish to submit a proposal and seeking their advice on matters they need considered. Box 19.1 provides some indication of the sorts of material that may be expected.

BOX 19.1 INFORMATION COMMONLY SOUGHT IN A BOOK PROPOSAL

- Book's title and subtitle.
- Summary of scope and content.
- Keywords to describe content.
- Compelling and concise description, written in layperson's language.
- Book category (e.g., monograph, reference, manual).
- Current form of the book (from 'ideas only' to a full draft).
- Table of contents.
- Chapter synopsis.
- Word count.
- Anticipated submission date.
- Number of figures, photos, illustrations and tables.
- Recommended peer reviewers.
- Sample material (e.g., a chapter).
- Market: who will read and buy this book?
- Competing or comparable books.
- Unique selling points (i.e., why would someone buy your book, not the competition; what does your book offer that others do not?).
- Opportunities for promoting the book (e.g., relevant conferences and professional societies; journals for review).
- Format in which you will provide the manuscript (e.g., hard copy or soft copy).
- Your biographical and contact details.

In your proposal you will need to justify your work and sell your capabilities to deliver a high-quality manuscript, on time. Be truthful. Do not exaggerate, but do not be unduly or overly modest about the book or your own capabilities. As Box 19.1 indicates, you will also need to point to the book's likely markets. Frost (2011) makes an interesting and counter-intuitive observation about this:

> The publisher will need to know which established markets your book will sell to. If you tell them it is like nothing else, you're actually telling them there's no established market. That is the last thing they want to hear because it takes a lot of time and money to create a market from scratch. If, however, you can describe your book as structured like Writer A's, or containing a discussion that counter-argues Writer B's, they know straight away who else they might sell to.

Write your proposal carefully. Especially if you are an author unknown to the publisher they will be assessing you and the quality of your work on the basis of the proposal.

When it's time to send your proposal to potential publishers (see Box 19.2), two important points need to be remembered. First, even if you have already written the book, do not send them the entire manuscript unsolicited. Send the proposal and a sample chapter or section, being sure it is a good one! Second, deal with one publisher at a time – or be upfront that your work is being considered elsewhere. Some publishers ask about simultaneous multiple submissions in their proposal form. If you really wish to approach several publishers at the same time, ask if they will consider your work under these terms or do they demand sole agency? Whatever you do – single publisher or several – let the publishers know. 'Keep in mind that if two or more presses like your book and want to offer you a contract after they have invested time in [reviewing] your manuscript, the ones you turn down are going to be unhappy, and you might want to work with them in the future' (Otis, 2008).

BOX 19.2   WHAT HAPPENS TO YOUR BOOK PROPOSAL?

- Editor conducts initial review of proposal.
- Editor may send the proposal to readers for ('blind') critical review. Appraisers are typically asked to consider matters such as:
  - What is the thesis of the work? Is the scholarship sound and up-to-date? Will the manuscript make a significant contribution to its field?
  - Is the presentation effective in terms of style and organization?
  - What is the primary audience for the work? To what extent is it likely to appeal to readers outside its main area of scholarship and to general readers?

- What are the major books published on this subject? How does this work compare with them?
- What revisions would you suggest? Do you recommend publication? Readers' identity is usually confidential.
- Assuming there is reviewer support for the proposal, the editor then negotiates aspects of the proposal with author.
- The proposal proceeds to the final stage of consideration: financial review and a decision from the publisher's review committee.

NEGOTIATE A GOOD CONTRACT

Good news! Your book proposal has successfully navigated the process set out in Box 19.2 and has been accepted by the publisher who has sent you a lengthy contract to consider and sign. What scope do you have to tailor this to suit your specific needs and ambitions?

The answer is, not much. Most reputable book publishers have standard contracts that specify their own responsibilities in the production of a book as well as those of the author (or editor). The contract usually assigns to the publisher the full and exclusive right to publish the work. It will stipulate the format and deadlines for the manuscript submission, including electronic details, numbers of figures, tables, photographs and other illustrations, and word count. It will also set out royalty rates, information about any advance payments, details of complimentary copies for the author, and describe the author's responsibilities for obtaining permissions, returning proofs and providing an index. Unless you are already well established as an academic superhero, you will probably find little scope to significantly amend important elements of a book contract – such as royalty levels, though there is a range of online advice available on areas in which there may be some opportunity to make your book more accessible to readers and/or to increase your financial returns (see, for example, Kara, 2018). Do not expect to make much if any – money out of publishing an academic book. Royalty rates usually lie between 5 and 15 per cent of publishers' *net* receipts and, as Berlatsky (2014) notes, many *successful* scholarly books sell only 350–1000 copies globally! Typically, contract negotiations are around the 'margins', such as who pays for indexing (you or the publisher), how many complimentary copies of the book you will receive, the timing of manuscript receipt and processing, who is to be involved in the important issue of cover design, and publisher support for marketing activities such as a book launch. Although there may not be too much scope for amendments to a contract, do remember that because it is an agreement between you and the publisher you are just as entitled to make specific demands as they are. Often a book contract will contain a clause noting that you will offer your next book to the publisher before presenting it to any other. You may be happy with this, or you may wish to keep your options open and so prefer to delete the appropriate clause. In my experience, publishers have never actually chased me for violating the 'next book' provision. Moreover, even if you did offer the publisher your next book without any desire to publish with them, you could always refuse to accept the terms of any second book contract.

Before you sign a contract, check to see if there is an appropriate lawyer at your institution who is able to cast their critical eye over it. Or you may wish to consult your relevant society of authors. There are many of these around the world (e.g., Australian Society of Authors; The Authors Guild (USA); The Irish Writers Union; New Zealand Society of Authors (PEN NZ Inc) Te Puni Kaituhi O Aotearoa; The Society of Authors (UK); The Writers' Union of Canada) and they may check your contract, as well as offering a range of author support and representation services.

You should also register with your relevant copyright or reproduction rights agency (Box 19.3). Their missions vary, but most work to ensure that appropriate payments are made to creators (e.g., authors) by government, educational bodies and other users of copyrighted materials. So, for example, material copied for classroom teaching purposes can be a source of revenue to the relevant author. Sometimes, these payments can be relatively generous. In my own experience, copyright agency payments often exceed publisher royalties.

BOX 19.3 COPYRIGHT AND REPRODUCTION RIGHTS ORGANIZATIONS AROUND THE WORLD

Access Copyright – Canada
AIDRO – Italy
Authors' Licensing and Collecting Society Limited – UK
Bonus Presskopia – Sweden
CADRA – Argentina
Copyright Agency Limited – Australia
Copyright Clearance Center – USA
Copyright Licensing Agency – UK
Copyright Licensing and Administration Society of Singapore Limited
Copyright Licensing New Zealand
CEDRO – Spain
CeMPro – Mexico
CFC – France

Copibec – Quebec
Copy-dan Writing – Denmark
DALRO – South Africa
Irish Copyright Licensing Agency
JACC – Japan
Kopinor – Norway
Kopiosto – Finland
Luxorr – Luxembourg
OSDEL – Greece
ProLitteris – Switzerland
Reprobel – Belgium
SIAE – Italy
Stichting Reprorecht – Netherlands
VGWort – Germany

Source: Copyright Agency Limited (Australia) (2023).

WRITE THE BOOK … 'SELL' THE BOOK

And now for the easy part – writing the book. Once you are contracted to produce a book you can set about the labour required to complete it. This is a time you will need to marshal all of the research skills, time management skills and other skills discussed in this book. When you have finished your manuscript *on time*, submit it to your commissioning editor. Surprisingly, because on-time delivery is quite uncommon, your punctuality may endear you to your commissioning editor and support your next book proposal!

After your manuscript has been submitted and checked, it will be copy-edited and moved through production. During this process, and as with journal articles, you will receive correspondence from the editor, copy-editor and others about the manuscript before it goes to print. You are also likely to be asked to provide more information to the publisher about marketing opportunities (Box 19.4), to write 'blurbs' for the cover and promotional material, to suggest the names of learned others who may be willing to provide quotes endorsing the book, and you may even be asked to contribute to a publisher's blog in ways that link the book to current events. Although it can be tedious, give careful attention to the publisher's requests for assistance on marketing matters. Your ambitions to maximize the book's audience are aligned!

BOX 19.4 EXAMPLES OF BOOK MARKETING QUESTIONS ASKED BY PUBLISHERS OF AUTHORS/EDITORS

- If you were researching in this general topic, which six keywords would you use to find books and articles of interest in Google?
- What are the five or six special features of the book? What distinguishes it from any existing books in the same subject area?
- Please list, in order of importance, the prime potential readership for your book and the reasons for their interest.
- Provide the names of key, relevant people who might be approached to write a short supportive statement about the book for its cover.
- What journals, both mainstream and specialized, might be interested in advertising or reviewing your book?
- Which blogs, online newsletters, or websites might be willing to review or promote your book?
- If your book could potentially be used as a text, for which courses do you feel it might be adopted, and in which departments and institutions might it be taught?
- Do you have any suggestions regarding the marketing of your book, for example a list of relevant conferences and professional groups or associations who may be interested in the book?

And do give thought to some of the many ways *you* can help to promote your book (Box 19.5). Do not be shy about letting others know that your book is available. Use LinkedIn, Facebook, on-campus media, professional body newsletters, The Conversation, local newspapers ... to get the message out. You will have spent a great deal of time and energy producing it. You have something worth saying. And people are so often busy with their own work and lives they may not be aware of the work that has consumed your every waking hour for months or years. Tell them about it.

BOX 19.5 SOME WAYS OF HELPING TO PROMOTE YOUR BOOK

- Work with the publisher to produce a great cover.
- Make sure the cover copy for the book is appealing. The publisher will probably ask for a paragraph describing the book in layperson's terms. This will be used on the back cover and on websites, brochures and

catalogues to promote the book. Be aware that the publisher is unlikely to modify the text you provide. So, make it really good, really clear and really engaging. Think about the importance of this kind of blurb in shaping your own decisions about which books to look at more carefully.

- Add details of the book (with a hyperlink to the relevant publisher's web page promoting the volume) to your email signature block and to your personal and institutional web pages.
- Arrange a book launch.
- Complete the publisher's marketing or author promotion forms to the best of your ability.
- Ensure review copies of the book go to appropriate journals with good book review sections.
- Send materials advertising the book to key colleagues, lecturers for whom the book might be useful, and other possible purchasers.
- Deliver public lectures highlighting the book's content on campus, at other institutions and to relevant community or professional groups.
- Circulate announcements on listservs, newsgroups and through discipline newsletters.
- Engage with mass media. Do radio interviews, newspaper articles, on-campus articles that may be picked up by broader media. Check with your institution's PR/media people to see how they can assist.
- Use social media such as Facebook, Snapchat or blogs to publicize your book.
- Provide details of relevant professional society meetings to the publisher so they can promote and sell the book at them.

20. Speak

Talking about your work is a significant career-supporting opportunity. Speaking at public fora and conferences is a way of letting colleagues and community members know about your work and why it is exciting, clarifying your ideas, and opening up the possibilities of collaborations with academic colleagues, business people and other citizens from the broader community (Box 20.1). Spoken presentations can also support your career more directly. For example, many scholars learn of new work from talks at professional meetings (Feibelman, 2011, p. 40), and referring to the US context, Berman (undated, p. 8) observes that some researchers do a '"tenure tour" (giving talks at institutions where prominent people in your research area work), the year before they are up for tenure so that potential reference letter writers will be "fresh" and knowledgeable about their work'. And in terms of more personal rewards, travelling to conferences and other speaking engagements can be a good way of getting to see your city, country or the world.

BOX 20.1 OPPORTUNITIES PRESENTED
BY CONFERENCES AND PUBLIC
PRESENTATIONS

- Promoting your current research to a group of interested colleagues.
- Receiving well-informed feedback on your work.
- Refining your thinking on your work by having to communicate aspects of it to others.
- Positioning yourself with colleagues, the public and the media as a person working in a particular area.
- Finding out about new developments, trends, ideas and emerging figures in your field (and sharing your observations about these when you return to your university).
- Listening to influential scholars.
- Making new friends and nurturing personal and professional relationships (e.g., potential research collaborations).
- Gauging the current and future state of the job market.
- Finding out about new books, journals and professional bodies.

- Setting yourself up to be approached to write papers, chapters, books or to serve in advisory or editorial capacities.
- Uncovering funding opportunities.
- Participating in expert-led field trips to areas of personal or professional interest.
- Recharging and revitalizing your scholarly interests by getting out of your everyday routine.

Source: Adapted from De Hertogh (2012); Gray and Drew (2012, pp. 140–41); Hay et al. (2005).

When you first take up an academic appointment or if you make a significant change to your research trajectory, give serious thought to speaking about your work to relevant local groups. Offer to give a seminar in your new school or in cognate disciplines. Contact local interest groups, learned societies, organizations, businesses, or teachers likely to be interested in your work, letting them know you are available to speak to them. Not only will you present yourself as an outgoing, dynamic person but you may also make useful and supportive connections. You will expose your work to interested colleagues and help expand your networks. It will be simplest to speak at universities and other agencies in your local area (e.g., local government, government departments, private enterprise) but you might also speak in more distant institutions if you happen to be visiting for other purposes. For them there is the advantage of having your talk included on their seminar and visitor schedules for less than the full travel costs. And you might be fortunate enough to receive some part-funding to help cover the costs of your trip. Of course, emerging conference and video technologies (e.g. MS-Teams; Tencent/Voov; Zoom) now mean that there is less need to of travel to be able to speak elsewhere, While this technologies diminish the networking potential of 'speaking tours' and departmental visits, they do can certainly extend the spatial extent of your speaking circuit.

If you are confident enough and believe your work has useful public and media appeal offer to speak to radio or television stations. Many universities and other research organizations now have public relations and media sections who can provide helpful guidance, as well as offering specific training on dealing with the media (see Chapter 9 for more detail). It is probably good to develop these sorts of media engagement skills as an early career academic, particularly if you believe you are destined for a distinguished academic career and the associated public attention or if you enjoy the publicity this kind of exposure can offer.

Even if it appears that nothing has come of your meetings or media engagements (e.g., no one calls to follow up or invites you back), this does not mean the work has been in vain. You will almost certainly have made an impression – hopefully a good one – and you will be remembered. And at some time in the future there is a chance you will be approached by a potential PhD student, a book editor seeking a chapter, a relevant organization looking for a board member, or a prospective co-author who was present at one of those talks or who has heard of your work from someone who was. Of course, all of this means that you do need to take any presentation you give seriously. I recall one sage arguing that it is good to treat every talk as a job interview. While this may be overstating the case, the general point is a good one. At every talk you will leave an impression; always try to make sure it is a good one.

There are only so many conferences you will have the time and the money to attend. Large national and international conferences may have thousands of attendees, offer amazing opportunities to develop extensive networks, be prestigious, dynamic and exciting, and yet be simultaneously anonymous and frustrating by virtue of their scale. Small, local conferences can offer greater scope to develop deep and productive relationships with close colleagues, but they may also become dull and predictable. Choose the conferences you attend very carefully, thinking about what you wish to achieve, and make the most of those you do go to. Contemplate the cultures and practices of the professional communities you wish to belong to: local, global, all-of-discipline-focussed (e.g., anthropology, history) or subfield-focussed (e.g., linguistic anthropology, Indian colonial histories). If necessary, speak to more experienced colleagues to gather their opinion of the value of specific conferences and assess available opportunities in light of your specific career needs.

Practise any presentation, making it consistent with the demands of the conference, the medium, or occasion (e.g., duration, use of audiovisual aids), for as Feibelman (2011, p. 40) remarks:

> [a]s the speaker, you are putting on a one-person show. Your listeners are investing … their valuable time. Of course they want to learn something from you, but like theatre goers, they expect to hear a good story, with a beginning, a middle, and an end. They don't want to squirm when you explain something poorly or wrongly, when you show a slide containing an egregious mis-spelling, or when the end … is approaching and you obviously have a lot left to tell. Disappoint your listeners at your peril.

Watch recordings of your rehearsals, a possibility now enhanced by the growing availability of audiovisual recording facilities from university teaching spaces to mobile phones. Get critical friends and colleagues to appraise both your rehearsals and talks frankly. It is all very well to make arrangements to speak so you can improve your profile but you must also perform well. A talk may be your first opportunity to make a good impression with people positioned to shape your future career. Take advantage of the great abundance of resources online, through community organizations (e.g., Rostrum, Toastmasters International), and in scholarly publications and blogs to help develop your speaking skills (for example, Albuquerque, 2015; Feibelman, 2011; Hay, 2012; IFERP, 2022; Tierney, 2015). Emulate good speakers. Learn from your own and others' mistakes. There are few excuses left today for not knowing the technicalities of a good talk. What remains is practising and refining your skills.

Bear in mind too that in this era of greater institutional demands for tangible outputs from your labours, attending a conference or even giving a paper at that conference may count for little. So consider participating in – or organizing – focussed conference sessions intended to yield special journal collections (see the discussion in Chapter 9 'Get known and networked'). Many scholarly journals publish special collections of papers, commonly with a guest editor. Though challenging, such a role can be an excellent way of helping to cement yourself as an emerging or key figure in your field. In the early stages of your career give some thought to teaming up with a more senior colleague to organize a special conference session and journal special issue. Although you might initiate the process and do a lot of the work, your colleague should be able to guide you through the process in ways that minimize risk and maximize success. Similar efforts could also yield an edited book. Such works tend not to have as much academic kudos associated with them as monographs, but they can certainly help establish or consolidate your place as a leader in your field and assist with the development of strong networks in your speciality area.

Finally, do remember that conferences and other meetings are not all about presentations and publications. There is an abundance of important networking and stimulating socializing to be done (see Ernst, 2004; Hay et al., 2005; Teperek, 2018). Stay at the conference for longer than the duration of your talk! Find out what others are doing. Take opportunities during breaks to mingle and extend your range of professional contacts. And if appropriate, follow up afterwards with short correspondence to the new colleagues in your expanding network.

21. Secure funding

As demands on university budgets grow, so grows the expectation that academics will strive even further to secure greater levels of research funding. Unfortunately, this is occurring in an era when many granting agencies themselves face straitened times (Margolin, 1983; Mongeon et al., 2016). Not surprisingly then, there is a great deal of advice emerging online and through institutional guidance programmes about where to find research funds and how to complete a successful grant application, detailing matters like: following the instructions carefully, ensuring you have a clear focus and strong justification, writing clearly and simply, choosing the right words, and so on (e.g., Churches, 2015; Gitlin et al. 2021; Madsen, 2007; *ResearchProfessional, 2023; Shaw, 2013). Almost every university now offers its own online advice on successful grant writing and there are abundant other online resources. While Box 21.1 provides an overview of such advice, the vast detail of sources and grant-writing processes are beyond the scope of this book. However, we can consider some very general advice on how to get funding.

BOX 21.1 SOME KEYS TO A SUCCESSFUL GRANT APPLICATION

1. Follow the instructions!
2. Make sure your project is aligned with the interests of the funding body.[a]
3. Choose a title that is clever (but not twee), that aligns with the funding programme and describes the research effectively.
4. Highlight your strong, promising track record.
5. Show that you are brilliant, original and ambitious in your research goals. Propose ideas that push the frontiers of knowledge, preferably with multidisciplinary approaches, but avoid overstating the possible outcomes.
6. Make clear the work's broad impacts and implications. Who or what will benefit?
7. Explain how you will resolve problems or controversies, rather than simply collect data.

8. Make clear how the momentum of the research subject demands support now.
9. Cite the relevant literature and discuss its significance to your proposed work.
10. Write the research plan concisely, with clear objectives, focus and a well-defined research strategy. What are you going to do, with whom, when, where, why, and how? Be realistic on the extent and feasibility of the project. Your great ambitions need to be matched by convincing methods and realistic prospects of success.
11. Include an accurate and appropriate budget request: ask for enough to do the work without waste.
12. Make sure the proposal is: written clearly and simply (e.g., grammar, spelling, straightforward language, no jargon); presented carefully (e.g., references, tables); and assembled logically.
13. Set out a clear plan for the dissemination of results.
14. Get critically constructive feedback before you submit your proposal.
15. Follow the instructions (see item 1).

Note: ªAs Scott (2006, p. 27) observed some years ago, 'the era of disinterested and unconstrained "blue skies" research is (apparently) over. Now researchers must learn to play the political gallery and/or "play the market"'.
Source: Belmonte (cited in Pain, 2007); Debowski (2012); Feibelman (2011); Gitlin et al. (2021); Johnson (2011); Shaw (2013).

You may be in the fortunate position where your research does not require large sums of money for support. Nonetheless, your supervisor, current employer and prospective employers will almost definitely expect you to be able to demonstrate your scholarly status by outcompeting others in the ever more spirited struggle for funds. Indeed, demonstrated capacity to do just this is an increasingly common and important criterion in academic appointment decisions (see Chapter 13). Moreover, although you may not need direct financial backing for your research, grant funds may be useful to support PhD and postdoctoral scholarships, travel to conferences, sabbatical, or to pay teaching assistants or research assistants to help with your work in ways that serve your ends as well as theirs. Funding can also allow you the luxury of doing the 'fun bits' of teaching for example, leaving the more onerous parts to others:

> If you're not doing enough research, you'll end up doing more teaching, you'll end up doing more dull teaching – whereas I get research grants which pay for somebody else to do my teaching, and I essentially get to choose which bits of my teaching I do. And I go, 'I'll have the fun bits please'. (Jules, New Zealand, in Sutherland, 2015, p. 11)

Grant writing takes a great deal of time and often has a low success rate. For instance, the 2017–18 success rate for applications to the UK's Economic and Social Research Council (ESRC) was 26 per cent from a total number of applications that had dropped by almost half since 2011–12 (UK Research and Innovation, 2022). In Australia, the success rate for Australian Research Council (ARC) 2022 Discovery Projects in the Humanities and Creative Arts was 18.7 per cent and in the Social, Behavioural and Economic Sciences it was 18.9 per cent (ARC, 2021). And in New Zealand, the 2020 Marsden Fund round had a success rate of 9.6 per cent in the Social Sciences and 11.2 per cent in the Humanities (Royal Society of New Zealand, 2022). Early in my own career I decided that my research could be conducted at relatively low cost and that, given the very low success rates for competitive national grants, I was better to: (1) seek out smaller, lower-profile, though not necessarily less prestigious, grants, and (2) spend more time writing books and papers than crafting grant applications. For me, this cost/benefit approach was fairly successful, though perhaps not the best approach. In retrospect I see that there may have been value in spending a little more time working on larger grant applications to secure funding that could have enlarged my research horizons. Moreover, the applications themselves may have provided the basis for some scholarly publications. In your own work give consideration to the balance of time you spend on grant-writing and how you can weave that together productively with your scholarly publishing and other activities. If appropriate, discuss your thinking and approach with a mentor or supervisor.

While it almost goes without saying, do make sure your grant application is well thought-through and well written. A mentor or supervisor may be able to assist with this. Remember, influential key colleagues working in *your* field will be reviewing your proposal very carefully. Do not damage your academic reputation with a poor-quality application.

Getting a grant will generally demand that you have a track record of success in your field. And typically this means that you have a number of publications to your credit, in good journals, and in a quantity appropriate to your career level. A grant proposal is unlikely to be successful if you cannot point to the generation of worthy outcomes from previous work.

Find out which organizations have got money, what they want to spend it on, and to whom they prefer to give it. Which agencies support the kind of work you do? Befriend those people in your university who oversee and advertise research grants and find out from them what may be available. Check funding agencies' websites and other sources. Check their aims and mission statements to see where the greatest alignments with your work exist. By way of example, the ambitions of a number of funding agencies are set out in Box 21.2 indicating support ranging from the very general (British Academy) to the quite specific (American Institute of Indian Studies).

BOX 21.2 EXAMPLES OF FUNDING AGENCIES' OBJECTIVES

The British Academy – http://www.britac.ac.uk/about-us
'The British Academy is the UK's national academy for the humanities and social sciences. We mobilise these disciplines to understand the world and shape a brighter future.'

The National Geographic Society – https://www.nationalgeographic.org/society/grants-and-investments/
'We fund individuals working on projects in science, conservation, story-telling, education, and technology that align with one or more of our focus areas', namely Ocean, Land, Wildlife, Human histories and cultures, and Human ingenuity.

The American Institute of Indian Studies – https://www.indiastudies.org/about-aiis/
'The American Institute of Indian Studies (AIIS) was formed to further the knowledge of India in the United States by supporting American scholarship on India. The programs of AIIS foster the production of and engagement with scholarship on India, and promote and advance mutual understanding between the citizens of the United States and of India. AIIS is committed to equity, inclusion and access to all communities in fulfilling its mission. It will promote wider diversity throughout the organization, in the interest of addressing the historical disenfranchisement of communities globally. AIIS will develop collaborations and initiatives with institutions that represent the diversity of the United States, including those serving communities that have not had access to India-focused programs.'

And then, if you are able, communicate with key people in the appropriate (typically smaller) agencies. This does not mean 'schmoozing' in the hope of winning some advantage in grant assessments! Because most agencies have independent, stand-alone review procedures, any time you spend in such activity will not only be wasted but it may also be regarded as inappropriate. Instead, develop well-thought-out written approaches to agency programme officers or executive directors advising them of your research agenda, background and ideas, and inquiring about opportunities that may be appropriate to your work.

Develop research credibility within your relevant community of scholars. The academic world has been argued to be made up of 'tribes' (for a detailed discussion, see Becher and Trowler, 2001) and although the significance of these groups may be weakening (see Trowler et al., 2012) you establish your place within your significant intellectual group's hierarchy by publishing well; giving high-quality conference presentations; asking insightful questions; meeting with key colleagues (the tribes' leaders); and otherwise presenting yourself in the best possible light. Through such activities and interactions you may be able to develop clearer views on emerging, fundable areas of work germane to your own. You will also be bringing your work to the attention of those likely to be involved in reviewing your grant applications. The opinion these colleagues form of you may stand your application in good stead during grant review.

If you are new to grant writing, collaborate with colleagues who have already had a good deal of success. While you may have to do much of the work involved in developing the proposal, your chances of succeeding may increase. Importantly, if you work with the right people, you should learn some key skills in grant writing (e.g., justifying the research; interpreting referees' responses). And once you have developed an early track record of securing grants, you should be better positioned to capture future funding. There is a dark side to collaborations, however. For instance, in jurisdictions such as Australia, some granting bodies' rules appear to have had the unintended consequence of turning junior–senior collaborations into exploitative relationships. Under Australian Research Council funding that supported 'science rather than salaries', any person named on a grant could not be paid from it (Phillips, 2015). What this meant is that junior academics on short-term contracts reportedly foresook their own chance to secure a grant, instead writing for their senior colleague in the hope that if the proposal was funded, they would be able to get a research position under the grant. Despite this particular unintended consequence, collaborations may generally offer productive introductions to successful grant writing and are worth developing.

Finally, be sure to let any agency you have received funding from know of relevant outcomes and products such as papers, books, reports and conference publications. The organization will value and perhaps publicize such information for it will help to justify its own existence. In fact, as part of broader shifts to performance management and research accountability, most agencies now demand progress reports and final reports on outcomes. Satisfactory completion of these is typically a requisite of continued or subsequent funding. Notwithstanding reporting mandates, evidence of research success will also help to cement your place as a key member of the scholarly community the agency is also a part of. That should help you to secure funding in the future.

22. Attract postgraduate students

Effective student supervision or advising is an increasingly common measure of academic research productivity and success. Some institutions use completed PhDs as an empirical marker of the adviser's research activity. Less formally, there are occasions when acclaiming a colleague's career in retirement speeches and other laudatory moments that speakers will refer to the number of doctoral students supervised and what those students have gone on to do as indicators of professional impact, connectedness and influence.

Developing a cadre of postgraduate students has other significance for a successful scholarly career. Enthusiastic and engaged postgraduate students working in overlapping and related areas can be energizing, mutually sustaining and attractive to other students and colleagues. A flourishing research group is something many aspiring and successful academics long to be associated with.

Moreover, many advisers co-publish with their postgraduate students. Not only can this relationship help students negotiate and learn about publishing processes and procedures, it also contributes to the adviser's publication record and scholarly career. As discussed in Chapter 18 this is not without its risks, however: some advisers fall into a trap of co-publishing almost exclusively. This may benefit the various students involved, but it does not reflect well on the independent career of the adviser.

Research student supervision is also a clear means of influencing students in ways that are more immediately evident than undergraduate teaching where student–teacher relationships are more detached and where developmental effects may be unnoticed in the short term. Supervising and guiding a new generation of scholars is part of the rewarding process of creating an intellectual legacy and helping to make a lasting contribution to human knowledge.

Supervising research students may also help you to learn and practise management skills. Every student has different needs and all require support and guidance (e.g. moral support, planning; determining priorities; setting timelines) to complete their research journey efficiently and effectively and in accord with explicit institutional guidelines and regulations. Through this work as a supervisor you will find yourself developing general management experience.

Finally, advisory relationships can yield rewarding lifelong friendships and productive collegial relationships. Indeed, they can be the most satisfying relationships of all in academic work, as you see a fledgling scholar emerge and develop, shape their career, and move on to great things.

However, some postgraduate supervisory relationships have a more sinister side. There is an emerging literature pointing, for example, to various exploitative and unethical relationships between postgraduate students and their supervisors (e.g. Bodewits, 2017; Cheng and Leung, 2022; Francis, 2001; Lee, 1998; Löfström and Pyhältö, 2017, 2020; Mitchell and Carroll, 2008). These include, for example, 'gift authorships' – whereby students are required to include their supervisor as an author on a paper (or talk) they wrote, even if the supervisor contributed little to the study on which the paper is based – and its close relative, research misappropriation. This involves the representation of aspects of another's research as one's own.

Advisory relationships can sometimes also be muddied by the intrusion of their romantic and sexual counterparts, presenting many personal, professional and ethical challenges surrounding issues including conflict of interest, tensions between personal compatibility and relevant research expertise, exploitation and inequitable treatment). Advisers who enter romantic or sexual relationships must tread very carefully indeed, taking cognizance of institutional policies as well as moral strictures.

To help negotiate such challenges and ensure that supervisory relationships live up to their rewarding promise many universities now have explicit policies on professional and personal relationships in the workplace that provide useful and clear guidance on how to manage problematic supervisory relationships. In general, it is the responsibility of the supervisor or adviser – not the student – to take charge of the situation and to negotiate outcomes that are procedurally correct as well as just and respectful. However, this does not work if you are the supervisee and for this reason the guidelines typically also offer direction on how supervisees might proceed. If they do not, and you find yourself in a difficult relationship, seek counsel from a mentor, a trusted colleague, a union representative, your head of department, or dean … And if you have any doubts about a particular state of affairs you are involved in or become aware of, ask yourself how you would feel if the behaviour or situation was to be described in dispassionate terms on the front page of a local newspaper.

HOW TO ATTRACT POSTGRADUATE STUDENTS

Numerous national and institutional strategies exist to attract and support local and international postgraduate students. These include schemes ranging from high-profile Commonwealth, Fulbright, and Rhodes international scholarships to national postgraduate awards to individual university funding arrangements. These are all well and good but what can you, as an individual, do to ensure that those who are supported by such schemes are encouraged to work with you in particular? There is a range of strategies that can be adopted, including self-promotion, professional skills development and luring local undergraduates!

First, develop your advisory skills. There is a vast range of published and online resources (e.g. Byrnes et al., 2019; Hill and Conceição, 2020; Huysmans, 2020) on how to be an effective supervisor, whose content I will not precis here. To develop advisory proficiency and maintain a good reputation, study how to be a good supervisor and take advantage of training programmes that your institution almost assuredly offers. Keep up to date with these and always keep in the back of your mind how your students might respond to the question: 'Would you select this adviser if you had your time over again?'

Second, develop high standing in your field of scholarship. This may help attract students. Keep publishing in well-regarded, good-quality outlets. Speak at conferences where prospective students may be present and give seminars in your own and other universities. If possible, build a profile in on-campus news media and perhaps the media more broadly.

Third, make sure you have a good, up-to-date web presence. For many potential students it may be through the web that you make your important first impression. Create entries for sites such as LinkedIn, ResearchGate, ORCID and Academia.edu (see Chapter 9). Your institutional web page should be current and as exciting as you can make it. And if you have the skills and inclination, consider developing a personal website that discusses your research in exciting, imaginative ways unconstrained by the formatting and content constraints of anodyne commercial and institutional sites. There are many good examples of personal sites on the web. Spend some time looking at the sites of some colleagues you admire and respect to see how they represent themselves there.

Fourth, work with a critical mass of active scholars on a coherent body of research (see Chapter 23). Not only is a group likely to attract the attention of more prospective students, it will also allow scope for enthusiastic exploration of a broad range of student interests and may lead to the reciprocal movement of students from one institution working in the field to another.

Fifth, take on projects that have appeal, relevance and significance – and find ways of ensuring that those characteristics are evident to students (e.g., through the ways they are presented on your personal or group web page). At the same time be sure there is scope within the group's focus for new arrivals to work on relevant problems that appeal particularly to them.

Sixth, seek ways to fund the work of students and advertise the opportunities through appropriate networks (e.g., newsletters, websites, listservs). Funds may be available through research grants that carry PhD stipends with them.

Seventh, although it is a chicken and egg proposition, have great students already! Good prospective students will want to work with others like themselves: people who are engaged, bright and enthusiastic.

Eighth, recruit and cultivate high-quality undergraduates and early postgraduate students (e.g., Masters students) at your own institution who are interested in your work. If possible, offer them PhD positions with you before they seek alternative opportunities elsewhere. This strategy is not favoured in all academic fields and indeed may be questioned in areas where there is an expectation that good upcoming scholars will complete a PhD in a different institution from the one in which their undergraduate or Masters degrees were obtained. However, if you and the student believe you offer the best opportunities realistically available, that student may be well served by continuing their work locally, irrespective of prevailing disciplinary mores. And, of course, in many instances students may be bound to a specific university by familial, social, employment and other ties which make options in other places illusory.

Ninth, enhance your reputation as a good supervisor. Advertise the successes of your PhD students (e.g., employment outcomes; awards they have received for their doctoral research and related activity; their key publications, conference presentations or community engagements) through your own websites and through institutional or disciplinary communications channels. Where they exist, apply for awards that recognize high-quality supervision. For instance, many universities such as Monash in Australia, Massey in New Zealand and Simon Fraser in Canada have annual awards for excellence in postgraduate supervision. Similarly, professional scholarly organizations, national bodies and some governments recognize high-quality supervision through prizes and awards. For example, since 2016 an award for 'Outstanding Research Supervisor of the Year' has been awarded in the UK as part of the annual Times Higher Education University Awards (UK Council for Graduate Education, 2016).

Finally, be sure to work somewhere that has broad geographical or disciplinary appeal! I hear that Hawaii is nice!

23. Join or start a research team

There is a proverb 'If you want to go fast, go alone, if you want to go far, go together' that has some application in a research context. You may certainly be able to make swift progress with many research projects in the humanities, arts and social sciences (HASS) if you work alone – and that is a common model of much HASS scholarship – but you may very well learn more and make greater long-term progress in your academic career if you are part of a research team.

Research teams take many different forms, depending on their purpose, funding, role and location and may comprise diverse groups including local and distant co-investigators, postdoctoral scholars, postgraduate students, professional and technical staff, industry representatives and so on. Nevertheless they have in common an identity as 'a group of people working together in a committed way towards a common research goal' (Vitae, 2022). Research teams are much more common in science, technology, engineering and maths (STEM) than in HASS disciplines that have a more established 'lone scholar' tradition, but they can be helpful where the research problem being explored requires multiple perspectives, interdisciplinary backgrounds, diverse capabilities (e.g., GIS [geographic information systems], qualitative research skills, statistical expertise) and more than one person to do the work. Indeed, there does also seem to have been a distinct growth in team-based approaches to scholarly work over the past half-century as Jones (2021, p. 190) observes:

> For example, while papers with two or more authors constituted only 19 percent of economics journal articles in 1960, this share rose to 44 percent in 2000 and 74 percent in 2018. Moreover, team-authored papers in economics have increasing impact advantages over solo-authored papers. By 2010, a team was three times more likely to produce a highly cited paper than a solo author, an advantage that has grown steadily with time. *These shifts appear not only within every subfield of economics, but also in virtually all fields of science, social science, and patenting.* (Emphasis added)

Given the growing complexity of many of today's 'human' problems (Hay, 2016a), the need for, and impact of, creative combinations through multidisciplinary HASS teams and joint STEM/HASS work seem likely to grow further (Shah 2020).[1]

Moreover, Johnson (2011, pp. 30–31) observes that, aside from bringing together strong multidiscipline groups, research teams comprising the right partners, with compelling and appropriate credentials, working *together*, promise: access to new tools, information and skills; an (inter)national perspective to your work; greater bidding strength for research grants and consulting; a heightened profile, locally, nationally or internationally; and greater research outputs. Collectively these yield personal and professional rewards, including achievement of project goals. Teams also allow the aggregation of individual expertise in an era of heightened specialization. 'As individual researchers become increasingly narrow, teams allow the aggregation of specialized knowledge and thus offer a line of continued attack on problems of wider application' (Jones 2021, p. 200). Research teams also help create and sustain long-term professional relationships that may allow you and your colleagues to support one another's work for many years to come.

But for career success and sustainability, research teams do need to comprise partners who are right not just professionally but also personally. As Crone (2010, p. 69) notes:

> Collaboration can be amazingly fruitful, energizing, and intellectually stimulating when it works, but it can also be a nightmare that makes you dread every meeting with your collaborators and make you wish you had never started the project. My personal rule is that I will only collaborate with people that I like. We have to get along and respect each other over the duration of the collaboration, and it is likely that there will be challenges to face and problems that will test the relationship. This is why I feel it is critical for the personalities of the collaborators to be compatible at a minimum, and best if you enjoy a friendship and camaraderie as well as complementary expertise. Once a good collaborative relationship is established, then I have found it often to be the case that we continue to look for excuses to work together even after the original project is completed. *It is these relationships that make it all worthwhile.* (Emphasis added)

On the other hand, research teams comprising difficult or lazy people managed poorly can be deeply frustrating and inefficient. Research teams can also divide and obscure credit, which is central to the reward system of science and to individual career progression (Jones 2021). And disturbingly, there is some evidence to suggest that women are less likely than men to receive tenure the more they coauthor (Sarsons et al. 2021).

Despite some drawbacks, on balance, and for much research, there is a compelling case for team-based research and a number of agencies such as Vitae (2022) and ReStore (2022) at the UK's National Centre for Research Methods offer useful practical advice on developing and managing effective research teams. Such counsel echoes well-rehearsed ideas set out in extensive literatures on leadership and management (see, for example, Cameron, 2013; DuBois et al., 2015). By way of summary, Box 23.1 describes operational issues and critical issues of team dynamics and engagement.

BOX 23.1 SOME CHARACTERISTICS OF A SUCCESSFUL RESEARCH TEAM

Operational issues

- Does the team have a clear and shared sense of purpose? Is there a plan?
- Does the team have the skills and knowledge to satisfy its aspirations?
- Do team members know their roles and responsibilities?
- Does the entire team have effective modes of formal and informal communication (e.g., email, listserv and/or meetings, Zoom/Teams, morning teas)?
- Are adequate resources available for the group to function effectively and are those resources distributed appropriately? If appropriate, how does the team cope with the unpredictable nature of research funding?
- How is progress towards achievement of the team's goals reviewed?
- Does the team fulfil its ambitions?

Team dynamics and engagement

- Are team members' views, capabilities and backgrounds recognized and valued? How?
- How is the team involved in decision-making?
- Do team members fulfil their roles? Are there hangers-on and 'free-riders'?
- Are disputes resolved quickly and effectively? How?
- Is team members' professional development supported?
- How are successes celebrated?

Before joining or initiating any research team, think about the questions posed in Box 23.1, using them to guide your decision to join the group or to shape your thinking about how to create an effective, cohesive and collegial research team supportive of high-quality collaboration. Ask yourself why you would wish to be involved, taking care to be specific about matters such as project aims, methods, locations, timelines and partners. If you do not think involvement is to your advantage or more significantly that it may disadvantage or hinder your work, step back. There will be other future opportunities (Johnson, 2011, p. 30).

NOTE

1. It is interesting to note that teams of different size may do different things. For instance, in their study of 65 million science and technology papers, patents and software products spanning the period 1954–2014 Wu et al. (2019, p. 378) suggest that smaller teams have 'tended to disrupt science and technology with new ideas and opportunities, whereas larger teams have tended to develop existing ones.'

24. Teach well

Teaching well is not only a key measure of academic success. It can also be one of the most emotionally challenging and rewarding experiences for many academics in their professional lives. For instance, delivering a well-received lecture to a class of 300 first-year students can be truly uplifting. On the other hand, a flop in front of the same group can really ruin your day! Despite significant recent transformations in modes of teaching it often – though not necessarily – involves presenting yourself and your ideas to large and small groups, week after week at specific times, irrespective of how good or prepared you feel.[1] That commitment cannot be circumvented. And on the line every day are your personality and your expertise, the way you talk, the way you dress, your technical prowess and digital savvy, and the ways you stimulate thinking and communicate ideas. Under this deeply personal scrutiny, many academics give disproportionate attention to the quality of their teaching (or they give up entirely), failing to negotiate successfully the balance between teaching and research and other aspects of their lives. The longer-term timeframes and the depersonalized character of much research mean that it can be put off – sometimes. If you do not feel like working on a project today, maybe you can do it tomorrow. And you often have the opportunity to revise your scholarly writing after thoughtful, measured review. But teaching is more often immediate, personal and can involve instant, unsympathetic assessments of credibility. It can lead to anxiety and self-doubt. Distinguished political scientist and university teacher David Kahane reveals some measure of this (2011, p. 17): 'I was miserably anxious starting out as a teacher. There was an exhilaration in sitting or standing at the front of a classroom, but also deep insecurity about my knowledge and competence.'

In my own experience as a graduate student in the United States I remember many of my high-achieving teaching assistant colleagues talked of their 'fear of being found a fraud'. They could not accept their academic success and were concerned that someday someone would challenge their expertise, revealing publicly that they really knew little at all. This so-called 'impostor' phenomenon (Imes and Clance, 1978) seemed most pronounced ahead of their teaching, major examinations and conference presentations. A tendency my colleagues shared with many other academics was to attempt to deal with this by being more diligent, by overpreparing, by trying to become the expert they thought they need to be and that everyone else appears to be (for revealing accounts see Bernard and Stone-Sabali 2022; Hay, 2011b; Jaremka et al. 2020; Kahane, 2011; Wesch, 2011). Yet one vital point that research on effective and successful university teaching has shown is that while subject mastery is of some importance, it is far from being the sole determinant.

In 2004, Ken Bain published his award-winning book, *What the Best College Teachers Do.* Available in at least a dozen languages this volume continues to offer enormously influential advice on the things that university teachers can do to encourage students to achieve remarkable learning results. On the basis of a 15-year study of nearly 100 tertiary-level teachers in the United States, Bain identified six key attributes of the best college teachers. Certainly, these scholars knew their subject extremely well. But there were other qualities behind their success. They treated all elements of teaching as serious intellectual endeavours, as demanding and challenging as their research. They expected 'more' (student high achievement), favouring objectives that embody thinking and acting expected for life. They created a natural critical learning environment in which students learn by confronting intriguing, beautiful or important problems and authentic tasks. They reflected a strong trust in students, believing students want to learn, and displaying openness. And finally, they adopted a systematic programme to assess their own efforts and make appropriate changes. Though useful, on the basis of more recent autoethnographies written by some of the world's best university teachers and published as *Inspiring Academics* (Hay, 2011a), Bain's observations can be further refined and extended (Box 24.1). The principles apply equally well to face-to-face and online learning environments.

BOX 24.1 WHAT THE BEST COLLEGE TEACHERS DO – BAIN MODIFIED

- Move beyond a focus on failure, fear and uncertainty.
- Know their subject extremely well, but appreciate that good teaching involves more than subject mastery.
- Appreciate that learning is different from teaching.
- Treat all elements of teaching as serious intellectual endeavours, as demanding and challenging as their research.
- Expect 'more' (student high achievement), favouring objectives that embody thinking and acting expected for life.
- Organize for risk.
- Create a natural critical learning environment (students learn by confronting intriguing, beautiful or important problems and authentic tasks).
- Acknowledge humanness – their own as well as students.

- Reflect a strong trust in students, believing students want to learn, and displaying openness.
- Replicate – and improve on – inspiring teachers.
- Have a systematic programme of reflection to assess their own efforts and make appropriate changes.

Good teachers have the willingness to move beyond failure, fear and uncertainty. Many of the great teachers in *Inspiring Academics* highlighted uncomfortable, yet transformational, experiences they had had as early-career academics. For example, Wendy Rogers recalled that: '[a]fter ... some disastrous student feedback, the onus was on me to develop imaginative teaching methods that would be educationally sound, informed by best practice ... and, most importantly, engage the students' (Rogers, 2011, p. 104). And Rhona Free, who went on to receive the 2004 US Professor of the Year Award from the Carnegie Foundation for the Advancement of Teaching and the Council for Advancement and Support of Education, noted that:

> [a]fter only a few semesters in the classroom there were signs that my teaching had to change. While I thought my lectures were full of exciting *voila!* moments, students just seemed relieved when I stopped talking. Their lack of enthusiasm and the minimal time their grades suggested they allocated to the course were discouraging, especially since I spent hours and hours preparing for each class. (Free, 2011, p. 70)

In each case, rather than being devastated by their failures, fears and uncertainties these great teachers reflected on them constructively and systematically and rethought their approach to teaching – comprehensively in many cases.

Next, good teachers realize that teaching involves more than subject mastery and that learning is different from teaching. Attention moves from teaching to student learning, which means changing teaching from a '"what will I teach" focus to a "why am I teaching this?"; "how should I teach?"; and "what should I teach?"' (Wesch, 2011, p. 27) as well as 'to whom am I teaching?' and 'what are the characteristics and needs of the learners?' And for Regan, the emphasis also includes creating a community of learners: 'Successful teachers do not simply transmit information; rather, they invest in creating a community of learners, a community based on mutual respect and dignity and dynamic exchange between students and teacher' (Regan, 2011, p. 136).

Good university teachers organize their teaching in ways that allow them to take 'risks'. So, for example, instead of thinking about a lecture or seminar as requiring a certain amount of material to be 'covered' or 'transmitted', a good teacher might have organized online or face-to-face learning resources in ways that allow space and time for impromptu learning-related issues to be discussed or for innovative teaching strategies to be explored. For instance, Lucas (2011, p. 168) remarked: 'On a good day, I now respond to a "dead" situation in a classroom by taking risks. I try out completely new activities, radically revise tried and trusted activities.' Inspiring academics also acknowledge their own humanness and individual characteristics as well those of their students. Political-economist Rhona Free recalled reshaping her teaching to play to her strengths: 'Not being good at leading discussions ... I replaced lecture time with in-class problem-solving exercises, analysis of cases and simple experiments about economic behaviour' (Free, 2011, p. 73). And New Zealand-based writing scholar Lisa Emerson suggested that no bag of teaching tricks can be effective unless the humanity of the classroom is acknowledged:

> None of these tools [plethora of teaching techniques and pedagogical tools] could have an impact unless the fundamentals were in place: that unless we honour the uniqueness of our students as individuals, understand and empathize with their fear, develop for ourselves an 'interpretive' role, and create our classrooms as communities, nothing else could empower our students to realize their dreams. (Emerson, 2011, p. 132)

Finally, good teachers replicate and improve on the qualities of other inspiring teachers. In some cases, as Cameron (2011, p. 79) recounts, inspiration came from poor role models! 'Some memories never leave you and I was determined not to replicate some of the practices inflicted on me, but instead to mirror those of the best, most dedicated teachers I had experienced.'

So, in short, teaching well involves a good deal more than merely developing and demonstrating subject expertise. The depth and breadth of a discussion about the constitution and practice of good teaching leaves it well beyond the scope of this volume but fortunately there are vast resources available on how to teach and foster learning effectively. These include classics such as Robert Boice's (2000) inimitable *Advice for New Faculty Members* and Parker J. Palmer's (2017) extraordinary volume *The Courage to Teach*. There are general and discipline-specific journals dedicated to the field (e.g., *International Journal of Teaching and Learning in Higher Education*; *Journal of Political Science Education*; *Teaching Anthropology*) as well as very many, very good 'how to' volumes (e.g., Biggs et al. 2022; Debowski, 2012, Chapters 7–9; Fink, 2013; Race, 2020) and guides on teaching tips and tricks (e.g., McKeachie and Svinicki, 2014; Patry, 2009; Revell and Wainwright, 2009) that provide helpful insights to the very many 'analogue' and digital forms that contemporary teaching and learning take (e.g., flipped classrooms,[2] online discussions, peer assessment). Be sure to incorporate such works into your professional development endeavours.

GET A TEACHING QUALIFICATION

On the path of academic success, you may not only need to be a good teacher but for appointment, tenure and promotion procedures you will also need to prove to others that you are. Indicators of your commitment to high-quality teaching include availing yourself of appropriate professional development opportunities and earning a relevant teaching qualification such as a Postgraduate Certificate in Learning and Teaching in Higher Education, a Master of Tertiary Education, or a Fellowship of the Higher Education Academy. Drawing from their research in Canada, New Zealand and Sweden, Sutherland et al. (2013, p. 65) sagely advocate obtaining a tertiary teaching qualification early in your career. It needs to be noted that this sort of encouragement is not shared comprehensively. A diminishing number of scholars – generally in private conversations – continue to suggest that academics cannot and should not develop teaching prowess through formal courses. Instead they should improve their professional practice through experience coupled with constant and enduring critical reflection. Aside from the irony of its implicit questioning of the value of formal educational qualifications altogether, this approach demands that students serve as guinea pigs for educational experimentation while exposing academics to an experiential approach to their own learning that can be psychologically harmful. Notwithstanding early misguided scepticism in certain circles about tertiary teaching qualifications (Hardy and Smith, 2006; Stewart, 2014), a graduate certificate, graduate diploma or Masters degree in higher education can certainly serve several useful ends.

First, in institutions where they are an option rather than a requirement, such a qualification marks you out as someone so dedicated to high-quality teaching that you have been prepared to invest the time and effort to develop appropriate skills and knowledge (see, for example, Advance HE, 2023). These qualifications provide 'proof of engagement in trying to improve teaching' (Hardy and Smith, 2006, p. 346). Having said this, it bears noting that many participants undertake these courses only to satisfy their university's promotion and professional development requirements rather than as the result of any intrinsic desire to improve learning and teaching. As one respondent in Hardy and Smith's (2006, p. 343) study noted, he did it 'for promotion – to demonstrate that I am learning how to teach'.

Second, if you work on such a qualification with a group of others from your own university, you may develop an informal network of teaching-interested colleagues from other disciplines with whom you can discuss teaching-related (and other) ideas, challenges and opportunities. These informal communities of practice can be tremendously useful for sharing good practice, creating new knowledge, and successfully negotiating or indeed shaping institutional procedures and systems in ways that enhance teaching individually and collectively. More than this they can also be helpful and supportive social networks that you can draw from and to which you can contribute. My own experience as a member of a formal teaching qualification class at Flinders University also yielded a productive professional relationship (with a criminologist) spanning more than three decades and yielding several teaching initiatives and scholarly publications (e.g., Hay and Israel, 2009, 2022; Israel and Hay, 2012).

Third, the study required for a university teaching qualification may illuminate the 'black box' of teaching. Educational principles, ideas and techniques can be clarified, and having the opportunity to explore these under expert guidance can mean that you do not waste time and energy over the longer run uncertain of, and fretting about, skills you are not sure you have. Course offerings may also allow you to explore ways to be more effective and efficient in your teaching. Do you really need to run two separate lectures each week? Can they usefully be consolidated? What is the value of lectures? Might flipped classrooms be helpful? Can electronic media be used to reduce your workload and improve teaching quality – or do they offer the opposite? Can non-electronic approaches be used to achieve the same ends? What innovative ways of using new technologies to support learning are emerging? How can you share teaching with others in mutually beneficial ways? Overall, a course can help hasten the rate at which you develop the confidence required to teach better (Stewart, 2014, p. 94) as well as providing some of the resources helpful to make you a more effective and efficient university teacher.

Finally, as your career develops into management and leadership roles, an initial tertiary teaching qualification can provide a useful stepping stone to subsequent certifications in a relevant field (e.g., Master of Educational Leadership).

Do be aware, however, that gaining a teaching qualification can also have a number of drawbacks. First and most obviously, the time required to complete it can reduce opportunities available for research (as well as other activities!) at a critical time in your career.[3] However, providers of many teaching qualification programmes are conscious of this and endeavour to mesh elements of the course as closely as possible with the teaching development challenges you are facing as you study (e.g., assigned work based on course or assignment development). Thus, you may actually save some time in your teaching, improve the pedagogy, and generate better courses for your own students! Moreover, you may be able to transform some of the assigned work required for your qualification into scholarly publications. Some academics elect to complete a tertiary teaching qualification at their own university rather than at another: this may allow a closer integration of programmed learning with day-to-day practice. But before you enrol locally do check programme requirements, relevance and assessment. If the course does not offer the flexibility, engagement and efficiencies you seek, enrol elsewhere (e.g., a nearby university or a reputable distance provider).

Second, in some so-called research-intensive institutions, completing a teaching qualification may mark you out as someone not quite fully serious about the serious business of serious research! And your manifest interest in developing teaching may see you burdened with teaching-related administrative tasks (e.g., arranging Open Day events; leading school groups around the department; coordinating degree programmes). If you find this happening, continue to be collegial but find ways to avoid being exploited.

FIND WAYS TO LINK TEACHING, RESEARCH AND SERVICE

Teaching well at university can be sustained by connecting it in efficient and mutually supportive ways with research activities – and even with service roles. Heightened levels of attention are being given to the scholarship of teaching (see Box 24.2) and to the so-called teaching–research nexus (e.g., Douglas, 2013; Geschwind & Broström, 2015; Gottlieb and Keith, 1997; Neumann, 1992). And there is good reason for this attentiveness. Teaching offers a wonderful way of clarifying and consolidating research ideas. There is little better for refining research ideas than trying to communicate them to a class of critical or confused students. Even teaching classic principles and first-year materials can be tremendously useful in helping to forge the links between your current work and key ideas in the discipline. As Fiske (2010, p. 123) remarks: 'Preparing and delivering lectures on a technical subject can bring intellectual insights, even on material you know by heart'. Sometimes, too, teaching can be a useful means of uncovering and overcoming shortcomings in one's own disciplinary education. Supervising the work of graduate students can help develop your research career. Through the engagement you have with graduate students' approaches to research questions and responses to specific research challenges, you may be able to expand your own array of research skills and knowledge. So, rather than regarding teaching and research as discrete activities, think about them as more or less equal partners and find ways to strengthen their marriage. This should support your research profile, perhaps even offering a 'scholarship of teaching' string to your academic bow, and also helping to ensure that your teaching is of high quality.

BOX 24.2 SOCIETIES AND AGENCIES SUPPORTING
THE SCHOLARSHIP OF TEACHING AND
LEARNING AND THEIR WEBSITES

- AdvanceHE – (formerly the Higher Education Academy [UK]) – https://www.advance-he.ac.uk/
- Ako Aotearoa: National Centre for Tertiary Teaching Excellence (New Zealand) – https://ako.ac.nz/
- Carnegie Foundation for the Advancement of Teaching (USA) – https://www.carnegiefoundation.org/
- Higher Education Research and Development Society of Australasia (Australia) – http://www.herdsa.org.au/
- International Society for the Scholarship of Teaching and Learning – https://issotl.com/
- Professional and Organizational Development Network (USA) – http://podnetwork.org/
- Society for Teaching and Learning in Higher Education (Canada) – https://www.stlhe.ca/
- Staff and Educational Development Association (UK) – https://www.seda.ac.uk/

The nexus between teaching and research has several dimensions. First, and probably most obviously, (your) research can be woven into and inform lectures and other modes of teaching, making classes vital and up to date. For many academics, being an active researcher is vital to their professional role (Douglas, 2013, p. 382) – a matter that many universities shifting to teaching-only positions do seem to disregard or discount. Research provides examples for teaching. And teaching offers a wonderful and often undervalued means of disseminating research findings and stimulating the interest of others in work you regard as meaningful and significant. Some scholars' enthusiasm for their work, as expressed through their teaching, can be so infectious that it encourages their students to pursue research higher degrees under their guidance.

Second, as one of the participants in Douglas's (2013, p. 381) study of social sciences professors in the United Kingdom remarked: 'I'd try and think of problems or projects where I could use in the first instance people that are around me as data givers.' That is, students can be engaged to gather data or, in some cases, to serve as research subjects. This latter practice appears to be very common in psychology where, for instance, large groups of undergraduate students are so commonly used as project samples that they have distorted the discipline to the extent that it is said to require structural reorganization (Henrich et al., 2010).[4] The technique of using students as 'data givers' is also employed in other disciplines where classes may be engaged to devise and distribute questionnaires or to conduct interviews and focus groups. For example, students in my early undergraduate classes conducted large-scale surveys on fear of violence and its implications for the use of urban space (Hay, 1995) as well as conducting (unpublished) work commissioned by a neighbourhood citizen group on local demand for recreational facilities. Such practices may still present their own challenges (e.g., health and safety for students; authorship and other concerns about academic exploitation), but they do offer valuable opportunities for students to engage first hand in some aspects of research as well as providing access to research data that would otherwise be difficult or costly to obtain.

Third, teaching itself can be the object of research. For example, you might conduct studies on the effectiveness of innovative or novel approaches to learning and teaching in your discipline. Not only do such publications contribute usefully to your tangible measures of scholarly output, they also demand careful reflection on learning and teaching, demonstrating your commitment to scholarly academic practice. Reflecting the growing demand for work at the teaching–research nexus, over the years a wide array of journals have emerged that focus on scholarly teaching in general (e.g., *Higher Education Research and Development*; *International Journal of Teaching and Learning in Higher Education*; *Teaching in Higher Education*) as well as within specific disciplines (e.g., *Journal of Geography in Higher Education*; *Teaching Philosophy*; *Teaching Sociology*).

Another way of connecting teaching very productively with scholarly output is to prepare a textbook. When establishing a new topic for teaching, many of us look to existing texts to provide some structure for the class and to offer students a helpful aligned learning resource. Often the search for an appropriate volume is frustrating and fruitless. An alternative approach – especially in areas where there are few appropriate or widely used texts – is to write or edit your own. So, when you are establishing a new topic for teaching, think about using the curriculum you develop as the structure for an authored or edited book. Many textbooks have such origins. For instance, Matthew Sparke aligned very carefully his 2013 book *Introducing Globalization* to his first-year class at the University of Washington entitled 'Introduction to Globalization'. Preparing your own textbook can be especially successful in large undergraduate classes where you will have a substantial ready-made audience for your new book – subject to the ethical considerations of prescribing your own book as a text of course! (for a helpful discussion on this see the still-current 2004 statement by the American Association of University Professors (2023)). As noted in Chapter 18, in some academic contexts, textbooks are not valued as highly as research monographs (e.g., for promotion purposes), despite the fact that they may sell many thousands of copies, influencing many fledgling scholars (Box 24.3). However, if you can produce a volume based on research that serves as a textbook, you will have very usefully satisfied two different ambitions.

BOX 24.3 WHEN LECTURES ENDED, THE TOPIC BECAME THE TEXTBOOK

I used to provide students in my 'Research Methods in Geography' class with a substantial (about 200 pages) collection of my 'lecture notes' for the topic. The idea behind this was to distract students from focussing on note-taking and concentrate instead on our discussions of more interesting and complex material. These notes provided the framework for a successful textbook, *Qualitative Research Methods in Human Geography*, published by a major international publisher and now in its fifth edition (Hay and Cope, 2021). An earlier edition of the book also became a key foundation for a fully online postgraduate research methods class.

As signalled earlier in this part of the book, community service can also be integrated into or aligned successfully with your teaching profile. For instance, during the 2010s, University of Washington geographer Michael Brown taught courses on Seattle, queer geographies, political geography, and research design. He worked collaboratively on a research project entitled 'Biopolitical Geographies' investigating the relations in the pre-AIDS era between Seattle's gay and lesbian community and health-promotion agencies. And he volunteered with the Northwest Lesbian and Gay History Project. The teaching and research of his University of Washington colleague at the time, Professor Victoria Lawson, incorporated 'theoretical and empirical material that illustrates and builds understandings of inequality, poverty and feminist care ethics across the Americas'.[5] And all of this work is bound in with the international Relational Poverty Network of which she is co-founder.

Teaching well is unquestionably a key to academic success and for many of us it requires a significant investment of time and emotion. Given the level of commitment required, those investments are best made wisely and advisedly and, where possible, in ways that help to sustain and draw from the research and even the service aspects of your academic career.

NOTES

1. Although other forms of teaching such as project-based learning are becoming increasingly common, lectures, tutorials and seminars continue to dominate at most universities.
2. These are an educational strategy in which students are first exposed to new concepts and ideas through videos, readings or other media outside the classroom and then class time, whether that be face-to-face or online, is used to discuss, analyse or work through those ideas. Flipped classrooms are generally regarded as a reversal of the 'traditional' approach to university education in which lecturers present new ideas in class and students work independently or in small groups outside class to understand and interpret them.
3. This is in no way intended to devalue teaching relative to research – as anyone who knows of the character of my own academic career will appreciate. It is simply an acknowledgment of the institutional understandings and pursuit of the particular forms of 'academic superheroes' introduced in Chapter 1.
4. Henrich et al.'s paper (2010) made the remarkable observation that behavioural scientists routinely publish broad claims about human psychology and behaviour in the world's top journals based on samples drawn entirely from Western, educated, industrialized, rich and democratic (WEIRD) societies and that many of these samples come from undergraduate student populations. As they note (p. 63), a randomly selected American undergraduate is more than 4000 times more likely to be a research participant than is a randomly selected person from outside the West!
5. See: http://faculty.washington.edu/lawson/professional-philosophy-practices/, accessed 6 January 2023.

25. Think about university service and leadership positions

As your career develops it is more or less inevitable that you will be offered or pressed into administrative roles that demand leadership and management skills – as well as a capacity to deal with everyday 'administrivia'! These roles might initially be as a degree coordinator, graduate student coordinator, or seminar series coordinator, for example. Such positions are difficult to avoid – even if you want to – especially if you are a woman working in disciplines or faculties where women are under-represented.[1] As Wolf-Wendel and Ward (2015, p. 23) observe, in the demands associated with service roles, for women in some disciplines 'there is no place to hide' and as part of a small cohort of female faculty members, some women also feel like they have to be on committees. Similar circumstances also shape the working conditions of members of identified minority groups.

Despite the negative overtones to this chapter's opening words, it is important to note that service and management roles are an accepted and often deeply rewarding part of being an academic in a contemporary university. Over and above the intrinsic value of contributing to the fulfilment of your university's mission, service roles offer three key benefits (Irish, 2021). First, they can enrich your professional life by building up important networks on and off campus. Moreover, the experiences gained such as running events, leading colleagues and generating policy may be regarded more highly than some additional papers on your publication record should you ever choose to move out of academia. Second, service activities can offer opportunities to support your teaching. For example, an across-university role will bring you into contact with colleagues from other discipline areas, raising the prospect of interdisciplinary research or teaching collaborations. Service work with student groups (e.g. honour societies, sustainable campus advocacy groups) may also provide opportunities to support student success and exercise your teaching skills. Third, service roles can support your research. Depending on your field consider applying a research focus to the service work in which you are involved. You may be able to write informed commentaries based on your experience. By way of example, my own university leadership experience ambitions led me to write 'Defending letters: a pragmatic response to assaults on the humanities' (Hay, 2016a). I found it a very helpful way to clarify and justify my responses to campus and community utilitarian criticisms of the humanities.

Participation in these service and leadership activities is almost always an expectation for appointments and promotions. Service functions can, as noted above, extend your local professional networks thereby affording insights to how and why things (do not) get done (Fiske, 2010, p. 123). As one participant in research conducted by Wolf-Wendel and Ward (2015, p. 28) observed: 'taking on service positions on key committees helps me to see what is going on … It also gives me the opportunity to participate at some very high levels.' However, the extent to which you accept or volunteer for these sorts of role should be thought through carefully and considered against other demands and obligations whilst taking account of your university's workload equivalence/ assignment measures (if they exist!).

Suitable service may support your promotion and other prospects, but too much can have the opposite effect. Indeed, in the United States there are some who go so far as to suggest that service is 'a dragon that must be slain to survive the hero's journey to tenure' (Irish, 2021). Some suggest that the 'ivory ceiling of service work' may adversely affect your career development ambitions (Wolf-Wendel and Ward, 2015, p. 29), even if those ambitions lie in university management. How might this happen? In some cases, so-called service roles have attached to them an institutionally agreed workload allowance. That is, there is formal acknowledgement by your employer that a particular service role is time consuming and so consideration is given to the extent of that by, say, a 0.2 release from other duties. What this example means is that your supervisor and university acknowledge that you need to spend 20 per cent of your time each week on this additional role and so your teaching and research commitments should be pared back to reflect this. This sounds very well in principle but in practice such allowances rarely reflect the real load associated with the new role and the other commitments rarely diminish sufficiently to compensate. So, if you are offered a workload allowance for service (or other) responsibilities, scrutinize it carefully. Does it seem to offer some fair compensation for the additional effort? Seek advice from others who have or have had a similar role. And, if the allowance seems inadequate and there is scope to do so, negotiate an adjustment that more accurately reflects the commitment you will need to make. Knowing these things, actively seek those roles that sit best with your other, broader plans (Chapter 16) and complete them to a high standard. If you find yourself dragooned into a position you are not too happy with, accept it with good grace, complete it well and move on to other things as swiftly as you are able.

Through your career, increasingly demanding functions, such as department chair, may present themselves. As leadership roles, these are a slightly different matter from the administrative positions discussed above. Commentators like Gray and Drew (2012, p. 136–137) are adamant that you should never accept the role of department chair unless you are already a tenured full professor. Quite rightly they point to significant burdens of management with the accompaniments of less time to do research, more mind-numbing email traffic than you can imagine, and the everyday challenges of herding the proverbial 'academic cats'. They also suggest that being head of department (or associate dean or some other similar managerial role) is unlikely to advance your academic promotion prospects. But this is not entirely true. First, some universities expect promotion applicants to have demonstrated institutional leadership through a position such as department chair. Second, being a successful department head is a key step if you aspire to even more senior management responsibility such as a dean, pro-vice-chancellor, or provost. Having said this, there remain many universities that do indeed attach less significance at promotion time to departmental leadership and service than they do to your ability to attract research funds and citations. So, if the opportunity to head your department or to take on some other management or leadership role presents itself, think and ask carefully about its place and time in your intended career trajectory.

Over and above any impediments to promotion, accepting a position of departmental head or associate dean can present other drawbacks. If you mishandle a major calamity on your watch, such as an industrial relations issue, a workplace safety incident, or a sexual harassment case, it may tarnish your career for a very long time. If you offend or disappoint your colleagues – and you are almost sure to upset some – they may ostracize you, excluding you from shared projects, co-authored papers and weekend parties. And if you do take on this kind of responsibility, you need to commit significant energy and effort to doing it well, effecting constructive change, improving research and teaching performance, or improving global rankings. While simply holding a sound departmental ship to its course may be extremely valuable – particularly during turbulent times – sadly it is unlikely to offer compelling evidence for an academic promotion either to professor or some other management role.

University leadership appointments do not always present themselves as a choice. There may come a time when you are 'tapped on the shoulder' and urged – almost certainly with some flattery and less commonly with some fine food – to accept such a position. If you are already a tenured full professor, give this serious consideration, if it appears to be a useful step on the ladder to more senior roles or because it provides the opportunity to shape a department or institution in ways you regard as important. But if you do not already have the benefits of seniority and tenure, ask yourself why you have been approached. While it may be a flattering acknowledgement of your innate or proven leadership skills, it may also be because there is simply no one else suitable to do the job or because other people are prepared to sacrifice your career for their own success or just because everyone else said no! And if everyone else did say no, ask yourself why.

Should circumstances be such that there is no way to avoid the offer, do all you can to make accepting it worthwhile. Just how do you wish to be compensated for potentially putting other aspects of your academic career into a state of suspended animation for three to five years?[2] Seek a pledge of tenure or promotion. Insist on a salary rise, supplementary research funding, reduced teaching, conference travel, a designated parking space, administrative assistance, sabbatical at the end of your term, leadership coaching, mentoring or any other benefit that will serve you well. And make sure you get everything that has been agreed set down in writing (see Chapter 15). Not only do senior administrators lie, they also forget, they move to other jobs, they die … Get it in writing!

If, by choice or coercion, you do find yourself destined for a leadership or management role (e.g., head of school, dean), avoid being one of the many people in positions of seniority who are manifestly poor at their job and unhappy in their position. This organizational flaw is sometimes explained by the 'Peter Principle', a popular – though not uncontested – concept (see, for example, Cohen, 2008, p. 172) suggesting that 'managers rise to their level of incompetence' (Peter and Hull, 1969, p. 8), and it is there that they stop being promoted. To minimize your chances of being one of the incompetent, look to academically linked leadership development organizations and programmes (e.g., the Academic Leadership Programme (ALP) run by Britain's Advance HE; Universities New Zealand's Women in Leadership programme; US Academy for Academic Leadership) or professional management associations such as the Australian Institute of Company Directors, the British Academy of Management, or the South African Institute of Management, to develop some of the financial, administrative and leadership skills and knowledge you will require. If they are available, participate in programmes tailored to the needs of academics. Many generic offerings cater largely for people in the private sector or government, both of which operate in different ways from universities.

And if you believe you can do so much better than the 'Peters' above you in the hierarchy and so seek additional leadership and management opportunities, let your supervisor (e.g., executive dean, pro-vice-chancellor) know of your ambitions and ask to be considered for, or included in, relevant pre-leadership career development opportunities (see Martin, 2022). If there are programmes outside the university that look interesting and appropriate, look for opportunities to secure the sometimes substantial financial or other support, such as leave, that will allow you to participate and support your leadership aspirations. It is well worth pursuing such opportunities for your own sake as well as for your university as a whole. Do not be shy about this. As Debowski (2022, p. 22) observes, even though universities are highly reliant on senior leaders to navigate through 'cataclysmic shifts in funding models, changes to student demand and workforce deployment' and even though '[t]heir impact on cultures, moral, well-being and strategic decisions is clear', 'many are thrust into key roles with little support or guidance'. Senior leaders can have 'profound consequences on thousands of individuals'. If you aspire to be one of these leaders, get prepared.

NOTES

1. The disproportionate and exhausting demands on women to serve as representatives on numerous committees and in other service roles have led to a phenomenon I have heard referred to as 'killing the Queen'. And, of course, similar demands are also placed on academics from under-represented groups.
2. This book does not examine the under-investigated and stressful transition from university manager back to an academic role. While the literature on that subject remains thin, some helpful recent contributions have been made by Bailey et al. (2016), Mallinger (2013), Martin (2021), Sale (2013) and Smith et al. (2012). Sale's work is especially helpful.

26. Find a voluntary role

Well, as if you didn't have enough to do already, what about adding a voluntary role to your workload?! Some scholars reject volunteering as a constituent of their career, with claims that they 'need to get publications out' or they 'don't have enough time' amidst all their other activities. Especially for an early-career academic these declarations may have some merit, but it is unwise to be completely dismissive of profession-related volunteer work as an element of career success and personal fulfillment.

People volunteer for three primary sets of reasons: altruistic (e.g. helping others, supporting a cause), utilitarian (e.g. developing skills, enhancing professional experience) and social (McFadden and Smeaton, 2017). Not only may volunteering provide relatively light relief from the sometimes seemingly relentless demands of teaching and research, it may also allow you to do some (professionally-enabled) good in communities meaningful to you while opening up other useful, enriching personal and scholarly opportunities and social networks. In short, as well as contributing to objective understandings of career success, volunteering locally and further afield can be a fundamental contributor to subjective career success, offering paths to life satisfaction and contributions to society.

Pragmatically, volunteering can enlarge and diversify personal and professional networks. The people you meet through your activities may know of job opportunities, useful cognate organizations and other people who may be interested in your work. For example, as Fiske (2010, p. 123) points out: 'Serving on the advisory board of a company or a local educational institution can help you connect to your community and unearth opportunities for consulting or collaboration. For example, volunteering at a science museum might turn into a collaborative science-education project.' Or, as Zoe Cournia discovered, volunteering to speak at her home country's universities during regular trips there from the United States and Germany eventually helped her land a good job in Athens (Box 26.1). While Cournia's disciplinary background is as a chemist there is no reason similar outcomes cannot be achieved in humanities, arts and social sciences (HASS) fields. Indeed, you may even find employment in the organization for which you voluteer. For instance, my own experience as a volunteer for a local community geographical organization led to paid part-time employment as its inaugural Director when I retired from full-time university work.

BOX 26.1   VOLUNTEERING TO STAY CONNECTED

Zoe Cournia is a Greek chemist who received advanced training abroad and desired to return to her home nation for permanent employment as a researcher. After graduating with her Bachelor's degree in chemistry from the University of Athens, she pursued her PhD at Heidelberg University, Germany and post-doctoral training at Yale University in New Haven, Connecticut. To stay connected to her country's academic community while away, she corresponded with her undergraduate mentors and asked for introductions to other scientists. Whenever she came home on holiday, she volunteered to give research talks at her alma mater and elsewhere. Pretty soon, she was receiving invitations from universities across the nation to give seminars. 'I may have left the country physically, but I never left the Greek academic system', she says. After five years of notable research that included publishing, presenting and mentoring combined with connecting with colleagues and lecturing activities in Greece, Cournia landed a job as an investigator (lecturer) in pharmacology and pharmacotechnology at the Biomedical Research Foundation Academy of Athens (Levine, 2013) where she remains today, though in a more senior role.

Through volunteering you may find opportunities to practise and develop valuable professional – and social – proficiencies. For example, as a novice researcher you could apply and refine your research abilities by conducting work for a local community organization trying to gauge demand for recreation facilities in their neighbourhood or assessing members' views on the relative worth of the organization's activities. The organization will probably welcome your talents and offer a wonderful mechanism through which to practise them. Many universities welcome staff involvement in such community-engaged research.

Of course, your own university may offer rewarding volunteering opportunities. Although most institutions tend to focus on volunteer opportunities for students, some coordinate programmes that invite academic staff for support. For example, Freie Universität Berlin (2022) directs a set of language and everyday life programmes intended to assist refugees.

If you have a desire to contribute to society even more broadly, an organization like Academics Without Borders (Universitaires sans frontières) may be of interest. AWB/USF is a Canadian-based consortium that works internationally to support developing countries improve and expand higher education.[1] Volunteers, who include working and retired professionals and academics from Canada and other medium- and high-income countries, work on a broad range of projects across disciplines and in countries such as Benin,

Chile, Ethiopia, Ghana, Indonesia and Nepal (AWB/USF, 2019). Given the level of time commitment required to participate in some of their projects (for which expenses are paid), this is the kind of work best undertaken as part of a sabbatical leave (see Chapter 30), other long break or even retirement.

EDITORIAL BOARDS

Your thinking about volunteering need not be confined to the community or development activities that the term is commonly associated with. It might instead be linked closely to service roles such as work with professional or disciplinary bodies or as a reviewer and editorial board member for a journal. While earlier chapters have discussed issues surrounding professional service and journal reviewing, less has been said about finding a place on an editorial board, an achievement that goes some way to signalling your particular expertise in a field as well as the regard you are held in by colleagues. Editorial board membership is generally volunteer work: it is remunerated very rarely. Typical roles of editorial board members are set out in Box 26.2. Experience on an editorial board can be very rewarding and interesting as well as a useful step on the career ladder (Haak, 2002). So, how does one become an editorial board member?

BOX 26.2 EDITORIAL BOARD MEMBER ROLES

- Providing expert advice to the editor or publisher on the journal's content and strategic directions.
- Lending credibility to the journal through their association with it.
- Writing editorials or other invited pieces.
- Working as handling editor, electing and inviting manuscript reviewers.
- Serving as (emergency) manuscript reviewer, especially for difficult or challenging papers.
- Acting as ambassador for the journal, promoting it in institutions and amongst colleagues and attracting high quality manuscripts.

Most commonly one secures a place on an editorial board by invitation. On the basis of your published work in a specific field, your contributions to conferences, and/or your thoughtful, timely refereeing of works submitted to a journal (Box 26.3), the editor may decide to approach you with an offer. Such offers are very pleasing to receive but you should be wary of the increasingly large number of offers circulating to join the editorial boards of journals you have never heard of! Associations with questionable publications such as predatory open access journals (see Beall and Anonymous, 2021) will do your career little good. Do your homework. Check the bona fides of the journal, its publisher, the editor and existing editorial board members.

BOX 26.3 HOW TO BE A GOOD REVIEWER FOR A JOURNAL AND WIN THE HEART OF AN EDITOR-IN-CHIEF

- Respond promptly to invitations to review.
- Where possible, accept those invitations you feel well qualified for; decline those outside your area of expertise.
- Suggest names of appropriate alternative reviewers if necessary.
- Declare any conflicts of interest.
- Follow instructions.
- Submit reviews before deadlines and without reminders.
- Provide detailed, well-justified and constructive comments.
- Make a clear recommendation about prospective publication consistent with your comments.
- Do not offer confidential comments to the editor that contradict those made to the author.
- Be prepared to review manuscripts you have read earlier and have been revised for resubmission.

Source: Adapted from Brown (2014).

Alternatively, though undertaken much less commonly, you can seek an editorial board role by submitting a statement (with CV) to the editor of a journal *that is aligned closely with your scholarly work* offering your services as a reviewer and possible editorial board member. The editor may appreciate the offer of refereeing support and will perhaps choose to test out your commitment and capabilities by sending you a number of manuscripts to review. However, your self-nomination to the board may be regarded poorly, being seen as presumptuous or otherwise inappropriate. Much will depend on factors such as your qualifications, your reputation, the need for editorial board members and the attitude of the editor-in-chief to self-nominations. So, if you do make an offer, you need to be highly competent and well informed, and if you accept an offer you must also be reliable and willing to carry through with the work for which you are volunteering. Be aware that the workloads for editorial board members can vary significantly from one journal to another: some require very little; others may demand extensive manuscript reviewing, editorial writing, and so on. Make sure you know what you are letting yourself in for. And if you take up a position on an editorial board, remember that editors-in-chief are not only busy; they are also influential and well connected and may have significant capacity to influence the shape of your career.

LEARNED SOCIETIES AND SCHOLARLY ASSOCIATIONS

In other activities closely related to your scholarly work, and as your career advances, there may be growing scope to take on rewarding and useful service leadership roles with learned societies and scholarly associations (e.g., Australasian Society for Classical Studies; New Zealand Historical Association; South African Archaeological Society). Such bodies provide numerous and regular opportunities for individuals to serve in voluntary, elected leadership positions (they are rarely paid) and on committees. Professional societies typically hold elections amongst their members for jobs such as councillor, secretary or president. If you see a call for nominations, give serious thought to putting up your hand. Aside from being able to do good works, such a role will almost certainly offer you fascinating insights into the broader professional community you are a member of. You will be better placed to meet and network with senior and distinguished colleagues as well as to support the development of junior scholars. And it may bring a higher profile to your research activities. Through such work, you may derive extensive personal as well as professional rewards that can reach well into your future. They can, for instance, help you secure interesting and rewarding leadership roles as you progress through your career and beyond into retirement.

To conclude, volunteering offers scope to contribute to society, to your university and to your discipline at the same time as it supports your career track record, demonstrating to current or prospective employers ways in which you can apply your research and related skills practically. Importantly, it offers the potential for immense personal satisfaction – as well as distinguishing you from other comparable candidates in the competition for future academic jobs.

NOTE

1. Another, though very slowly emerging, organization with similar objectives is the International Professors Project (IPP, 2023), 'a non-profit worldwide network of volunteer professors, professionals, graduate and college students interested in development, especially in education'.

27. Consider consulting

Some scholars apply their professional skills to consulting as ways of extending experience and networks; gaining insights to the broader value of their scholarship; and 'doing good' in the wider community. These can be noteworthy benefits of incorporating consulting into an academic career. Moreover, for those who consult for fees, the financial rewards can be significant. Certainly some humanities, arts and social sciences (HASS) fields such as archaeology, economics, planning, geographical information systems, environmental impact assessment and higher education attract more paid consulting opportunities than others, but the opportunities to consult span almost all disciplines. It is not just established, full-time scholars who find value in consulting. There is clearly scope for academics who find themselves in precarious employment relationships (e.g. short-term contract, casual employee) to use consulting as a means of securing additional income. This might be done alone, in partnership with other academic colleagues, or even with students. For instance, in an innovative development, a group in Singapore has developed a not-for-profit social change agency called Conjunct Consulting,[1] which simultaneously employs and trains Singaporean university students in all aspects of consulting while providing consulting services to non-profit organizations and social enterprises. Following compulsory training, teams of five students, working under the direction of appropriate professionals, provide consulting to clients in areas such as financial sustainability, strategic planning and impact measurement.

Many prospects for consulting work can be found through personal and professional networks but there are increasing opportunities to find consulting opportunities through other means, notably the Internet and the commercialization arms of some universities. As universities and research agencies look for ways to better connect with 'industry', so they have established services intended to bridge any gap between scholars and broader society and to act as clearing houses for consulting capacity. Examples include Flinders Partners Pty Ltd, which is the commercialization agent for Flinders University in South Australia; University College London Consultants Ltd; and the University of Washington's University Consulting Alliance.

Some examples of the more global, profession-based or web-centred opportunities to find consulting are listed in Box 27.1. Aside from helping to connect consultants and clients, such sites offer useful, sometimes jurisdiction-specific,

guidance on consulting, including how to price your services, preparing proposals, ownership of intellectual property, developing a résumé appropriate
to consulting, how not to get sued, and designing a good website for your
consulting business.

BOX 27.1   SOURCES OF INFORMATION ON CONSULTING OPPORTUNITIES AND SUPPORT

Below is a short list of some of the organizations offering opportunities and
resources for consultants (and their clients). A quick search of the Internet
will reveal others that may be related more closely to your specific disciplinary interests.

- American Historical Association (https://www.historians.org/) offers
  advice for historians as consultants and contractors.
- Australian Association of Consulting Archaeologists Inc. (https://www
  .aacai.com.au/) is the professional association for consulting archaeologists in Australia, AACAI develops best practice, promotes training and
  communication and provides support for its members.
- IdeaConnection (http://www.ideaconnection.com/) claims to offer
  clients access to a worldwide network of experts, leaders and industry
  veterans.
- InnoCentive (https://www.innocentive.com/about-us) crowdsources
  innovation problems to consultants who compete to offer their services to help resolve business, social, policy, scientific and technical
  challenges.
- Maven (http://www.maven.co) comprises thousands of consultants from
  a huge array of professional backgrounds in over 150 countries. Their
  consultants are said to include doctors, lawyers, teachers, social media
  experts, polymer scientists and goldminers.
- Planning Institute of Australia (https://www.planning.org.au/) supports
  and represents the interests of consultant planners in Australia.
- Strategic Sustainability Consulting (http://sustainabilityconsulting.com)
  is a network that brings together consultants with clients seeking to
  manage social and environmental impacts.

Professional consulting is not without its costs and challenges (see Box 27.2).
Consulting can cause issues if you use, for example, university resources
and facilities to support what is effectively a private business. Hence many

universities demand that staff declare details of their consulting work and the proportion of their time dedicated to it. Such matters need to be thought about carefully. Another prospective challenge lies in the reactions of colleagues to your consulting. Some may begrudge the additional income you achieve. Others may feel that you are spending time on consulting at the expense of teaching, research and service activities and feel aggrieved if they have to 'pick up the slack'. Obviously the requirements of any consulting can cut significantly into the time available to work in any primary employment or on other scholarly endeavours and so these relationships need to be managed carefully. Consulting often demands a good deal of expensive and time-consuming travel to meet with clients and research partners or participants. Liability or malpractice insurance costs may be substantial. You may also need to develop and apply appropriate business and legal skills to run your consultancy properly.

BOX 27.2   SOME ADVANTAGES AND DISADVANTAGES OF CONSULTING

Advantages

- 'Flexible' work hours.
- Sustaining productive connections between academia and relevant communities.
- Broad range of satisfying work opportunities.
- Lucrative pay.
- Opportunities to extend networks.

Disadvantages

- Unreliable pay and irregular hours.
- Dealing with conflicts of interest.
- Managing the consultancy's business and finance affairs.
- Cost of insurances (e.g., income protection; professional liability).
- Need for strong self-motivation: 'get up and go'.
- Maintaining boundaries between work and personal life.

There are other considerations. You may think that consulting can allow you to be paid extra while generating data for your publications. However, in many instances the data derived from consulting may not be used for scholarly research outputs, if that data are understood to legally belong to the agency that commissioned the work – irrespective of who gathered or produced it.

Moreover, many universities, research agencies and governments do not recognize consulting reports as research outputs, typically because they are not
generally subject to peer review. There remain questions at the back of some
people's minds about the impartiality of work conducted by a 'gun for hire'
and the risk of conflicting interests.

For example, the US NIH was exposed in the 2000s to intense scrutiny
following media reports suggesting that its scientists' consulting arrangements
posed conflicts of interest (Marris, 2004, p. 497). In some instances too, as
a consultant you may be legally bound not to publicly reveal the results of your
work (e.g., works that are confidential, secret, or involved in legal proceedings)
and so there is no product to report anyway! For example, work conducted as
part of the US Natural Resource Damage Assessment (NRDA) of BP's 2010
Deepwater Horizon oil spill in the Gulf of Mexico is not available for public
scrutiny. As one researcher observed: 'When you collect data for the [NRDA]
and agree to analyse them, you are essentially foreclosing on your ability to
publish those data because they're going to be involved in court cases and
they're subject to all kinds of sequestering and gag orders' (Ian MacDonald,
cited in Mascarelli, 2010, p. 538).

Finally, consulting for one agency may preclude you from working with
another or from applying for government funds. Again, in the case of the
Deepwater Horizon spill, some scholars found that consulting for BP under the
NRDA process raised the serious prospect that they would be prevented from
applying for federal funding (Mascarelli, 2010, p. 538).

Notwithstanding its clear challenges, consulting can be a useful, beneficial
and lucrative adjunct to a successful university career as well as offering
a plausible way of beginning to move out of an academic career or transition-
ing to semi-retired status (see Chapter 35).

NOTE

1.   See: http://conjunctconsulting.org/, accessed 23 June 2022.

28. Get recognized

In the development of your successful academic career, an important adjunct to getting known and networked (discussed in Chapter 9) is achieving favourable recognition for your work. Fellowships, awards and other markers of peer esteem are not only rewards for work done and very good for the ego (as well as for your institution), they can also lend support to your continuing career advancement efforts. Some awards may come to you unexpectedly; others may demand some effort on your part.

From the outset of your academic career it pays to pursue career grants and fellowships (e.g., British Academy, Churchill Fellowships, Leverhulme Trust, Nuffield Foundation) and travel awards. Many organizations offer research and travel grants to emerging scholars. For instance, in the United States, the National Science Foundation offers prestigious awards through its 'Faculty Early Career Development Program' (CAREER):

> in support of early-career faculty who have the potential to serve as academic role models in research and education and to lead advances in the mission of their department or organization. Activities pursued by early-career faculty should build a firm foundation for a lifetime of leadership in integrating education and research. (National Science Foundation, 2022)

In Europe, the EUTOPIA Science and Innovation Fellowship Programme offers the opportunity to high-profile young researchers to develop their own research project with the aim of fostering the fellows' entrepreneurial spirit, tangible research impact and innovation (EUTOPIA, 2022). And the Institute of Australian Geographers makes substantial awards available to early-career scholars to present papers at International Geographical Union congresses. Apply for such awards as well as scholarly prizes (e.g., journal and society awards for your work). An increasing number of journals (e.g., *British Journal of Criminology*; *Economic Geography*) and organizations (e.g., Australian Institute of Urban Studies; Society for the Study of French History) offer prizes for exemplary scholarship. There are also awards for high-quality conference presentations, sometimes specifically for doctoral students[1] and early-career researchers. As you become more senior in your field maintain your lookout for fellowships and awards for which you may be eligible. These will be offered by, for example, learned societies, international bodies, scholarly journals, and community organizations.

Ask colleagues and mentors about extant opportunities. Become close friends with those staff in your university's research office who can tell you about them. Submit your own applications or nominate colleagues. If you do put someone else's name forward, they will probably be delighted, given that such collegial recognition is a remarkably rare commodity. Having said this, do not be shy about nominating yourself if you believe you have the credentials for a credible case. Egotistical as it may seem, self-nomination for awards is a common practice – even being expected in some cases – and may be likened to the grant application process.

In your pursuit of support and recognition, do persevere. Some 'stars' have only a few setbacks (although this is very rarely the case), but for most 'lesser mortals', repeated applications for grants and prizes are the norm (Stefan, 2020). If you find yourself despairing, think back to Abraham Lincoln's terrible record of failure on the way to the White House and one of the great US presidencies or of Robert the Bruce's reputed utterance: 'If at first you don't succeed, try, try and try again'. And once you start to be recognized, additional and greater recognition is likely to follow, assuming you continue to do good work of course.

When you are recognized through an award or when you do something remarkable like publishing a book, receiving a rare grant, or being appointed to an influential committee, let people know. Of course, there are good and not so good ways of doing this! A not-so-good way is to walk along the departmental corridor shouting out loud that you have just received a major grant or award. A slightly better way is to let people know through your social media presence (e.g. LinkedIn). And perhaps an even better way is to contact your university's public relations unit. They specialize in disseminating success stories, which reflect well not only on you as an individual but also on your department and the institution as a whole. Typically, unit staff will get some background information from you and possibly some photographs or audiovisual materials that will be used as the basis of a story of your good tidings for a large and interested audience. And if you are blessed with a good public relations team, they will even give you the opportunity to review and remark on their story before it goes public.

Public recognition for scholarly work is not merely an outcome of a successful career. It contributes to that success by indicating your status in the field and supporting promotion and tenure claims. And it can also be supportive of job and life satisfaction, making you happier and more confident in your work. Seek out opportunities for recognition but also remember to make a point of recognizing and acknowledging the achievements of your colleagues.

NOTE

1. Though not for conference presentations per se, the Three Minute Thesis competition is an important emerging professional development and recognition activity for PhD students. It began in 2008 at the University of Queensland to celebrate the research conducted by Doctor of Philosophy students. According to the University of Queensland's (2023) website, 3MT cultivates students' academic, presentation and research communication skills. The competition supports doctoral students' capacity to effectively explain their research in three minutes, in a language appropriate to a non-specialist audience. Since its inauguration 3MT has diffused internationally and is held in over 900 universities across more than 85 countries worldwide.

PART V

PRESERVING YOUR ACADEMIC SUPERPOWERS

29. Review your performance

Performance review and associated changes to the ways you do things are critical means of preserving and improving your academic capabilities. Most universities have now formalized a raft of review processes for students and academics. These include, for example, student and peer evaluations of teaching, regular assessments of research output, and annual performance reviews. Such evaluations are often vital components of appointment, promotion, tenure and other career-related decision-making processes. However, many of these forms of evaluation have intrinsic problems (see, for example, Chávez and Mitchell, 2020; Esarey and Valdes, 2020; Kreitzer and Sweet-Cushman, 2022; Rubino, 2022; Shevlin et al., 2000; Spooren et al., 2015) and have sometimes become so 'routinized' as to lose much of their meaning and foundational purpose (see Spiller and Harris, 2013). Nonetheless, they can be useful formative assessment tools for your professional development (Ballantyne et al., 2000). So, instead of joining those of your colleagues who regard the various expressions of formal reviews as an unfortunate, time-wasting and flawed imposition from your university's human resources or 'people and culture' division, look at them as providing an opportunity to gather intelligence about how your students, supervisors and colleagues regard your relative performance and to uncover ways of improving that performance.

One of the most common forms of review used in universities are course evaluations or student evaluations of teaching (SETs). SETs commonly take the form of anonymous/confidential surveys comprising closed and open-ended questions which are intended to evaluate and deliver feedback on teaching effectiveness and course content. There is extensive criticism of SETs, suggesting they reflect student biases around matters including age, gender and race (e.g. Heffernan, 2021) and that they are otherwise unreliable but there is also a view that despite their flaws, and if used in conjunction with other indicators of quality, SETs can offer some helpful insights to students' experiences with university teachers (e.g. Esarey and Valdes, 2020). Many universities demand the use of SETs and have established prescribed means by which they are conducted. So, there is every possibility that you will have to deal with SETs whether you want them or not. It is helpful therefore to know how to respond to them and Box 29.1 offers some detailed advice on how to do that. Try to use the results of such reviews as general advice on ways to enhance your teaching practice. But if you find comments that are distressingly offensive (e.g. racist, ageist) and inappropriate consider raising your concerns with your supervisor.

BOX 29.1 HOW TO RESPOND TO STUDENT EVALUATIONS OF TEACHING

- Focus on the recurring themes. Try not to dwell on the outliers – either positive or negative – unless something in them genuinely resonates with you. Remember too that different teaching styles appeal to different people and so yours may not appeal equally to everyone.
- Consider the possible reasons for any negativity. A poor comment may be because the student is angry or disappointed (about a grade) or that they find there is more work in the class than they had counted on or they are stressed because they are having money problems. Though sometimes more insightful than the quantitative component of SETs anonymous commentary in some SETs allows students to make misogynist, misandrist, homophobic, ageist, racist and other slurs that are much more a reflection of the author than they are of your teaching.
- Revisit the evaluations a day or two after you first receive them. By then you may be better positioned to reconsider good/poor reviews more dispassionately and to apply an analytical perspective to the results.
- Work out how what aspects of your teaching/curriculum warrant change (e.g. perhaps one particular assignment is regarded by many students as poor; students don't like that your classes start later than scheduled or that they run over time). Set about making those changes.
- Do the evaluations differ significantly from those of previous years or other classes you teach? What has changed? What is different? What is to be learned from this?
- Especially if there are specific areas you want to amend consider seeking feedback more frequently during a teaching term so you can adjust your teaching as you go rather than at the end of a semester. It may be helpful to ask students in short anonymous surveys: what is going well about the class?; what needs improvement?; and what should you stop?
- Seek teaching advice and support if the evaluations suggest it may be required. This might include asking a colleague to sit in and observe your class(es).
- If you make changes to your practice on the basis of evaluations, let students know acknowledging that you are responding to feedback to help improve learning and teaching.

- And, just in case you receive negative feedback, remember that even the best professors have that experience (see Chapter 24)! Reflect on the feedback and use what you can to make constructive changes to your practice.

You may wish to consider running your own appraisals to complement or supplement institution-initiated instruments. For example, your university's SETs may not present an opportunity to evaluate specific teaching initiatives or aspects of your teaching that you seek special consideration for. You may be interested to know which aspects of your courses students value most highly and which they would like to see revised. You can conduct this kind of assessment easily with a simple anonymous survey administered in class or online. Or if you want to get a broader sense of how things are going, ask a skilled professional developer (e.g., from your university's centre for teaching development) or trustworthy senior colleague to meet with your class to run – in your absence – a short discussion/focus group to find out what aspects of your teaching and the curriculum they regard as especially strong or weak. Some universities offer this kind of intervention as part of their teaching development services.

You can also formalize your independent review activities by engaging in scholarship related to that work (e.g., scholarship of teaching). In other words, apply your research skills to the careful and systematic analysis of your teaching, service and other professional activities. There is a strong tradition of such activity in the area of teaching, with numerous journals in the field (e.g., *Art Education Journal*; *Feminist Teacher*; *The Journal of Economic Education*; *Journal of Planning Education and Research*; *Teaching Sociology*); scholarly societies (notably the International Society for the Scholarship of Teaching & Learning [ISSOTL]), and international conferences. Through this kind of endeavour, you can turn thoughtful, high-quality reviews of your professional activities into tangible aca demic output.

Finally, if you move from academic to management ranks, give serious consideration to the value of 360-degree (or multi-rater) reviews, if these are not already part of institutional practice. These reviews generally entail: (1) soliciting (anonymous) direct constructive feedback on your strengths and weaknesses from subordinates, peers, supervisors and other interested parties; and importantly (2) acting on the feedback. Most academics in teaching/research roles are already involved in 360-degree reviews, receiving comment from peers, students and supervisors. Somewhat ironically, however, many university managers – including heads of department, deans, pro-vice-chancellors and so on – are reviewed only by their supervisor. While 360-degree reviews are not without their drawbacks (Church et al., 2019; Lawrence, 2015; Peiperl,

2001), they may forestall management problems and signal difficulties or strengths in your management style or interpersonal communication skills. By conducting regular 360-degree reviews of your work you offer colleagues the opportunity to provide critically constructive feedback in a way that is non-confrontational and before any issues become toxic and unmanageable. And what you learn may stand you in good stead if you move upward through academic hierarchies.

30. Take sabbatical

Despite increasing institutional thrift, or even austerity, some universities and research organizations continue to offer sabbaticals (increasingly known as study leave to better reflect their changing intent and expectations [Scott and Scott, 2022a, p. 16]) to academic staff. Sabbaticals are periodic opportunities to set aside teaching and management responsibilities and concentrate on academic and professional development and to enhance or re-establish personal well-being (Badenhorst et al. 2022, p. 167).

Sabbaticals are typically six months to a year in duration and usually – though not necessarily – involve conducting work at another institution, often abroad. Sadly, as universities become more and more hardnosed the duration allowed for sabbatical is sometimes diminishing and the qualifications required to 'win' this form of leave are increasing (e.g. length of service; academic seniority). Sabbatical is also almost exclusively open to staff on 'permanent' or 'tenured' appointments. As larger proportions of academic staff find themselves in limited-term contracts and other forms of impermanent employment, fewer have access to the rewards sabbatical affords. Even for those who are eligible to apply, sabbaticals are becoming more and more difficult to receive and in some cases their award is highly competitive. And so, in starting this chapter, let me say that if you wish to take sabbatical at some stage in your career, read your institution's sabbatical rules years before you expect to apply! Interrogate the regulations to work out how to maximize your chances of securing this valuable opportunity. This may see you poring over an Enterprise/Collective Agreement, studying university policies and procedures, and speaking with experienced colleagues and perhaps union officials (Scott and Scott, 2022a, p. 220).

Though not intended to be a holiday or opportunity for you to paint your house sabbatical can be a tremendously refreshing – and demanding – opportunity (see Handford and Sibbald, 2022 for an insightful collection of papers on many aspects of sabbaticals). On the plus side, sabbatical offers many benefits to individual academics as well as to their universities (Box 30.1).

BOX 30.1 BENEFITS OF SABBATICAL

- *Rejuvenation and renewal.* As the aphorism suggests, 'A change is as good as a rest'. Simply getting out of your usual routine can allow a real renaissance in your work and attitude to it. It may enhance your mental and physical well-being, reduce stress and moderate depression.
- *Time for reflection.* Escaping the everyday demands of 'administrivia' and meetings allows opportunity for contemplation on matters such as your research themes, career direction and publishing plans. During sabbatical make yourself scarce in your home institution. Stay away from your office and, where possible, do not answer emails. You are absent. If people have any inkling that you are around you can be assured that they will find urgent, important things for you to do!
- *A fresh perspective.* You may have the opportunity to take a different view of shifts and trends in your discipline.
- *New professional relationships.* This really is an important part of any sabbatical experience, with new collegial and productive relationships sometimes lasting for many years.
- *Enriched cultural experiences.* This is particularly likely if you have the opportunity to spend 3–6 months in another country or cultural context.
- *Becoming or staying current in the discipline.* In the midst of other everyday pressures on time it can be easy to fall behind with technical and theoretical developments in your area of interest, a matter sabbatical can help remedy.
- *Opportunity for skills development.* An extended break away from usual commitments can allow opportunities to dedicate time for career enhancing skills development (e.g. educational management; learning to use complex new software).
- *Increase research productivity* by allowing opportunity for conducting research, undertaking analysis and writing.
- *Enhancing teaching* by, for example, introducing new pedagogical approaches supporting curriculum development and heightening enthusiasm.
- *Improved morale* – but perhaps only if all staff have abundant access to sabbatical opportunities!

Source: Adapted from Zahorski (1994) and Scott and Scott (2022b).

A period of sabbatical can be deeply rewarding, but your own anticipation and expectations of it can also make it debilitating! Very often scholars look forward to sabbatical as an extended research idyll, failing to take proper account of the challenges they may face during the time. A common mistake is overestimating what can be done in the time away. So, to begin, when you consider your ambitions for sabbatical leave, or set them out in an application to take leave, be as realistic as possible. Indeed, it may even pay to understate your objectives, focusing on your major aspirations and putting aside some of the minor outcomes as supplementary goals.

Bear in mind too that when you start sabbatical you may be quite exhausted from the preceding years of work that were required to earn or entitle you to the opportunity. Indeed, some universities will expect you to enable your absence for part of the teaching year by 'bringing forward' all of that year's teaching! This may leave you so worn out that the initial stages of your sabbatical are spent recovering (see, for example, Handford, 2022).

Arranging sabbatical and setting everything in order before you begin it, and adjusting to new work and living arrangements, can be stressful and much more time-consuming than you anticipate. Susannah Mintz colourfully discloses a deeply unsettling disjunction between expectation and reality in her wonderful and revealing paper 'The dirty little secret of sabbatical':

> My friends had had adventures on their sabbaticals. They lived in Europe for a year, burrowing into important foreign archives. They spent semesters at universities and libraries in nearby vibrant cities, making coffee dates with scholars whose names anyone would know and hooking up with other intellectuals for smart conversations and sex. They made it sound so glamorous, so revitalizing, I couldn't imagine, starting out, how low my own sabbatical would bring me: I felt sure I would do important work. I didn't yet know how much the time off would confuse the connection between doing and being, working and/as the self, how much my discomfort would crystallize around a sense of not belonging and of not getting something right. (Mintz, 2009)

She wishes she had known before her sabbatical how much others had suffered during theirs. Exhaustion, high expectations of one's own performance, romanticized and unrealistic views of one's stamina for work; relationship traumas, and separation from the 'grounding' effect of a regular routine can all lead to unexpected and debilitating anguish:

> Most of all, I wish I'd known that others had also suffered on their sabbaticals – a fact I didn't realize until I began to confess to my friends how dangerously low I'd gotten, and some, to my surprise and relief, reported similar experiences of lonely struggle. So much extended isolation is madness in itself. (Mintz, 2009)

The tribulations one encounters on sabbatical may also have other origins as Handford (2022, pp. 75–6) illustrates in her review of a six month leave period:

> In mid-February, my husband experienced two serious health events, just as the COVID-19 pandemic was gaining strength. Everything stopped as we managed specialists, tests, family concerns, and our own anxieties .... I was highly aware that my husband, with his lengthy list of risk factors, was vulnerable in ways beyond his health events. I cancelled plans to attend conferences where I was presenting in April, May, and June .... By the end of the month, I had cancelled all conference registrations and presentations scheduled to the end of August.

Finally, although sabbatical can relieve you of the everyday university demands, you do actually have to (be able to) disengage from those quotidian pressures during sabbatical if you are to accrue and preserve well-being benefits of the respite (Badenhorst et al. 2022, p. 168; Davidson et al., 2010; Flaxman et al. 2012). It is possibly for this reason that scholars who take their sabbatical outside their home country seem to enjoy more enhanced well-being than those who do not (Davidson et al., 2010).

So, sabbatical is not without its pitfalls. However, forewarned of some of the risks, you may be better placed to manage them by allowing yourself time for rest and recuperation at the beginning of the leave and not imposing unnecessarily onerous or high expectations on yourself – perhaps as a way of convincing your supervisor that you should be granted leave! It is probably better to underplay that hand and trust that you can achieve more than agreed.

Despite its challenges, most scholars find sabbatical to be an invigorating and rewarding experience presenting unparalleled career-supporting and life-satisfying opportunities. As Box 30.1 suggests, sabbatical can be mentally stimulating and invigorating, offering chances to develop new ideas, explore old ideas more fully, complete a book, wrap up those projects that have been haunting you for ages, and develop new professional relationships with colleagues. Notwithstanding these and other rewards, time as a visitor at another institution can look very good on your CV.

Having considered some of the pros and cons of sabbatical, what of some of the practicalities? Your university will certainly demand that you consider and accommodate scholarly practicalities such as how your customary teaching will be handled in your absence and what arrangements have you made for the supervision of your graduate students? They will 'guide' you though this process as part of the sabbatical application process, prompting you to provide advice on how you will manage these matters. However, personal practicalities can be a little more opaque, potentially challenging, and gendered (e.g. Smith et al., 2016). If you are single, relatively unconstrained and involved in research with few major, specific infrastructure requirements, sabbatical can be relatively easy to arrange. If, on the other hand, you have a spouse in paid employment, children in schools, ageing relatives, a cat or dog that needs caring for, a house that needs to be occupied, a car that needs to be driven and research that ties you to your institution, taking sabbatical somewhere else can be rather more of a challenge! Some – but obviously not all – of these problems can be overcome by having other academics take over your home, caring for your garden, making sure your car gets driven and looking after the pets. Again, from Mintz (2009): 'Go to Italy, they said, for six months, as if I could afford such a lark on half-pay, and no one ever explained to me who would feed my cats.' Leaving the cat aside (so to speak), there is at least one useful website called Sabbatical Homes[1] that facilitates sabbatical accommodation exchanges globally. According to the website, Sabbatical Homes is 'dedicated to providing temporary home rentals and home exchanges to our community of academics, writers, artists and friends'. It has been operating since 2000. There are other sites that can assist with the issue of accommodation, including Sabbatical.com and Academichomes.com[2] and some universities offer assistance to visitors in the form of relatively inexpensive, conveniently located accommodation. You can usually find details on university websites. If you are visiting a colleague already known to you or arranging your leave through a section of the university dedicated to facilitating such visits (e.g., the University of Edinburgh's Institute for Advanced Studies in the Humanities) they may be able to direct you to useful local resources.

While sabbatical is typically supported through the continued payment of salary and a supplement to contribute to any travel and accommodation costs, you may find it helpful or necessary to seek out additional funding. Speak with colleagues in your research office or at the institution you are visiting to see if there are any opportunities you are eligible for. Some universities and granting bodies (e.g., American Council of Learned Societies; British Academy; Open Society Foundations) have attractive schemes for this very purpose. Of course, there are also opportunities available in the form of fellowships offered by international organizations (e.g., Churchill, Fulbright or Leverhulme) as well as individual universities (e.g., Bristol's Benjamin Meaker Visiting Fellowships; National University of Singapore's Isaac Manasseh Meyer Fellowships). Not only do those provide additional funding, but some of the more prestigious agencies and institutions may also lead to other opportunities and career connections. On the matter of money, it is important to be aware that in some jurisdictions sabbatical and its funding can have significant and challenging tax implications, particularly where work-related expenses can be applied against earned/won income. As Scott and Scott (2022b, p. 29) suggest, seek the expertise of a good taxation accountant in such cases.

When your study leave is over you will almost certainly be expected to write a report outlining your activities and achievements (benchmarked against those things you said you were going to do when you applied for sabbatical).

Do not treat this lightly. Write a strong, comprehensive report and submit it on time. Often, future entitlements to sabbatical hinge on successful completion of the last.

Notwithstanding the availability of various sabbatical funding opportunities, in this extended 'age of austerity' for universities many institutions seek to eliminate or minimize study leave prospects to save money. Arguably this cost-saving strategy is misguided for the institution given that sabbaticals offer the prospects of increased staff efficiency, versatility and productivity; fortified institutional programmes; enhanced learning environments; better staff morale; heightened loyalty to the institution; a better intellectual climate; and an enhanced academic reputation (Zahorski, 1994). If you find that your institution seeks to wind back its study leave opportunities, for your own sake as well as that of your colleagues present and future, point out these benefits as counterpoints to budget-driven cutbacks.

NOTES

1.   See: http://www.sabbaticalhomes.com, accessed 21 January 2023.
2.   See: http://sabbatical.com/ and https://www.academichomes.com, accessed 21 January 2023.

31. Get refreshed

Long summer holidays, job autonomy, social status and flexible work arrangements are all characteristics that make life as a scholar appear attractive to many people outside the academy. But most observers generally do not see the pressures and strains in universities that are, without question, growing in intensity and damaging employees and, in some instances, their loved ones. Moreover, anxiety, stress, depression and other mental health problems afflict career academics and those preparing for such work (Flaherty, 2022; Mula-Falcón et al., 2022; Wiegel et al., 2016; Wilcox, 2014; Winefield and Jarrett, 2001). For example:

> In 2010 I started a PhD ... A year on, and the pressure began to build, reaching the point where I had a nervous breakdown. I spent time going to counselling for help, but then decided to take a 10-month break from the research I was doing. Upon returning I was able to work for a few months before falling back into depression because I felt I had no chance of gaining the qualification I desired. I eventually got to the stage where I felt I was going nowhere and cleared my desk late one Saturday, saying nothing to anyone that I was leaving. While suffering from depression, I felt isolated, as everyone around me was able to get on with their PhDs. I felt I was the problem. I feel I received some support for my issues but more could have been done to ease me back into full-time study after returning. (Cited in Shaw and Ward, 2014)

While explanations for specific, individual problems vary, the broad phenomena of stress and psychological distress are almost certainly intensified by a challenging combination of perfectionist scholars with unremitting demands from student 'consumers' for round-the-clock responses to email queries; falling public regard for academics and universities (Arum and Roksa, 2011; Heller, 2012); increasingly precarious employment relationships (González-Calvo, 2020; Shaw and Ward, 2014; Wilcox, 2014; Winefield et al., 2003); and heightened demands from university representatives for academics to increase measurable 'output' – even to the absurd extent of demanding celibacy, or childlessness at least:

> At the beginning of my PhD, the director of the department gave our entire cohort a lecture about not getting pregnant and told one of my friends when she applied for maternity leave that the PhD should be a time of celibacy. Some of our supervisors publicly and proudly exchanged stories of failed marriages as if this was the ultimate

proof of their devotion to research. Others gossiped about promising colleagues who 'would have achieved so much more' had they not had children. All of these subtle and not so subtle hints guaranteed that no graduate student, especially those with families, would ever sacrifice enough for their research and would thus, by implication, always be a failure in some respect. (Cited in Shaw and Ward, 2014)

Moreover, working with stressed colleagues can be 'infectious', with strained and breaking relationships creating new tensions. And all of these problems are likely to be made worse by the fact that because many scholars work in areas they love, they find it difficult to separate work from other aspects of their lives.

United States biologist Elizabeth Haswell has colourfully likened the situation many academics find themselves to that of overworked topsoil on a farm. She opines:

> Like the topsoil on a farm, a scientist's ability to produce thoughtful and creative teaching, research and service must be protected in order to ensure long-term productivity and to prevent damage to the ecosystem. Too often we sustain constant productivity with the inorganic fertilizers of coffee and wine, and generate toxic run-off like negativity, competition and self-doubt. (Haswell, 2017)

As other chapters of this book discuss, some pressures can be dealt with – or the 'topsoil remediated' – by means such as managing your time effectively (Chapter 17) or employing a range of behavioural tactics to stay happy and healthy (Chapter 34). Another way of coping with the stresses of the job is by actively seeking ways of staying energized and enthusiastic about your work. Several ways of staying 'fresh' as an academic are set out in Box 31.1. While some of these require incorporating additional tasks to your already very busy schedule, by unsettling and adding variety to your routines they offer the promise of reinvigoration and renewed dynamism.

BOX 31.1 SOME WAYS OF STAYING 'FRESH' AS AN ACADEMIC

- Visit other departments in your own and cognate fields. See how things are done differently administratively, in teaching and in research. If you feel a bit jaded or disenchanted with your own department, a visit to another may either make you feel better about where you are currently or provide ideas about ways of making life better where you are.
- Go to conferences. Be energized by the intensity of activity, new ideas, catching up with old colleagues and meeting new ones.

- Get involved in external workshops, seminars and continuing education programmes. Refresh and extend your skills.
- Converse with colleagues about your teaching and research as well as about sport, politics and the weather: 'the act of just talking with colleagues about what they are doing in the classroom can open you to new ideas' (Tulloch, 2012, p. 17).
- When you can, say no to 'invitations' that distract you from your main goals. Maintain your focus on the things you love and really want to do.
- Co-teach. Rather than simply dividing and partitioning a course, work with colleagues to find ways of enhancing it and invigorating your teaching (Buchanan and Childerhouse, 2012, pp. 15–16).
- Stay fit and healthy. Avoid developing problems like occupational overuse syndrome (OOS) (also known as repetitive strain injury – RSI), from spending long hours in front of a computer. Move – often. Seek advice on appropriate ways of dealing with any of the hazards associated with your research and fieldwork. If you find that you are uncomfortably stressed or anxious, seek help. Get exercise.
- Create and maintain clear boundaries between work and personal life.
- Take regular breaks – short (e.g., 15 minutes for coffee or a walk) and long (e.g., weekend away at the beach). Brief diversions from a task can improve our ability to focus on that task for prolonged periods (Yates, 2011) as well as allowing us to retain information and make intellectual connections (Oakley, 2014).
- Make time for activities you enjoy outside work. Go to the movies, go fishing, read a novel, or paint a portrait.
- Use your annual and holiday leave for recreational purposes, not work.
- Do not sacrifice sleep, meals or exercise.
- Develop social relationships with people outside academia (e.g., through sports clubs, special interest groups, religious organizations).
- Keep in touch with your friends.
- And if you still find that everything is getting overwhelming, seek support from professional sources, friends and family.

While these behavioural approaches can certainly support mental and physical health, I know from personal experience that they can sometimes feel like additional burdens atop an already huge load. The sense that one *has* to exercise or *has* to have a hobby or *has* to spend time with friends and family or *has* to look after a garden to somehow maintain a balance against the other demands on our time can simply compound existing problems, forcing you to try to squeeze more and more into each day. So, think about the workloads you might be able to jettison – and do not to replace them with other forms of work!

Try to acknowledge and understand your mental self-flagellation. And, if you are able, perhaps try a tactic employed by engineer, athlete, and mindset coach, Turia Pitt, who suggests rephrasing internal 'I have to' demands to 'I get to' opportunities (Imber, 2022). To better make sense of this it helps to understand a little about Pitt. According to her website:

> In 2011, I was a mining engineer, living my dream life in the Australian outback. Then, while competing in a 100km ultra-marathon, I was caught in a grassfire. I was choppered out of the remote desert barely alive, with full thickness burns to 65 percent of my body. I lost seven fingers, had over 200 medical procedures and spent two gruelling years in recovery. (https://www.turiapitt.com/my-story/)

Knowing this about her, it is easier to appreciate and apply the distinction been 'have to' and 'get to' that Pitt makes.

Despite all your best efforts, if you continue to feel that work is overwhelming, do not hesitate to admit that. Know that you are not alone. Many others in your own department and university almost assuredly are having similar experiences. And once you have accepted that there is an issue in need of resolution, seek help, taking care to do this sooner rather than later. You might start with your local medical practitioner, naturopath, or psychologist. Some universities also offer free or subsidized (and anonymous) access to appropriate mental health care services. These are sometimes known as Employee Assistance Programmes (EAPs) or Faculty and Staff Assistance Programmes (FSAPs). Check for them on your institution's website.

We sometimes forget that individuals' work-related challenges are not always handled best by an individual-focussed response. As Haswell (2017) observes, group-focussed responses may be helpful. She suggests, for example, that allowing individuals to pursue their passion for teaching, research or service as they choose may be much more effective, efficient and innovative than current practices emphasizing excellence by all in each aspect of the job. If you find yourself in a position where you are able to help effect such an organizational orientation do consider it.

There may also be related systemic problems that are affecting you as well as other colleagues. These may include inappropriate workload models or expectations, poor communication practices that cause you and others to feel bewildered about your work, or even a culture of bullying (e.g., Farley and Sprigg, 2014). If such problems exist, you are likely to need powerful allies to guide you through appropriate ways of responding and, where necessary, to step in and take over the 'fight'. Enlist the support of your union (e.g., Australia's National Tertiary Education Union, Britain's University College Union, New Zealand's Tertiary Education Union), relevant discipline group (e.g., a national or professional society you are affiliated with), or other organization representing the interests of scholars (e.g., the American Association of University Professors). Remember, you are not alone.

32. Sustain collegiality

The term collegiality circulates widely around many universities and other academic institutions. It is upheld as a vital characteristic of being a good scholar and 'corporate citizen'. It is critical to job and life satisfaction and supportive of academic effectiveness. And it is a key part of the 'glue' that 'binds ... members of a common scholarly community and helps connect them with the larger world' (Lewis and Zelinsky, 1987, p. 75).

Collegiality thrives on individual thoughtfulness, awareness of and recognition of one another's efforts, as well as productive institutional rituals such as regular events and gatherings (e.g., shared morning or afternoon tea,[1] a weekly seminar, end of week drinks). It is about being part of a community: mingling, listening, conversing, supporting and helping out.

You can go a long way to making yourself part of a collegial community by participating in the (positive) rituals: attending or leading seminars, buying a sweepstake ticket, or going to morning coffee. For all the small talk about sport, the weather and political calamities, these informal social gatherings can yield valuable spontaneous insights to your colleagues' research, the workings of the department, as well as helping to resolve everyday issues before they escalate into more significant problems.

But, of course, collegiality is not all about getting involved in casual social engagements. It may also require some effort on your part. For example, you may be asked to support someone by covering their class so they can attend a conference; offer a second opinion on problematic assessment; or help supervise a student. To the best of your abilities, try to help out. As Gray and Drew (2012, p. 117) note astutely: 'The web of obligations is two-sided and you will receive reciprocal favors over time'.

Do be aware that collegiality can be exploited and misunderstood. First, as a proven good colleague, you may find yourself being asked for too many favours. Try to avoid being caught up in and paralysed by the web of obligations. Second, some people seem to regard collegiality as demanding unqualified support for their pursuits, irrespective of any concerns you may have. If a co-worker asks for your opinion on some matter, be reasonable and honest – and tactful! In the long run, your fairness and integrity will be more highly valued and will serve you well across your career.

Of course, collegiality is also about the relationships you have with administrative staff, technicians and librarians, people who are vital – but often underappreciated – contributors to scholarly work. Develop good professional relationships with them and they may grant you access to their extensive institutional networks and to their profound appreciations of the mysterious ways in which the university works. They can smooth rocky roads. But should you irritate these colleagues, you may find that they can make your life frustrating and miserable. So, for their sake and yours, be nice. Respect their expertise. Acknowledge good work.

Likewise, treat tutors, 'casual' teachers, and research assistants with respect, if not admiration. In their vital labour-intensive work most slog away conscientiously and unselfishly, all the time eking out an existence on shamefully low incomes. Provide them with support. Help minimize frustrations. Offer clear instructions. Be available to answer their queries and address their concerns. And thank them for their work. Acknowledge their efforts and always remember, that if they are your delegates, it is not them but *you* who is responsible for their actions.[2]

Collegiality is not without its dark side. Certainly, gender, 'race', age, employment status and seniority have their influence in the shaping of collegial relationships (Breeze et al., 2019). And some people simply do not warm to companionship and cooperation with their fellow workers. They may remain on the margins either feeling unwelcome or simply eschewing workplace camaraderie. As a result, certain individuals and/or groups may find themselves ignored, abandoned, ostracized or othered; outcomes which are supportive of neither workplace harmony nor productivity. So, particularly if you find yourself in a senior position explore some of the approaches departmental leaders can take to create more inclusive environments (see, for example, Misra et al., 2022). And even if you are not a formally designated departmental leader, do what you can to engage with your colleagues. Try to ensure that others are made to feel welcome and part of a community that supports mutual encouragement and inspiration.

Collegiality extended and reciprocated, can do much to nurture academic success. It provides useful foundations for research and teaching collaborations. It buttresses respectful and friendly management relationships. And it can also support individual academics' happiness, reduce stress and buoy confidence. It is critical to developing and sustaining successful academic careers.

NOTES

1.   For decades Penn State's Department of Geography has run a legendary weekly 'coffee hour', which involves refreshments followed by a guest lecture. According to Lewis and Zelinsky (1987, p. 75) 'it has proved to be a major force in creating and preserving a sense of intellectual and social community within the department'. It still runs today.

2.   For example, grade distributions across classes are usually the responsibility of the lecturer/professor, not the teaching assistant. Likewise the integrity of research work conducted by an assistant is ultimately the responsibility of the research leader.

33. Preserve your public reputation

As an academic you are something of a public figure. Semester after semester, year after year you may stand before classes filled with tens to hundreds of students. Your video-recorded or Zoom lectures may be viewed by students you may never actually meet face to face. All of these people will have had opportunity to find out quite a bit about you: your name, your background, your interests, and maybe even some of your pet peeves. They may even check out your professional and social media profiles. They will remember you. And when you are out and about – especially if you live in a small town or city dominated by a university – current students and past students will see you and covertly (or even obviously) make a point of watching you go about your day-to-day activities. Although I live in a fairly large city of well over one million people, many of my undergraduate students learned of my low-profile wedding because one of them happened to walk past my home on the day it occurred. So, if you are someone who frequents dodgy bars, dens of iniquity, nudist beaches, or if you put your profile on an online dating site, you should expect that your students will come to know this and they may share that information with their friends and classmates. In this era of social media such 'sharing' includes online photographs, video-, or audio-recordings you may find embarrassing.

Social media present tough new challenges to professional reputations and to any distinctions between academics' private and public lives. For example, a professor at St Xavier's University, Kolkata, was forced to leave her job after a parent lodged a complaint over a social media post in which she was pictured wearing a swimsuit. Apparently 'the complainant mentioned that her/his 18-year-old son was caught looking at the "obscene, vulgar, improper" pictures which were shared on her personal space' (Banerjee, 2022). And, some years ago, but in the kind of occurrence that the India case suggests continues today, sociology professor Gloria Gadsden of Pennsylvania's East Stroudberg State University, 'thought she was talking only to close friends and family as she vented on Facebook about her students, but ... since learned the hard way that her frustrated musings were viewable by some [of her] students' as a result of changes to Facebook's default settings (Stripling, 2010). The outcomes included being placed on administrative leave by her employer and a controversy Gadsden felt would damage her career and her chances of gaining tenure. In light of this kind of challenge, many US universities (e.g., American, Ball

State, Clark, DePaul, Washington State) have developed formal social media policies for their staff, acknowledging that social media sites blur distinctions between personal voice and institutional voice. Not surprisingly, that wave of controversial policy (Lough and Samek, 2014) is diffusing further afield (e.g., Monash University and Flinders University in Australia; Carleton University in Canada; University of Otago in New Zealand; University of Edinburgh in Scotland).

Even electronic mail, straightforward and benign as it seems, can present reputational or personal problems. For example, in late 2013, a University of Iowa teaching assistant mistakenly sent sexually explicit images of her and her male partner to her class as an email attachment (Jacobs, 2013). And I shall never forget the heart-stopping moment when I realized I had inadvertently sent a private letter intended for family and close friends to almost 500 colleagues via a disciplinary listserv. While it is fairly obvious that you should take care about the things you distribute by means of social media and email, there are other strategies to help preserve your public, online reputation. Some of these are set out in Box 33.1.

BOX 33.1 PRESERVING YOUR ONLINE REPUTATION

- Avoid choosing awkward or easily misinterpreted 'private' email addresses (e.g., hotchick@aol.com; slutz@gmail.com). If your institution has a standardized way of generating email account names that turns up something inappropriate for you (e.g., adick@university.edu), insist on having it changed. An inappropriate email address will not reflect well on either you or your university and may be remembered long after some of your significant scholarly achievements.
- Check your privacy settings on social media. Applications such as Facebook change user privacy settings often and those changes can mean that you are inadvertently revealing much more about yourself to the public than you intended). Err on the side of greater privacy than less. Mark your profiles as private.
- Safeguard your passwords. Consider subscribing to a password manager, some of which are free.
- Only accept friend or contact requests from people you know and trust.
- Learn how to block offensive or ill-intentioned users from your social media sites. Search for online advice on how to do this if required.
- Delete your unused social and professional media accounts (e.g., Facebook, Instagram, Tumblr).

- Keep all of your electronic communications polite and honest. Accidental or deliberate broadcast of your emails or online posts may be deeply embarrassing and harmful to your career, particularly if they are offensive, inaccurate, or discourteous.
- Think carefully about anything you post online. For example, how will pictures of you winning the annual Pigsknuckle Beer Drinking Championship endear you to a prospective employer – who is very likely to turn to a search engine to check you out.
- Monitor online reports of you and your activities. Use a search engine or two periodically to search for your name. If you prefer to be more systematic, register with a service such as Google Alerts (www.google.com/alerts). This service can provide daily or weekly notice of items that refer to you, allowing you to track and try to resolve harmful or inaccurate communications.
- Check other people's online posts that include you. If someone else posts a picture of you on Facebook that you find embarrassing, remove the 'tag' that identifies you. Also do not hesitate to ask others to take down pictures of yourself that you think could compromise your reputation.
- Watch out for so-called digital doppelgangers, that is, people who share your name and also have an online presence that may be confused awkwardly with your own. This possibility is more common than you might imagine. For example, I have at least three digital doppelgangers working in Australian universities (see Chapter 33 for more information). In difficult cases, you may need to change your 'identity' by, for example, including a middle name or initial in your electronic presence.

Over and above the challenges presented by email and social media sites, the ways you use academic social networking platforms can have both positive (see Chapter 9) and negative implications for your academic reputation (see, for example, D'Alessandro et al. 2020). Sites like Academia.edu, Google Scholar, Mendeley, ORCID, ResearchGate, and ResearcherID are being used increasingly as 'objective' representations of academics' reputations and are now sometimes considered during recruitment and promotion processes (Orduna-Malea et al., 2017). However, scholars can very clearly influence the ways they are represented on these platforms. And there are suggestions that the capacity to manipulate one's academic profile online may feed from and sustain narcissistic tendencies (D'Alessandro et al., 2020). So, rather than being impressed by a highly active, well-curated, and comprehensive LinkedIn profile, for instance, an external observer may actually regard it as a reflection of time-wasting narcissistic tendencies and be sceptical of the substance behind the shine.

Your public reputation or profile can also be compromised, though not necessarily sullied, by online namesakes. This occur on academic social networking sites as well as on social networks. For instance, I have found that there is a remarkable number of scholars who share my name and its slightly uncommon spelling together with some of my research interests. If you find yourself in this position, it will be helpful to seek ways within relevant platforms to distinguish yourself from your same-name colleagues (e.g. specifying the institution your work for; adding more details of your research). And if there is a way you can claim 'precedence' to your identity over someone else who shares the same name, consider that. For example, Google has a feature that enables you to do this under a 'Claim this knowledge panel' feature.

There is no doubt that the Internet and various social media platforms have significantly expanded the opportunities to promote yourself to a wide audience at little or no cost, but it also exposes you simultaneously to risk of significant professional damage. The text, photos and other material you – and others – post on sites like Facebook, Instagram, LinkedIn or Tinder may call into question your at-work face of scholarly sanctity and studious sobriety. So when you are online, type and post with care. And remember that even in your everyday activities in the supermarket, at the beach, or in a hotel, while you may know no one, people may know you. You work hard to develop your professional reputation. Be sure to act in ways that preserve it.

34. Stay happy and healthy

As we saw in the first chapter of this book, staying happy and healthy are critical components of academic career success. Much of an individual's happiness may be determined by genetic character and external circumstances, such as salary, work location, office space and material possessions (Lyubomirsky, 2008; Martin, 2011) but a great deal is also affected by beliefs and behaviours. There is little we can do about our genetic make-up and the effect that has on our happiness. And external circumstances typically have fairly short-term consequences for happiness, for, as Martin (2011, p. 51) reminds us, there appears to exist a 'hedonic treadmill', a tendency in people to adapt to positive and negative changes in their external circumstances and revert to their longer-term, stable levels of happiness. Martin (2011, p. 51) also notes that most people 'misperceive what will make them happier' and continue to strive for external rewards such as a higher salary or heightened professional rank, which in the long run will do little to make them happier.[1] So, rather than engaging in this futile pursuit, 'the most reliable way to increase happiness is to change one's own beliefs and behaviours' (Martin, 2011, p. 51).

Though Martin's exposition of the three dimensions of happiness is helpful – and we shall return shortly to the matter of changing beliefs and behaviours – he does appear to overlook the fascinating insights of thinkers and scholars like Pink (2009) and Duncan et al. (2015) who point to the centrality of *autonomy*, *mastery*, and *purpose* as key foundations of both motivation and happiness. That work suggests that the autonomous academic is free to set the goals they have for their teaching and research as well as the means by which those are achieved. Many academics have chosen their career precisely because it does offer an unusual amount of autonomy. Mastery involves development of scholarly skills to interrogate questions and resolve challenging problems. Academics work long and hard through postgraduate degrees, postdoctoral fellowships and other early career roles to secure appointments that allow them to continue to nurture and employ their professional mastery. Purpose means that an academic feels their work is personally meaningful but that it is also valued by their university or employing institution. Most scholars select their research areas and teaching focus because it involves activities in which they see worth and significance. Upholding these three foundations of autonomy, mastery and purpose is critical to maintaining happiness and motivation in academic work. Very sadly, however, many of the changes that are being

forced upon, and which are taking place within, universities around the world
are serving quickly and ruthlessly to diminish each of these three dimensions
(e.g. Bergan et al., 2020).

In some instances you may have to change your external circumstances to
defend these three foundations. For example, if your employing institution
erodes your professional autonomy to an extent you consider untenable, consider reviewing your outlook on autonomy, engaging in action to restore your
professional standing, or looking to alternative employment. If your school,
faculty, or university aims to change its mission in ways inconsistent with your
own sense of purpose, you can speak out against the changes or look elsewhere
(including outside universities) for employment that will continue to give you
contentment. And if you find that you are losing sight of your own sense of
purpose, you may need to reconsider some of your own beliefs and behaviours.[2] Some of the 'solutions' to affronts to autonomy, mastery, and purpose
imply fairly drastic remedial steps, which might be likened to significant
course changes by the skipper of an ocean-going yacht. Fortunately they are
required fairly infrequently and instead, more frequent, minor 'sail trimming'
and course adjustments can support happiness and motivation in academic
work. And it is here that we return to my earlier point about changing, or
perhaps more accurately adopting, particular beliefs and behaviours.

With Martin (2011), numerous scholars and self-help authors (e.g., Foster
and Hicks, 2004; Matthews, 1990; Seligman and Csikszentmihalyi, 2014)
describe behavioural tactics held to be supportive of happiness. These include:

- expressing gratitude;
- being forgiving;
- being optimistic;
- being mindful;
- creating and deepening relationships;
- helping others;
- entering a state of flow.

The significance of expressing gratitude (e.g., for being in a job with some
security of tenure; having more professional autonomy than many people
enjoy); being forgiving (of students who are late with assignments or journal
editors who take ages to respond to your paper submission); or being optimistic
and mindful (especially in academic environments where, as Hodgins, 2012,
makes clear, it is easy, if not encouraged, to be cynical) is not to be denied, but
for academics the final three of the points listed above stand out as being areas
being most germane and appropriate for detailed attention.

CREATE AND DEEPEN RELATIONSHIPS

In some fields, especially within the arts, social sciences and humanities, academic work can be or become a fairly solitary affair. The picture is clear from the acknowledgements pages of Paul Starr's Pulitzer Prize-winning work, *The Social Transformation of American Medicine* (1982, p. xiii), 'This book was written in the old-fashioned way: the lone scholar pecking away at his word processor.' Such solitude can stifle social relationships that are a key component of life satisfaction and happiness for many people. And the growing need for scholars to be wedded to computers and other devices further erodes opportunities for social – rather than virtual – interaction. It does take some initiative to disconnect from devices, step out of the office, and to reconnect personally with students and colleagues near and far – as well as with your partner, spouse, children, parents and friends – but for many of us it is critical to happiness and career success.

Of course, relationships at work may be found with research collaborators, co-teachers, university bureaucrats, students and professional community members. Collectively these relationships constitute a personally and professionally rewarding web of influence and support, and they do demand time, care and diligence to maintain. Particular relationships with specific individuals or groups may not work out or may be fleeting, but the overall web of relationships you develop is a key to being a happy and successful academic.

HELP OTHERS

Martin (2011, p. 53) reminds us that 'helping others is a reliable way to feel better yourself'. Academic work may not be regarded commonly as 'helping work'. It is not like medicine, nursing, veterinary medicine, social work, the ministry, or even law, where there is a fairly clear public perception that the profession's focus is on caring for or helping others. And yet, much of our teaching and research is indeed about helping. Perhaps attention to the helping character of our work has been diminished as electronic media have disconnected us from meaningful face-to-face interactions with students; as institutions have purged our capacities for independent, personalized, professional judgement; and as the measures of research have shifted from the process of engaging productively in meaningful work to empirical inputs (e.g., grant dollars) and outputs (e.g., published papers). A consequence of this too is that many of us have become emotionally and spiritually separated from the good we do.

Notwithstanding these disturbing developments, teaching is fundamentally about helping students to learn. And a great deal of research in the social sciences focuses on helping others by, for example, seeking ways of making people's lives better; reducing inequality; and understanding and minimizing exploitation, violence, powerlessness and marginalization. The existence of these dimensions of helping is worth recalling and emphasizing as part of any strategy to sustain a successful academic career. And if you seek still further opportunities – and have the energy to do so – remember that volunteering and professional and community service (see Chapter 26) offer rewarding prospects for helping others and developing relationships with colleagues and community members you might not otherwise have met.

ENTER A STATE OF FLOW

There are times in some academics' careers when, in their everyday work, they enter 'the zone' or a state of 'flow' (Csikszentmihalyi, 1990; Seligman and Csikszentmihalyi, 2014). Such moments occur when a person with a high skill level working on a high-challenge task finds themselves fully engaged with and absorbed by that task, energized, working as if instinctively, and with a heightened level of ability. Such moments can even make it seem as if someone else, much more capable, has taken over your intellect and your body is simply the conduit for their work. Flow can be associated with the conduct of research (e.g., interpreting research results, writing) and also in teaching-related tasks. As Martin (2011, p. 52) notes: 'To increase prospects for continued flow, teachers can set themselves challenges, for example, up-dating the curriculum, using innovative teaching methods, or finding new ways to present material and communicate to students. The idea is to turn teaching into a thrilling on-going challenge instead of a dutiful necessity'. As noted in Chapter 31 one way of approaching this is to follow Turia Pitt's sage advice to rephrase internal 'I have to' demands to 'I get to' opportunities (Imber, 2022).

   Martin (2011, p. 52) observes that achieving a state of flow can be so reward-ing that people strive hard to repeat it. To do this, at least three elements seem to be required. First, one must have appropriate, high-level skills to undertake the task. Second, the task should be neither too dull nor too challenging. The former leads to boredom and distraction; the latter to anxiety. Third, the con-ditions that allow flow to occur need to be fostered by eliminating distractions and interruptions such as email, phone calls, or knocking at the door (Duncan et al., 2015, p. 7). Creative workers need time to think (Mintzberg, 1998). This can be achieved by quarantining uninterrupted time for research and teaching each day or week. A risk associated with longer timeframes is that any post-ponement is likely to lead to a long break between activities. Prolonged inter-ruptions may make it difficult to regain mastery of the challenge. The shorter timeframe offers strength in that it may be progressively quicker and easier to 'warm up' to the task, to recapture one's position in it, and get into the 'flow'.

In reviewing this material on staying happy it might be argued there is an apparent inconsistency between the importance of developing and sustaining relationships – which may require throwing open one's office door to engage with colleagues and students – and the potential need for isolation to enhance the prospects of finding 'flow'. While a tension does indeed exist, it is not irresolvable. For many, the solution lies in pursuing both engagement and flow through thoughtful time management strategies (see Chapter 17) that set aside clearly demarcated occasions for interaction and equally well-delineated opportunities to find moments in the 'zone'.

CELEBRATE

Finally, and in a point overlooked by several of the scholars and self-help authors referred to earlier in this chapter (e.g., Foster and Hicks, 2004; Martin, 2011; Matthews, 1990; Seligman and Csikszentmihalyi, 2014), do make opportunities to celebrate your teaching and research successes. When you complete your PhD, throw a monster party. You have joined an exclusive club. When you send a paper to a journal, bake a cake to share with your colleagues. If it is accepted, bake two! When you (re)design a new course, have drinks with tutors and co-teachers. Revel at the end of semester with colleagues (and students). If you have a book published, be sure to arrange a book launch, with some esteemed colleague to laud your work. Often, academics forget to applaud noteworthy moments and successes. Celebrating marks happy moments in our academic careers; it rewards effort with some joy; and reminds each of us about what we are doing and why.

NOTES

1. There is something of a paradox here. Achievement of some of the objective understandings of academic career success such as grant funding and prestigious publications (see Sutherland, 2015 and the discussion in Chapter 1 of this book) may do little to support their subjective counterparts.
2. This can involve personal crises demanding care and assistance from counsellors and psychologists, as well as thoughtful colleagues and family.

35. Manage disruptions, interruptions and transitions successfully

There is an 'ideal' model of an academic career in the arts, social sciences and humanities. This typically imagines a healthy, able, youthful, footloose and well-resourced individual, unencumbered by binding family and friendship networks who can proceed full-time through a doctoral degree before moving to a university position, or possibly several, where they (usually he) work more or less uninterrupted to rise through academic ranks. A good deal of individual and institutional thinking continues to rest on this model that effectively ignores scholars' increasingly precarious employment conditions (Burton and Bowman, 2022) and our very humanness with all its complexities, positioning matters like pregnancy, childrearing, bereavement, or mental illness, for example, as 'disruptions' (see, for example, Khoo, 2013; McElrath, 1992). The model also takes little account of the personal and professional challenges associated with moving from one position to another and fails to attend to the concerns of scholars looking to transition successfully out of the university at the end of their career. This chapter does not promise to deal comprehensively with these important matters – each warrants a book in its own right. Instead, the aims here are to signal some of these so-called disruptions, interruptions and transitions and to suggest a few keys to their successful management.[1] Bear in mind that you do not need to handle the matters discussed here alone. Colleagues, friends and family will be able to offer advice and support, as should your adviser, manager or mentors (see Chapter 4).

MOVING FROM ONE ACADEMIC POSITION TO ANOTHER

Academic careers increasingly involve reluctant (e.g., as the result of a compulsory redundancy or the termination of a short-term contract); opportunistic (e.g., as the result of a call from a headhunter as described in Chapter 12); or deeply desired shifts from one institution, or even country, to another – or even within an institution (Enders and Kaulisch, 2006, p. 85). These moves can be extremely fulfilling, bringing new stimuli, extending your network of colleagues, and offering professional and personal rewards. Indeed, mobility can be critical to movement up the academic hierarchy (e.g. Mantai and Marrone,

2023). At the same time a move can be distressing, disappointing or unsettling, requiring you to make new social connections, find housing, surmount language barriers, adjust to new ways of doing things, establish different financial arrangements and so on. You may even experience culture shock, homesickness, or some other psychological issues.

The potential personal and social consequences of relocation should not be underestimated. Culture shock, for example, with symptoms including depression, inability to concentrate, irritability, insomnia and loss of confidence (Briones and Bush, 2015, p. 4; Oberg, 1960, pp. 177–8), can be personally and professionally debilitating. Such symptoms do not result necessarily from an international relocation between quite dissimilar places. Quite subtle differences between locations may also spark significant issues that may manifest themselves sneakily. A key is to be alert to the possibility that any relocation or employment dislocation may trigger troublesome maladies requiring professional, familial or collegial support. Be aware too that the early stages of a relocation may seem to demand such a focus on work (e.g., preparing new classes, setting up local research projects, learning about new administrative procedures) that other, vital dimensions of life are neglected, perhaps to your detriment, as well as to those around you. As Crone (2010, p. 87) notes sagely: 'Pay attention to developing a balance between your professional and personal life early – right after moving to the new city – and don't put it off until feelings of loneliness and isolation set in.' Over and above these important psychological and social issues surrounding relocation there are other important concerns that demand attention.

Before you relocate, work with your new employer to secure the resources required to support your move.[2] Most universities will outline clear policies and practices on such relocation matters (e.g., costs of disposing of your existing home, removal expenses, family and pet relocation assistance, temporary housing support). Work also to get what you require to re-establish yourself in your new context (e.g., local start-up funding, reduced teaching in your first year or two, mentoring, access to sabbatical), recalling that it is in the institution's best interests for you to be successful (Chapter 15 provides some suggestions for specific things to consider). These are fairly straightforward matters. More difficult are some of the other career-related challenges of relocating.

First, depending on the nature of your research, you may need to adapt it to reflect your new location and context. This may be a relatively simple matter of exchanging one set of case study sites for another, or it may require a much more substantial transformation, taking up local issues of significance, cultures, histories and politics. Consult with your supervisor, colleagues and mentors to find people and means to help hasten the process. There are some other more hardheaded research issues you may wish to consider. For instance, once you are sure you will be moving, don't hasten publications that will be attributed to your former institution. Instead, do what you can to ensure your affiliation is with your new academic home (Perks and Ruffer, 2019).

Second, you will probably need to employ quite different examples in your teaching to make content more significant and engaging to students. Depending on your disciplinary field, students may welcome some illustrations drawn from distant or diverse contexts you are familiar with, but they will generally not appreciate it if there are few local cases they can relate to. Your very approach to learning and teaching may also require rethinking. Students more accustomed to authoritarian approaches may find your flipped classrooms (see Chapter 24) and lecturer–student partnerships disorienting and disquieting. When you arrive at your new institution, find out who the best teachers are and observe their practices, perhaps asking if you can review curricula or sit in on classes. Consult too with local academic development staff, perhaps letting them know what you intend to do or having them (or discipline-based colleagues) attend some of your classes and review your learning-and-teaching approach and resources. Then modify your teaching practice in ways that best suit local circumstances and challenge local practices to achieve high standards. You may also find it useful to scrutinize your new institution's means of evaluating teaching and to arrange a midsemester course evaluation seeking student feedback (Perks and Ruffer, 2019). These may provide helpful insights to local cultures, practices and expectations that offer to make you a more effective teacher.

Third, you will certainly need to learn about and adapt to local institutional cultures and practices. Departments, schools, faculties and universities all have unique ways of doing things. Some of those practices will amaze you. Others will almost certainly annoy and frustrate you. And while you may be able to effect some constructive change, for the most part you will have to accept and work with local practices. Few of your new colleagues will be particularly interested in how (much better) things were done at your last university. So, rather than denouncing the system – however tempting that may be – and irritating colleagues, try to work amiably and conscientiously to negotiate your way through the organizational confusion that confronts you. Administrative allies will help things run much more smoothly. Embrace the positive aspects of your new location and work around its less appealing aspects. Later, once you have settled in and come to terms with local ways of doing things, you may be better placed to spark change in bothersome policies and procedures, maybe drawing from your prior experiences to point to models of better practice.

Fourth, strive to make a good impression quickly. First impressions count – colleagues and students will be observing you closely, so work to make a positive impact. To some degree, relocating means you will be starting with a 'blank slate'. Little of the authority or credibility you had at your previous institution will carry positively into your new position. You will need to earn all of that status again. So, be animated and engaging in your teaching. Get some research runs on the board quickly – and get them publicized (see Chapter 28). Seek out departmental and institutional service roles that appeal to you – before you get tasked with less attractive others – and find out how you can get yourself involved with them (Perks and Ruffer, 2019). Demonstrate through your everyday interactions that you are a good, productive and sensible colleague. This will go a long way to ensuring a successful relocation.

Finally, do not forget those colleagues and friends you have 'left behind'. Relocating can undoubtedly allow you to extend professional and social networks locally, nationally or internationally, including valuable collaborators for research projects or referees for promotion and appointment letters. But you must work to sustain those networks. So, keep your associates posted on your activities by calling them, writing to them, congratulating them on their achievements, including them on your professional social media sites (e.g., LinkedIn), sending them copies of any new publications and so on – but not to the extent that they think you cannot 'let go' of the past. And perhaps also maintain institutional links by staying on relevant listservs and social media sites, continuing your inclusion on mailing lists and occasionally reviewing relevant local websites to keep abreast of any developments. There is a short-term risk that retrospection will aggravate homesickness or longing for the past – especially at times when the transition to your new location is proceeding less than smoothly – but with appropriate support and assistance these should pass and the long-term collegial and social rewards may be much greater and of longer endurance.

PREGNANCY, CHILDREN AND OTHER MAJOR LIFE EVENTS[3]

To state the obvious, many academics have children. While this affects women and men, the biology of fertility and the common coincidence of childbirth and childrearing with gaining a doctoral degree and early career development remains especially challenging for women (Mason et al., 2013; Tower et al., 2015). And as authors such as Mason and Ekman (2007) and Philipsen and Bostic (2008) make clear, the question about when is the best time to have a child is an especially knotty one (Box 35.1).

BOX 35.1   WHEN IS THE BEST TIME TO HAVE A CHILD IN AN ACADEMIC CAREER?

There is probably no general best or perfect time. For every possible moment there will be an argument about why it is awkward or inconvenient. And, of course, in some cases there is no choice about timing to be made! Best times may be affected by the availability of a partner or family members well positioned to contribute to childrearing activities. Depending on the kind of research activity associated with your PhD, as well as your sources of income, the PhD's flexibility offers opportunity for pregnancy and childrearing. Any additional time required to complete the doctorate is likely to be of less long-term career significance than an interruption of the same duration while you are working. But flexibility will demand good time management skills to ensure timely progression towards completion (see Chapter 17). If you wait until you have an academic job, you will have a reliable income and are likely to have access to forms of institutional support (see Box 35.2) that may be unavailable to doctoral students (e.g., maternity leave). However, less flexibility, more uncertainty and much greater work demands typically distinguish early-career work from a PhD, particularly if you are a pre-tenure academic in North America or a short-term contract academic elsewhere. If you wait until you have a permanent appointment, you will have some valuable job security but you (and your partner) are likely to have reached an age that makes having healthy children difficult. Moreover, it may be more difficult to cope with the physical and mental challenges associated with raising those children.

As Wolf-Wendel and Ward (2015, p. 20) observe of the US context:

> the tenure and the biological clock tick simultaneously. The average age for women academics who earn a doctorate is 34. Assuming the average female professor moves through the tenure ranks in the typical six-year period, she will earn tenure at around age 40. Waiting until one earns tenure to have children could be difficult for women as female fertility significantly declines after age 35.

Having children, raising teenagers and managing other family responsibilities (e.g., caring for elderly parents or disabled siblings) profoundly affect the choices that academic staff – and particularly women[4] – make (see Rosa, 2022). These include whether to undertake a doctoral degree, move to another university, return to one's home town or country, or accept a leadership position. 'Many women [and I suspect more than a few men] anticipate incompatibility between having a family and living up to ideal worker norms, so they avoid career decisions such as going up for promotion and seeking higher level administrative positions' (Wolf-Wendel and Ward, 2015, p. 32).

While very significant challenges remain, such as advisers unwilling to write letters of reference for pregnant graduate students; students maintaining silence about their identity as a mother; colleagues who suggest abortions to facilitate career advancement; and academic leaders unfamiliar with their institution's mechanisms to meet academics' on-going parenting needs (Hardy et al., 2016; Mason et al., 2013; Mirick and Wladkowski, 2018), most universities and related organizations now at least acknowledge the engagements of biology, family and career, taking some account of them in promotion and tenure decisions as well as through a range of other supportive policies and procedures (Box 35.2). Of course, this is not to deny that universities remain deeply 'gendered organizations' (Acker, 1990) where many of the accommodations to biology and balance fall to individual academic employees (and their colleagues) rather than to the employing institution. Clearly, there remains room for improvement.

BOX 35.2   ACCOMMODATIONS TO HELP OFFSET CAREER 'DISRUPTIONS'

- Paid and unpaid maternity and paternity leave.
- Revised or lighter duties during pregnancy.
- Adoption leave.
- Carer's leave.
- Access to preferred parking facilities.
- Flexible hours on return to work.
- Breastfeeding/lactation facilities.
- Childcare and holiday care facilities on campus.
- Conference funds that include financial support for childcare.
- Conference crèches.
- Fellowships for parents whose research momentum has been affected by caring responsibilities.
- Gender-specific leadership initiatives (e.g., Universities New Zealand's Women in Leadership [NZWiL] Programme; Adelaide University's Women's Professional Development Network).
- Provisions in promotion, research assessment and grant procedures to acknowledge activity 'relative to opportunity' (e.g. circumstances such as child-rearing, administrative responsibilities, illness or disability, which have delayed or interrupted studies or research, or otherwise affected the performance on which an assessment is being made).

214 How to be an academic superhero

But leaving institutional inadequacies to one side, the assistance and advice available through collegial social relationships and informal and professional networks can be of great value. It can be helpful and assuring to be connected personally and/or online[5] to others in a similar developmental phase (e.g., raising toddlers, managing teenagers, caring for elderly parents), as part of a network supportive of individual and collective well-being (Tower et al., 2015, p. 526):

> I found myself at my personal limits a few years ago when I was pregnant … It turns out that I was not nearly as strong and enduring as I thought I was. Dealing with the nausea and fatigue I faced in the first trimester of my pregnancy day after day, week after week was mentally debilitating. I became despondent because of the relentless and gruelling nature of the symptoms even though I knew eventually it would come to an end. After all, a pregnancy can't last much longer than 9 months.
>   What really helped was seeking out emotional support. We started a new moms' group in the college for faculty women who were pregnant or recently started a family … [T]hose meetings and the email exchanges with the other new moms really helped me to focus on the light at the end of the tunnel. (Crone, 2010, p. 89)

As this quotation suggests it is important to sustain social relationships and professional networks. Seek out help when you need it. Find people to talk to.

Notwithstanding the emergence of helpful institutional measures and presence of informal support networks, and acknowledging research that shows how motherhood is not an entirely negative experience in the workplace (Huopalainen and Satama, 2019), having children or assuming other caring roles restrains, restricts or limits opportunities for the development of an academic career in a wide variety of ways (Baker, 2012; Hardy et al., 2016; Jean et al., 2015). Several coping strategies can be identified, ranging from complete reconsideration of career course, to revising the pace at which you shape a successful career, to refining the focus of your research.

First, for many, the coincidence of starting a family and critical formative years in a scholarly career demands a comprehensive recalibration of priorities. How do family and children figure in *your* picture of a successful happy life?[6] Just what is *your* understanding of success (see Table 1.1 in Chapter 1) and how do you plan to translate this into action?

Second, and on a related theme, matters of aspiration and time become central. The career path for scholars bearing and raising children is likely to be different, more difficult and slower than it is for most of their childless colleagues. Means of dealing with this and of minimizing stress levels associated with unrealizable expectations, include: (1) abandoning promotion aspirations altogether, effectively 'parking' one's career (Hardy et al., 2016, p. 12); (2) stepping away from an academic role for an extended period (e.g., through leave without pay) and endeavouring to return later; or (3) extending self-imposed timeframes for achieving career milestones (e.g., aiming to reach professorial rank within 15 years of PhD rather than ten years). Each of these may involve trading off short-term research productivity, access to some time-limited research opportunities (e.g., research fellowships that are available within a certain period after PhD completion) and promotion, in return for life satisfaction rewards such as a better balance between work, family and leisure – as well as the mental well-being of you and those around you. Stepping away completely from an academic role for several years can make the return very difficult as fields change, your knowledge dates, technology shifts and professional skills dull. And in the last of these approaches, extending self-imposed timeframes, day-to-day time management and work–life boundaries will be more critical than ever before when children are drawn into the complexities of satisfying personal, family and employment demands (see Chapter 17). Time/aspiration strategies are challenging in other more testing ways. As noted throughout this book, universities are characterized by escalating, uncompromising and measurable demands on staff to publish, teach and commit to service roles. They are bursting with driven and competitive people, many of whom regard career parking or slowing as an anathema. As one of those highly motivated people, to work against institutional demands and what is likely to be your very own character is, to say the least, confronting.

Third, you may be able to, or indeed need to, reshape work and home patterns to accommodate the requirements of each. Despite growing 'flexibility' facilitated by electronic communications, there certainly remain some temporal and spatial rigidities in academic employment (e.g., teaching times and places). Nevertheless, the work typically offers much greater flexibility than many other careers to accommodate or respond to caring commitments (e.g., call from a crèche to say your child is sick; collecting children from school). But, as discussed in Chapter 17, it also demands careful time management and self-discipline. You can certainly work with your supervisor and colleagues to negotiate teaching and other responsibilities that will allow you to meet your familial commitments as well as your work obligations, but do be aware there may not be a lot of sympathy for your position:

> The self-referential mindset of 'I did it (or didn't) and you should (or shouldn't) too', is a pervasive one in academe and part of the faculty mystique … Historically, in many instances, senior women remained childless to succeed; and their reactions and interactions with junior women who took a different path within their careers and in their personal lives were not always positive. (Wolf-Wendel and Ward, 2015, p. 28)

Moreover, as Wingfield (2011) suggests, except in extreme cases, avoid using family responsibilities as an excuse for failing to get things done. She notes that your colleagues, working for the same pay in the same kinds of role, will not appreciate it. The onus will be on you to manage relationships between work and family effectively.

Finally, to accommodate familial caring roles it may also be helpful, if not necessary, to reconsider the very location, emphasis or form of your research. In some fields, such as the humanities, where scholarship is often individually focussed, it is possible to create 'work patterns that meet ... work and family needs while achieving the outcomes valued by [the] discipline and institution' (Wolf-Wendel and Ward, 2015, p. 30). However, in other fields that require fieldwork in remote or risky locations, extended periods in distant archives, or international collaboration with research partners, this may entail, for example, searching for short-term or enduring substitutes. This decision may even be made early in a research career, in anticipation of the arrival of children.

To close this section, life events other than pregnancy and child-raising, such as the death of a spouse, partner, child or parent, can have a substantial impact on a scholar's emotional state and career. In these times, some people find solace in their work and turn their attentions to that, perhaps becoming more academically productive than ever before. Others respond differently, questioning the value of their endeavours in the face of significant life events. Whatever your reaction, remember that your scholarly work is simply a part of your life and identity, not all of it. Be sure to look after your own well-being and that of your family and close friends first. Find people to talk to. Take advantage of any institutional support mechanisms. Consult with mentors before any parental or carer's leave, during it, and afterwards. Stay connected. Ask for help. And if you feel the need to take a break, remember there will long be classrooms, journals and books – in whatever form – and field sites and laboratories. They will wait for you.

TRANSITIONING OUT: LEAVING THE UNIVERSITY/ RETIRING

In many jurisdictions, life as an academic has become very much harder than in the past (Altbach, 2004b, 2005). As noted earlier in this book workloads have increased; expectations have changed and risen; and workplaces are more and more unstable. As Crone (2010, p. 102) observes: 'Faculty life can often-times seem like a long series of battles in an entrenched war' and we can be so worn down or disenchanted that we want to leave. But as she goes on (p. 102):

> In many ways academia is a bit like a cult. Many of us faculty have never ventured outside the university walls since beginning as freshmen. We believe – because we have been told over and over again – that academia is the best place to be and that we have wonderful privileges here ... that we will find nowhere else.

But this is simply not true. There are other roles that may pay more, treat you better, offer greater personal satisfaction and allow for better work–life balance (see, for example, Ernst, 2020). So, if your life as an academic is not taking the superhero form you had dreamed of, do not discount the merits of looking elsewhere or indeed of setting up your own business or consultancy (see de Moor, 2009 for some excellent preliminary guidance and Chapter 27 of this volume). Ransack the Internet; seek help from your university's human resources section (if appropriate); use your professional, personal and community networks; and contact headhunters (see Chapter 12). The grass may indeed be greener in other fields.

For those who do remain within the academy, there does ultimately come a time to bow out and 'retire'.[7] The causes are varied, with individuals' decisions perhaps being shaped by their experience of centrifugal and centripetal career forces set out by Crow (2021a) and shown in Table 35.1.

Table 35.1   Centrifugal and centripetal forces in career trajectories

Centripetal forces	Centrifugal forces
Affirmation of the value of one's work	Stress and/or poor health, possibly induced by sense of underperformance in context of audit culture
Social connection with colleagues/ students	Diminution/breakdown of collegial relationships/growing sense of age gap with students
Enjoyment from engaging with ideas	Dislike of new academic trends, feeling superseded, and running out of ideas/running out of steam
Sense of purpose (perceived duty to contribute and be useful, possibly hubristic)	Alienation from bureaucratic organization; compulsory or Employer Justified Retirement Ages; desire to 'make way' for the next generation
Continuing financial recompense	Appeal of 'comfortable' retirement
Absence of alternatives ('what else would I do?')	Retirement as a time to re-set work–life balance and focus on broad well-being

Source: Adapted from Crow (2021a, p. 48).

Some scholars retire completely and quickly, washing their hands of both the institution and many of their colleagues. One interviewee in Crow's (2021a) UK study:

> told the story of a former colleague, a successful and well-published Professor, who announced on the day of his retirement that 'I am never going to think another academic thought'; having left work he was said to have devoted his time to cultivating his garden, following in the footsteps of Voltaire's *Candide*.

Some fear retirement, like one of the respondents in Davies and Jenkins's (2013, p. 332) study of British academics:

> I dread it. I absolutely dread retirement ... I have a little flat down by [names area]. It will be desperate. What will I do? I haven't got the faintest idea. I haven't got new hobbies. Work has always been my hobby. It is really frightening. I'm in total denial. I can't imagine not coming to work. I can't even imagine it. I want to keep going on as I am now.

Others wind down gradually, perhaps moving to reduced work weeks through flexible retirement schemes and then to 'full' retirement, maybe with honorary or emeritus status, taking on only those roles they truly desire and seeking out other activities of interest (e.g., art collecting, board memberships, community service, consulting, University of the Third Age, gardening, fishing) (see, for example Crow, 2021b). Some academics are so passionate about their vocation they continue to research and teach, 'acknowledging that the only practical changes brought by "retirement" might be a changed job title (e.g. from Professor to Emeritus Professor) and no longer being paid' (Crow 2021a, p. 17). As 71-year-old writing professor Donald R. Gallehr of George Mason University remarks: 'If I go several days without teaching, I long for it ... I miss my students. I wish I was in the classroom' (in Hicken, 2013). Others find activities involving a period of less sustained commitment (e.g., writing guest editorials; delivering plenary addresses) or opportunities to contribute time and considerable experience to major service roles in their discipline (e.g., secretary or president of a national body). Fortunately – and perhaps because they have come to realize they have responsibilities to, and the prospect of benefiting from, retired academic staff – some universities have begun moving towards providing organizations and programmes for retired academics (e.g. voluntary boards, emeritus colleges). These offer benefits such as 'harnessing retiree experience for academic work, volunteer service, community outreach, mentoring, institutional history, fund-raising, and more' (Brown and Jones, 2018, p. 47). Notwithstanding some of the important issues of uncertainty and identity associated with moving to 'retirement' that Crow (2021a) so coherently sets out (e.g. sense of disengagement; threats to understandings of self and purpose; dismissive treatment by younger colleagues) the years of transition really can be a golden era in one's academic career, freeing you to pursue those teaching, research and service activities you are most passionate about and taking up or rediscovering hobbies and interests set aside in pursuit of your career.

Acknowledging that transitions from work to retirement are increasingly complex and that the possible ends to working life are multiplying, Davies and Jenkins (2013) categorize five different types of academic retiree. Their typology corresponds well with more recent excellent work conducted by Crow (2021a) in the UK. The categories and some of their key characteristics are set out in Table 35.2.

Table 35.2   Selected characteristics of academic retiree groups

	Clean Breakers	Continuing Scholars	Opportunists	The Reluctant	Avoiders
Significance of retirement	End of working Beginning of new life phase Retirement as a 'third age'	Gradual withdrawal from university world Maintain academic/research interests but diminishing over time	Time to develop new professional interests, using the skills, contacts and networks already developed	Loss of most highly valued activity; period of frustration Loss of role and status	No clear plans about retirement
Dominant emotions during the transition period	Excitement Satisfied Sense of completion	Acceptance	Excited Enthusiastic Revitalized Sense of freedom	Anger Powerlessness Disheartened	Anxiety Uncertainty
Attitude towards work	In many cases unsatisfying; in others, satisfying but pressured and draining Irritation with day-to-day pressures	Enjoy parts of the job, but job has changed Will be pleased to refocus on a narrower spectrum of activities and lose the more bureaucratic and 'institutional' activities Welcome the opportunity to focus on own interests	Enthusiastic in job Enjoyed the variety Sense of agency	Main source of self-definition and identity	Normally highly positive

	Clean Breakers	Continuing Scholars	Opportunists	The Reluctant	Avoiders
Relation of retirement to sense of self	Allows emergence of new part of self	Limited change – continuity of self; in fact, allows a more individual self	Golden opportunity to develop new career activities and face new professional challenges	Retirement represents loss of valued part of self	Retirement is a future event that has not been contemplated
Extent of change in overall life focus	Significant life change	Limited	Moderate	Significant	Not expressed
Focus of expected post-retirement	Largely leisure/ domestic	Combines academic with domestic activity	Combines university, external professional work and leisure	Limited domestic activities; attempts to recreate academic role	Not contemplated
Continued academic activity	Very limited; in some cases, hourly paid teaching	Selected academic work undertaken	Selected academic work undertaken	Academic activity continued to the extent possible	Not contemplated

Source: Adapted from Davies and Jenkins (2013, pp. 328–9).

Irrespective of one's style and pace of exit from an academic career, planning for a successful retirement is beneficial. Although it falls increasingly to individuals to take responsibility for their retirement (Davies and Jenkins, 2013, p. 335), universities do often make information sessions and resources available to staff on the disquieting issue of planning to safeguard a continuing source of income in retirement, commonly through their own pension plan arrangements or through referrals to independent financial advisers. Details are usually available through institutional websites or human resources departments. Making provisions for ongoing income is one aspect of retirement planning that should begin as early as possible so that savings are built up and compounded and income streams arranged.

   While there is some advice and assistance available on retirement saving and income, there is less guidance on other critical matters such as: managing your new identity as a retiree, rather than an academic; making arrangements to stay connected with colleagues and friends; establishing where you will live when freed from the constraints of your employment location; determining what you will actually do in the days and years ahead; and planning for activities to maintain your physical and mental well-being. Elaboration on these is beyond the scope of this book but fortunately there is a growing array of publications offering advice on planning for both the financial and non-financial dimensions of retirement (Baldwin, 2018; Fraunfelder and Gilbaugh, 2009; Manners, 2016; Roiter, 2008; Schultz et al., 2015). And as Davies and Jenkins (2013, p. 335) suggest, retirement coaching and life planning support may offer helpful tools. All of these published and applied resources are well worth considering to help ensure that you are able to transition smoothly and gracefully from a successful career to an equally successful retirement.

NOTES

1. Critics might suggest that the sectioning off of this material as a discrete chapter located at the end of the book supports the continuing marginalization of these significant issues. However, the messiness and unpredictable nature of the human condition mean that matters such as institutional relocations, pregnancy and career shifts may occur at almost any occupational stage (e.g., setting out, refining your powers, performing as an academic) and so a likely alternative would require discussing them repetitively and tiresomely in every chapter.
2. In their work on postdoctoral fellowships in HASS, Jones and Oakley (2018) point to a distressing challenge associated with mobility and short-term contracts: 'many "serial postdocs" hold successive short-term jobs, often resulting in a situation where they carry half-completed outputs with them from one postdoctoral project to another. These can include monographs, single-authored publications, and/or co-authored publications' (pp. 5–6). A solution they propose is that employers 'should allocate time at the project design stage for postdoctoral researchers to complete publications at the beginning of their contract, and to apply for their next position towards the end' (p. 10).
3. As a man with no children I write this section as an observer rather than as a participant-observer – and with some degree of apprehension. I do thank colleagues Bev Clarke, Andrew Millington and Graziela Miot da Silva for their thoughtful comments on earlier versions of this chapter.
4. It is telling, for instance, that Rosa's (2022) comprehensive review could find only three publications on academic fatherhood!
5. See, for example, the Facebook group, 'Mothers in Academia'.
6. Other caring roles, such as looking after elderly parents, which often fall most significantly to women, raise similar issues.
7. For comprehensive and quite different discussions on academic retirement see Crow (2021a) [focusing on the UK] and Baldwin (2018) [attentive to the USA]). Crow, in particular, observes how difficult it is to actually define 'retirement' for career academics.

36. Conclusion: acknowledging dual strands of success for your academic career

Despite its inevitable flaws and omissions, this book has been written with the best of intentions. It is meant to help guide early-career academics (ECAs) and other more senior academics developing their careers in increasingly challenging times. It aims to ease the paths for scholars looking to secure good academic employment – or indeed any work; struggling to meet the escalating demands of their employers; and grappling with ways of 'staying sane'. But in doing this, the pages of this book are characterized by an individual-focussed approach: what can you, as a more-or-less lone scholar, do to succeed in more and more challenging academic environments? The volume does not inter-rogate the origins, validity, rationale or wisdom of those growing demands. It does little – if anything – to question or change the circumstances within which academics find themselves working. Indeed, there is a paradoxical risk that by supporting scholars to better satisfy institutional demands, this book and others like it will actually encourage the ratcheting up of expectations by universities, contributing in the long run to even more testing professional academic environments for individuals. But at the very same time as scholars wrestle with heightening institutional expectations, universities find them-selves dealing with their own masters' requirements for 'improved standards', evaluated by external international ratings agencies and often made more difficult to achieve by increasingly watchful, frugal funding bodies. As a result many institutions now expect more and more of their staff (hence the quest for 'superheroes') and, despite their best efforts and any of their own good intentions, find themselves unable or unwilling to provide academic support and resources commensurate with those heightened expectations. Very sadly, it seems that until circumstances change in ways that allow both better working conditions and employment demands to be matched by appropriate levels of staff support and resources, the onus will be on individual academics to find ways to establish and sustain superhero careers. It is to the immediate service of such scholars that this second edition of this book continues to contribute.

Two key strands to a successful, fulfilling academic career are threaded through this volume. The first, and perhaps the most obvious, is that associated with meeting institutional or objective demands for academic superheroes. What are some helpful strategies for achieving high research productivity, exemplary teaching, and constructive university service – bearing in mind that there are only 168 hours in a week?

The second strand is much more about satisfying those criteria that you may personally attach value and meaning to. What contributions do you wish to make to society? How much autonomy and influence do you have? Are you in control of the balance between your work life and personal life? And how satisfied are you in your job? Both strands are significant, but their relative importance to establishing and sustaining your academic career will almost undoubtedly vary with your age, sex, ambitions, stage of career, and even your physical and mental health. A result is that parts of this book may have more or less significance at different times in your career. This is not intended to be a volume focussed on a single point in your career. Instead, by codifying and communicating experiences gained through deeply interested participant observation over more than 35 years, it offers preliminary guidance and triggers to action and strategy that may be helpful across your career. In doing this it also seeks to diminish individual professional anxieties and check unfortunate forays into academic cul-de-sacs.

Across the planet, many scholars are struggling to establish and sustain successful academic careers, let alone meet demands for so-called academic superheroes. While this book cannot change the challenging contexts and circumstances in which we find ourselves, it is my genuine desire that it goes some way to illuminating your pathway through an academic career in the arts, social sciences and humanities, making the challenging journey less stressful, more successful, and truly rewarding.

References

Aarhus University (2018), 'Agreement on working hours at the Faculty of Arts (finalised on 28 April 2017)', accessed 13 January 2023 at https://medarbejdere.au.dk/fileadmin/www.medarbejdere.au.dk/hovedomraader/Arts/Politikker_og _delstrategier/working_hours_agreement_for_Arts_2018.pdf.

Academics Without Borders/Universitaires sans frontières (AWB/USF) (2019), 'About', accessed 30 June 2022 at https://www.awb-usf.org/about/.

Acker, J. (1990), 'Hierarchies, jobs, bodies: A theory of gendered organizations', *Gender & Society*, **4**(2), 139–58.

Advance HE (2023), 'Fellowship', accessed 6 January 2023 at https://www.advance-he.ac.uk/fellowship/fellowship.

Albuquerque, U.P. (2015), *Speaking in Public About Science: A Quick Guide for the Preparation of Good Lectures, Seminars, and Scientific Presentations*, New York: Springer.

Allen, K.-A., S.R. Jimerson, D.S. Quintana and L. McKinley (2023), *An Academic's Guide to Social Media*, Abingdon, Oxon: Routledge.

Almeida, S., M. Randle, Z. Norzailan and M. Cropley (2022), 'Job crafting behavior and the success of senior academic women: An international study'. *Educational Management Administration & Leadership*, https://doi.org/10.1177/17411432221124747.

Altbach, P.G. (2004a), 'The costs and benefits of world-class universities', *Academe*, **90**(1), 20–23.

Altbach, P.G. (2004b), 'The deteriorating guru: The crisis of the professoriate', *International Higher Education*, No. 36, Summer, 2–3.

Altbach, P.G. (2005), 'Academic challenges: The American professoriate in comparative perspective', in A. Welch (ed.), *The Professoriate: Profile of a Profession*, Dordrecht: Springer, pp. 147–65.

American Association of University Professors (2023), 'On professors assigning their own texts to students', accessed 6 January 2023 at https://www.aaup.org/report/professors-assigning-their-own-texts-students.

Arad, A., O. Barzilay and M. Perchick (2017), 'The impact of Facebook on social comparison and happiness: Evidence from a natural experiment', *SSRN*, 13 February, accessed 13 January 2022 at https://ssrn.com/abstract=2916158 or http://dx.doi.org/10.2139/ssrn.2916158.

Archer, L. (2008), 'Younger academics' constructions of "authenticity", "success" and professional identity', *Studies in Higher Education*, **33**(4), 385–403.

Arthur, M.B., S.N. Khapova and C.P.M. Wilderom (2005), 'Career success in a boundaryless career world', *Journal of Organizational Behavior*, **26**(2), 177–202.

Arum, R. and J. Roksa (2011), *Academically Adrift. Limited Learning on College Campuses*, Chicago, IL: University of Chicago Press.

Australian Research Council (ARC) (2021), 'Selection Report: Discovery Projects 2022', 24 December 2021, accessed 21 June 2022 at https://www.arc.gov.au/grants/

grant-outcomes/selection-outcome-reports/selection-report-discovery-projects -2022.

Badenhorst, C., A. Doyle, J. Hesson, X. Li, H. McLeod, S. Penney and G. Young (2022), '"Sabbatical tales" expectations and experiences', in V. Handford and T.M. Sibbald (eds), *The Academic Sabbatical: A Voyage of Discovery*, Ottawa: University of Ottawa Press, pp. 165–94.

Bailey, D.N., M.F. Lipscomb and F. Gorstein et al. (2016), 'Life after being a pathology department chair: Issues and opportunities', *Academic Pathology*, **3**, 1–8.

Bain, K. (2004), *What the Best College Teachers Do*, Cambridge, MA: Harvard University Press.

Baker, E. (2022), 'University of Tasmania academic Vadim Kamenetsky under investigation for criticising the institution on Facebook', *ABC News*, 17 March, accessed 10 January 2023 at https://www.abc.net.au/news/2022-03-17/university-of-tasmania -academic-under-investigation/100915586.

Baker, M. (2012), *Academic Careers and the Gender Gap*, Vancouver, BC: UBC Press.

Baldwin, R.G. (ed.) (2018), *Reinventing Academic Retirement*, New Directions for Higher Education, no. 182, Hanover, PA: Wiley.

Ballantyne, R., J. Borthwick and J. Packer (2000), 'Beyond student evaluation of teaching: Identifying and addressing academic staff development needs', *Assessment & Evaluation in Higher Education*, **25**(3), 221–36.

Banerjee, P. (2022), 'Xavier's controversy: Women post swimsuit pictures on social media in solidarity with ousted professor', *The Times of India*, 11 August, accessed 13 January 2023 at https://timesofindia.indiatimes.com/city/kolkata/ xaviers-controversy-women-post-swimsuit-pictures-on-social-media-in-solidarity -with-ousted-professor/articleshow/93491254.cms.

Baron, N. (2010), *Escape from the Ivory Tower: A Guide to Making Your Science Matter*, Washington, DC: Island Press.

Beall, J. and Anonymous. (2021), *Beall's List of Potential Predatory Journals and Publishers*, accessed 13 January 2023 at https://beallslist.net/.

Becher, T. and P.R. Trowler (2001), *Academic Tribes and Territories. Intellectual Enquiry and the Culture of Disciplines*, 2nd edition, Buckingham, UK: The Society for Research into Higher Education and Open University Press.

Belcher, W.L. (2019), *Writing Your Journal Article in 12 Weeks. A Guide to Academic Publishing Success*, 2nd edition, Chicago, IL: University of Chicago Press.

Bergan, S.,T. Gallagher and I. Harkavy (eds) (2020), *Academic Freedom, Institutional Autonomy and the Future of Democracy*, Council of Europe Higher Education Series No. 24, accessed 28 June 2022 at https://rm.coe.int/prems-025620-eng-2508-higher -education-series-no-24/1680a19fdf.

Berlant, L. (2011), *Cruel Optimism*, Durham, NC: Duke University Press.

Berlatsky, N. (2014), 'What is the point of academic books', *Pacific Standard*, 17 December, accessed 30 June 2022 at http://www.psmag.com/books-and-culture/ point-academic-books-publishing-writing-literature-96610.

Berman, F. (undated), 'Building a research career', workshop presentation, accessed 10 February 2023 at https://math.mit.edu/wim/links/articles/careerbuilding.pdf.

Bernard, D.L. and Stone-Sabali, S. (2022), '5 – Impostor syndrome in graduate school', in M.J. Prinstein (ed.), *The Portable Mentor: Expert Guide to a Successful Career in Psychology*, 3rd edition, Cambridge, UK: Cambridge University Press, pp. 102–18. https://doi.org/10.1017/9781108903264.006.

Bernard, H.R. (1994), *Research Methods in Anthropology: Qualitative and Quantitative Approaches,* 2nd edition, Thousand Oaks, CA: Sage.

Biggs, J.B., C. Tang and G. Kennedy (2022), *Teaching for Quality Learning at University*, 5th edition, Maidenhead, UK: Open University Press.

Blumberg, P. (2014), *Assessing and Improving Your Teaching: Strategies and Rubrics for Faculty Growth and Student Learning*, San Francisco, CA: John Wiley.

Boden, R., D. Epstein and J. Kenway (2007), *Building Your Academic Career*, Newbury Park: Sage.

Bodewits, K. (2017), *You Must Be Very Intelligent: The PhD Delusion*, Springer, https://doi.org/10.1007/978-3-319-59321-0.

Boice, R. (2000), *Advice for New Faculty Members – Nihil Nimus*, Boston, MA: Allyn and Bacon.

Bonnell, A.G. (2016), 'Tide or tsunami? The impact of metrics on scholarly research', *Australian Universities Review*, **58**(1), 54–61.

Bostock, J. (2014), *The Meaning of Success: Insights from Women at Cambridge*, Cambridge, UK: Cambridge University Press.

Breeze, M., Y. Taylor and C. Costa (eds) (2019), *Time and Space in the Neoliberal University: Futures and Fractures in Higher Education*, Springer.

Briones, S. and K. Bush (2015), 'A campus professional's guide to understanding culture shock in international students', *Counseling Concepts and Applications for Student Affairs Professionals* (CNS 577), accessed 30 June 2022 at http://digitalcommons.wku.edu/cns_apps/39.

Brown, J.C. and D. Jones (2018), 'Structures and strategies to enhance academic retirement', in R.G. Baldwin (ed), *Reinventing Academic Retirement*, New Directions in Higher Education, no. 182, Hanover, PA: Wiley, pp. 47–56.

Brown, V.J. (2014), 'From early career researcher to editor-in-chief in 5 steps', accessed 30 June 2022 at https://www.elsevier.com/authors-update/story/career-tips-and-advice/from-early-career-researcher-to-editor-in-chief-in-5-steps.

Brunn, S.D. (1988), 'The manuscript review process and advice to prospective authors', *The Professional Geographer*, **40**(1), 8–14.

Buchanan, J. and P. Childerhouse (2012), 'Co-teaching invigoration', *TDU Talk*, No. 1, April/May, 15–16.

Burkeman, O. (2016), 'Why time management is ruining our lives', *The Guardian*, 22 December, accessed 30 June 2022 at https://www.theguardian.com/technology/2016/dec/22/why-time-management-is-ruining-our-lives.

Burton, S. and B. Bowman (2022), 'The academic precariat: understanding life and labour in the neoliberal academy', *British Journal of Sociology of Education*, **43**(4), 497–512, DOI: 10.1080/01425692.2022.2076387.

Byrnes, D., L.J. Uribe-Flórez, J. Trespalacios and J. Chilson (2019), 'Doctoral E-mentoring: current practices and effective strategies', *Online Learning Journal*, **23**(1), 236–48, http://dx.doi.org/10.24059/olj.v23i1.1446.

Cameron, I. (2011), 'Destinations and pathways: The curriculum challenge', in I. Hay (ed.), *Inspiring Academics. Learning with the World's Great University Teachers*, Maidenhead, UK: Open University Press, pp. 79–86.

Cameron, K. (2013), *Practicing Positive Leadership: Tools and Techniques that Create Extraordinary Results*, San Francisco, CA: Berrett Koehler.

Cantwell, R.H. and J.J. Scevak (2010), *An Academic Life: A Handbook for New Academics*, Camberwell, VIC: ACER Press.

Carlson, S. (2014), 'Mapping a new economy', *The Chronicle of Higher Education*, 12 May, accessed 30 June 2022 at https://www.chronicle.com/article/mapping-a-new-economy/.

Carrigan, M. (2019), *Social Media for Academics*, 2nd edition, London: Sage.

Chase, J.-A.D., R. Topp and C.E. Smith et al. (2013), 'Time management strategies for research productivity', *Western Journal of Nursing Research*, **35**(2), 155–76.

Chávez, K. and K.M.W. Mitchell. (2020) 'Exploring bias in student evaluations: Gender, race, and ethnicity', *PS: Political Science & Politics*, **53**(2), 270–74. doi:10.1017/S1049096519001744.

Cheng, M.W.T. and M.L. Leung (2022), '"I'm not the only victim…" student perceptions of exploitative supervision relation in doctoral degree', *Higher Education*, **84**, 523–40, https://doi.org/10.1007/s10734-021-00786-5.

Cheplygina, V. (2021), 'How I fail', accessed 13 January 2023 at https://veronikach.com/category/how-i-fail/.

Church, A.H., D.W. Bracken, J.W. Fleenor and D.S. Rose (eds) (2019), *Handbook of Strategic 360 Feedback*, New York, NY: Oxford University Press.

Churches, O. (2015), 'The words that make a successful research grant application', *The Conversation*, 27 February, accessed 30 June 2022 at http://theconversation.com/the-words-that-make-a-successful-research-grant-application-37699.

Clark, A. and B. Sousa (2018), *How to be a Happy Academic*, London: Sage.

Clauset, A., S. Arbesman and D.B. Larremore (2015), 'Systematic inequality and hierarchy in faculty hiring networks', *Science Advances*, **1**(1), DOI: 10.1126/sciadv.1400005.

Cohen, W.A. (2008), *A Class with Drucker. The Lost Lessons of the World's Greatest Management Teacher*, New York: American Management Association.

Conrad, L. and D. Padula (2022), '5 scholarly publishing trends to watch in 2022', 31 January, accessed 13 January 2022 at https://blog.scholasticahq.com/post/scholarly-publishing-trends-2022/.

COPE Council (2021), COPE Flowcharts and infographics – How to recognise potential authorship problems – English. https://doi.org/10.24318/cope.2019.2.22.

Copyright Agency Limited (Australia) (2023), 'International affiliates', *Copyright Agency*, accessed 16 January 2023 at https://www.copyright.com.au/about-us/international-affiliates/.

Cornell University (2023), 'Research statement', accessed 11 January 2023 at https://gradschool.cornell.edu/career-and-professional-development/pathways-to-success/prepare-for-your-career/take-action/research-statement/#:~:text=What%20is%20a%20Research%20Statement,and%20potential%20of%20your%20work.

Crone, W.C. (2010), *Survive and Thrive: A Guide for Untenured Faculty*, Williston, VT: Morgan and Claypool Publishers.

Crow, G. (2021a), 'Academics retiring, scunnered or otherwise', Extended working paper, School of Social and Political Science, University of Edinburgh.

Crow, G. (2021b), 'In search of role models of successful academic retirement', *Contemporary Social Science*, **16**(5), 604–17, DOI: 10.1080/21582041.2021.1983204.

Csikszentmihalyi, M. (1990), *Flow: The Psychology of Optimal Experience*, New York: Harper & Row.

D'Alessandro, S., M. Miles, F.J. Martínez-López, R. Anaya-Sánchez, I. Esteban-Millat and H. Torrez-Meruvia (2020), 'Promote or perish? A brief note on academic social networking sites and academic reputation', *Journal of Marketing Management*, **36**(5–6), 405–11.

Davidson, O.B., D. Eden, M. Westman, Y. Cohen-Charash, L.B. Hammer, A.N. Kluger, M. Krausz, C. Maslach, M. O'Driscoll, P.L. Perrewé, J.C. Quick, Z. Rosenblatt and P.E. Spector (2010), 'Sabbatical leave: Who gains and how much?', *Journal of Applied Psychology*, **95**(5), 953–64.

Davies, E. and A. Jenkins (2013), 'The work-to-retirement transition of academic staff: Attitudes and experiences', *Employee Relations*, **35**(3), 322–38.

Day, A. (2007), *How to Get Research Published in Journals*, 2nd edition, Burlington, VT: Gower.

De Cruz, H. (2016), 'Happily ever after? Advice for mid-career academics', *Times Higher Education* [blog], 24 March, accessed 30 June 2022 at https://www.timeshighereducation.com/blog/happily-ever-after-advice-mid-career-academics.

Debowski, S. (2012), *The New Academic: A Strategic Handbook*, Maidenhead, UK: Open University Press.

Debowski, S. (2022), 'Shifting sands: Navigating being academic in an evolving sector', *Higher Education Research & Development*, **41**(7), 7–20.

De Hertogh, L.B. (2012), 'Four good reasons to attend conferences', *Hastac* [blog], 4 November, accessed 30 June 2022 at https://www.hastac.org/blogs/dehertoghlb/2012/11/04/four-good-reasons-attend-conferences.

Delgado López-Cózar, E., N. Robinson-García and D. Torres-Salinas (2014), 'The Google Scholar experiment: How to index false papers and manipulate bibliometric indicators', *Journal of the Association for Information Science and Technology*, **65**(3), 446–54.

de Moor, A. (2009), 'Research consultancy: Taking the plunge?', *Making CommunitySense: For Working Communities*, 21 May, accessed 30 June 2022 at https://communitysense.wordpress.com/2009/05/21/research-consultancy-taking-the-plunge/.

Detsky, A.A. and M.O. Baerlocher (2007), 'Academic mentoring – how to give it and how to get it', *Journal of the American Medical Association*, **297**(19), 2134–6.

Douglas, A.S. (2013), 'Advice from the professors in a university social sciences department on the teaching–research nexus', *Teaching in Higher Education*, **18**(4), 377–88.

Dr. Karen (2016), 'Dr. Karen's rules of the academic cv', *The Professor is In*, accessed 30 June 2022 at http://theprofessorisin.com/2016/08/19/dr-karens-rules-of-the-academic-cv/.

DuBois, M., J. Hanlon and J. Koch et al. (2015), 'Leadership styles of effective project managers: Techniques and traits to lead high performance teams', *Journal of Economic Development, Management, IT, Finance, and Marketing*, **7**(1), 30–46.

Duffy, M. (2015), 'You do not need to work 80 hours a week to succeed in academia', *Times Higher Education* [blog], 28 October, accessed 30 June 2022 at https://www.timeshighereducation.com/blog/you-do-not-need-work-80-hours-week-succeed-academia.

Duncan, R., K. Tilbrook and B. Krivokapic-Skoko (2015), 'Does academic work make Australian academics happy?', *Australian Universities' Review*, **57**(1), 5–12.

Dyer, S., H. Walkington and R. Williams et al. (2016), 'Shifting landscapes: From coalface to quicksand? Teaching geography, earth and environmental sciences in higher education', *Area*, **48**(3), 308–16.

Else, H. (2015), 'Too many PhDs, not enough tenured positions', *Times Higher Education*, 28 May, accessed 30 June 2022 at https://www.timeshighereducation.com/content/too-many-phds-not-enough-tenured-positions.

Elsevier (2015), *Understanding the Publishing Process: How to Publish in Scholarly Journals*, accessed 30 June 2022 at https://www.elsevier.com/research-intelligence/resource-library/understanding-the-publishing-process-how-to-publish-in-scholarly-journals.

Elsevier (2023), 'Writing an effective academic CV', accessed 12 May 2023 at https://researcheracademy.elsevier.com/uploads/2017-11/ECR_Academic_CV_070912.pdf.

Emerson, L. (2011), '"I am a writer": Unlocking fear and releasing possibility in the classroom', in I. Hay (ed.), *Inspiring Academics. Learning with the World's Great University Teachers*, Maidenhead, UK: Open University Press, pp. 127–34.

Emerson, R.M., R.I. Fretz and L.L. Shaw (2001), 'Participant observation and fieldnotes', in P. Atkinson, A. Coffey and S. Delamont et al. (eds), *Handbook of Ethnography*, London: Sage, pp. 352–68.

Enders, J. and M. Kaulisch (2006), 'The binding and unbinding of academic careers', in U. Teichler (ed.), *The Formative Years of Scholars*, London: Portland Press, pp. 85–95.

Ernst, M. (2004), 'Attending an academic conference', July, accessed 30 June 2022 at https://homes.cs.washington.edu/~mernst/advice/conference-attendance.html.

Ernst, Z. (2020), 'Leaving academia for the private sector: Seven years later', *Medium*, 15 May, accessed 15 February 2023 at https://zacernst.medium.com/leaving-academia-for-the-private-sector-seven-years-later-fbb7849182f6.

Esarey, J. and N. Valdes (2020), 'Unbiased, reliable, and valid student evaluations can still be unfair', *Assessment & Evaluation in Higher Education*, **45**(8), 1106–20, DOI: 10.1080/02602938.2020.1724875.

EURAXESS Australia and New Zealand, L. Batrouney and V. Stephens. (2022), 'How to publish your first (or next) academic book', accessed 13 January 2023 at https://www.youtube.com/watch?v=qdD9qYe9g1A.

EUTOPIA (2022), EUTOPIA-SIF – Post-Doctoral Fellowships, accessed 23 June 2022 at https://eutopia-university.eu/english-version/research/sif-post-doctoral-fellowships.

Fargotstein, L. (2014), '9 publishing basics for anyone submitting to a scholarly journal', *Social Science Space*, 19 March, accessed 30 June 2022 at https://www.socialsciencespace.com/2014/03/9-basics-for-anyone-submitting-to-a-scholarly-journal/.

Farley, S. and C. Sprigg (2014), 'Culture of cruelty: Why bullying thrives in higher education', *The Guardian*, 4 November, accessed 30 June 2022 at http://www.theguardian.com/higher-education-network/blog/2014/nov/03/why-bullying-thrives-higher-education.

Feibelman, P.J. (2011), *A PhD is Not Enough. A Guide to Survival in Science*, revised edition, New York: Basic Books.

Ferguson, H. and K.L. Wheat (2015), 'Early career academic mentoring using Twitter: The case of #ECRchat', *Journal of Higher Education Policy and Management*, **37**(1), 3–13.

Fertig, A. (2015), '5 tips for recruiting a headhunter', *US News and World Report*, 24 March, accessed 30 June 2022 at https://au.finance.yahoo.com/news/5-tips-recruiting-headhunter-132310722.html.

Fink, L.D. (2013), *Creating Significant Learning Experiences. An Integrated Approach to Designing College Courses*, 2nd edition, San Francisco, CA: John Wiley and Sons.

Fiske, P. (2010), 'Side target', *Nature*, **465**, 6 May, 123.

Fitzgerald, T., J. White and H.M. Gunter (eds) (2012), *Hard Labour? Academic Work and the Changing Landscape of Higher Education*, Bingley, UK: Emerald Publishing.

Flaherty, C. (2022), 'Calling it quits', *Inside Higher Ed*, 5 July, accessed 25 January 2023 at https://www.insidehighered.com/news/2022/07/05/professors-are-leaving -academe-during-great-resignation.

Flaxman, P. E., J. Menard, F.W. Bond and G. Kinman (2012), 'Academics' experiences of a respite from work: Effects of self-critical perfectionism and perseverate cognition on post respite well-being', *Journal of Applied Psychology*, **97**(4), 854–65.

Flinders University (2015), 'Academic profiles. Levels A to E', December, accessed 13 January 2023 at https://staff.flinders.edu.au/content/dam/staff/pc/academic -profiles-levels-a-to-e.pdf.

Forgues, B. and S. Liarte (2013), 'Academic publishing: past and future', *M@n@ gement*, **16**(5), accessed 30 June 2022 at https://www.cairn.info/revue-management -2013-5-page-739.htm.

Foster, R. and G. Hicks (2004), *How We Choose to be Happy*, New York: Penguin.

Francis, L. (2001), *Sexual Harassment as an Ethical Issue in Academic Life*, Lanham, MD: Rowman and Littlefield.

Fraunfelder, F.T. and J.H. Gilbaugh Jr. (2009), *Retire Right*, New York: Avery Publishing.

Free, R. (2011), 'On scholarly teaching – a personal account', in I. Hay (ed.), *Inspiring Academics. Learning with the World's Great University Teachers*, Maidenhead, UK: Open University Press, pp. 70–78.

Freie Universität Berlin (2022), 'Academic offerings and services for refugees', accessed 9 September 2022 at https://www.fu-berlin.de/en/sites/welcome/index .html.

Friedersdorf, C. (2015), 'Stripping a professor of tenure over a blog post', *The Atlantic*, 9 February, accessed 30 June 2022 at http://www.theatlantic.com/education/archive/ 2015/02/stripping-a-professor-of-tenure-over-a-blog-post/385280/.

Frølich, N., K. Wendt, I. Reymert, S.M. Tellman, M. Elken, S. Kyvik, A. Vabø and E. Larsen (2018), *Academic Career Structures in Europe. Perspectives from Norway, Denmark, Sweden, Finland, the Netherlands, Austria and the UK*, Report 2018:4, Oslo, Norway: Nordic Institute for Studies in Innovation, Research and Education (NIFU).

Frost, C. (2011), 'Getting published: What academics need to know', *The Guardian*, 28 April, accessed 30 June 2022 at http://www.theguardian.com/higher-education -network/blog/2011/apr/27/getting-published-academics.

Furstenberg, F.F. (2013), *Behind the Academic Curtain: How to Find Success and Happiness with a PhD*, Chicago, IL: University of Chicago Press.

Gaillard, S., T. van Viegen, M. Veldsman, M.I. Stefan and V. Cheplygina (2022), 'Ten simple rules for failing successfully in academia', *PLoS Computational Biology*, **18**(12), e1010538. https://doi.org/10.1371/journal.pcbi.1010538.

Gans, J. (2011), 'Quelle surprise: Academics gaming the system sank the ERA journal rankings', *The Conversation*, 31 May, accessed 30 June 2022 at http:// theconversation.com/quelle-surprise-academics-gaming-the-system-sank-the-era -journal-rankings-1575.

Gasman, M. (2021), *Candid Advice for New Faculty Members. A Guide to Getting Tenure and Advancing Your Career*, Gorham, ME: Myers Education Press.

Gelles, R.J. (2006), 'Watson's Syndrome', *Inside Higher Education*, 19 June.

Germano, W. (2013), *From Dissertation to Book*, 2nd edition, Chicago, IL: Chicago University Press.

Germano, W. (2016), *Getting it Published. A Guide for Scholars and Anyone Else Serious About Serious Books*, 3rd edition, Chicago, IL: Chicago University Press.

Gertenschlager, B. (2016), 'Ten publishing tips for young academics', accessed 30 June 2022at https://www.academia.edu/1782619/Ten_Publishing_Tips_for_Young _Academics.

Geschwind, L. and A. Broström (2015), 'Managing the teaching–research nexus: Ideals and practice in research-oriented universities', *Higher Education Research & Development*, **34**(1), 60–73, DOI:10.1080/07294360.2014.934332.

Gitlin, L.N., A. Kolanowski and K.J. Lyons (2021), *Successful Grant Writing. Strategies for Health and Human Service Professionals*, 5th edition, New York, NY: Springer.

Gladwell, M. (2000), 'The new-boy network', *The New Yorker*, 21 May, accessed 30 June 2022 at https://www.newyorker.com/magazine/2000/05/29/the-new-boy -network.

Gold, R.L. (1958), 'Roles in sociological field observation', *Social Forces*, **36**(3), 219–25.

Goldsmith, J.A., J. Komlos and P. Schine Gold (2001), *The Chicago Guide to Your Academic Career: A Portable Mentor for Scholars from Graduate School Through Tenure*, Chicago, IL: University of Chicago Press.

González-Calvo, G. (2020), 'Programmed agar.io in higher education: Fundaments of the dynamics of overproduction and superproduction', *Qualitative Research in Education*, **9**(2), 160–87. https://doi.org/10.17583/qre.2020.5412.

Goodier, S. and L. Czerniewicz (2014), *Academics' Online Presence: A Four-Step Guide to Taking Control of Your Visibility*, Cape Town: OpenUCT, accessed 30 June 2022 at http://wiki.lib.sun.ac.za/images/5/5d/Online_Visibility_Guidelines.pdf.

Gornall, L., C. Cook and L. Daunton et al. (eds) (2014), *Academic Working Lives: Experience, Practice and Change*, London: Bloomsbury Academic.

Gottlieb, E.E. and B. Keith (1997), 'The academic research–teaching nexus in eight advanced-industrialized countries', *Higher Education*, **34**(3), 397–419.

Grant, W. and P. Sherrington (2006), *Managing Your Academic Career*, Basingstoke, UK: Palgrave Macmillan.

Gray, P. and D.E. Drew (2012), *What They Didn't Teach You in Graduate School 2.0*, Sterling, VA: Stylus.

Grove, J. (2016), 'THE university workplace survey 2016: results and analysis', *Times Higher Education*, 4 February, accessed 30 June 2022 at https://www.timeshighe reducation.com/features/university-work place-survey-2016-results-and-analysis.

Guzman, A. (2022), 'Anything to confess? Dean at Texas Catholic college who once served as Swiss Guard to Pope John Paul II and met Mother Teresa resigns after fabricating PhD and bachelor's degree qualifications', *Daily Mail Australia*, 18 August 2022, accessed 7 January 2023 at https://www.dailymail.co.uk/news/article -11122309/Tenured-Houston-business-school-dean-FIRED-claims-qualifications .html.

Haak, L. (2002), 'Editorial boards: A step up the academic career ladder', *Science*, 1 February, accessed 30 June 2022 at http://www.sciencemag.org/careers/2002/02/ editorial-boards-step-academic-career-ladder.

Handford, V. (2022), 'The sabbatical voyage: A triptych of renewal, reflection, and research', in V. Handford and T.M. Sibbald (eds), *The Academic Sabbatical: A Voyage of Discovery*, Ottawa: University of Ottawa Press, pp. 71–88.

Handford, V. and T.M. Sibbald (eds) (2022), *The Academic Sabbatical: A Voyage of Discovery*, Ottawa: University of Ottawa Press, doi:10.1353/book.94978.

Hardy, A., J. McDonald and R. Guijt et al. (2016), 'Academic parenting: Work–family conflict and strategies across child age, disciplines and career level', *Studies in Higher Education*, accessed 8 September 2022 at http://dx.doi.org/10.1080/03075079.2016.1185777.

Hardy, I. and E. Smith (2006), 'Contesting tertiary teaching qualifications: An Australian perspective', *Teaching in Higher Education*, **11**(3), 337–50.

Hare, J. (2013), 'Professor tag "wasted on pollies", says Phil Honeywood', *The Australian*, 30 October, accessed 30 June 2022 at http://www.theaustralian.com.au/higher-education/professor-tag-wasted-on-pollies-says-phil-honeywood/story-e6frgcjx-1226749191778.

Harvey, M., T. Ambler and H. Cahir (2016), 'Spectrum approach to mentoring: An evidence-based approach to mentoring for academics working in higher education', *Teacher Development*, **21**(1), 160–74. https://doi.org/10.1080/13664530.2016.1210537.

Haswell, E. (2017), 'Point of view: The sustainable professor', *eLife*, **6**, e31083, https://doi.org/10.7554/eLife.31083.

Haushofer, J. (2016), 'CV of failures', accessed 13 January 2023 at https://www.uni-goettingen.de/de/document/download/bed2706fd34e29822004dbe29cd00bb5.pdf/Johannes_Haushofer_CV_of_Failures[1].pdf.

Hay, I. (1995), 'The strange case of Dr. Jekyll in Hyde Park: Fear, media and the conduct of an emancipatory geography', *Australian Geographical Studies*, **33**(2), 257–71.

Hay, I. (ed.) (2011a), *Inspiring Academics. Learning with the World's Great University Teachers*, Maidenhead, UK: Open University Press.

Hay, I. (2011b), 'Opening doors', in I. Hay (ed.), *Inspiring Academics. Learning with the World's Great University Teachers*, Maidenhead, UK: Open University Press.

Hay, I. (2012), *Communicating in Geography and the Environmental Sciences*, 4th edition, Melbourne, VIC: Oxford University Press.

Hay, I. (2016a), 'Defending letters: A pragmatic response to assaults on the humanities', *Journal of Higher Education Policy and Management*, **38**(6), 610–24.

Hay, I.M. (2016b), 'Why edit a journal? Academic irony and paradox', *The Professional Geographer*, **68**(1), 159–65.

Hay, I. and D. Bass (2002), 'Making news in geography and environmental management', *Journal of Geography in Higher Education*, **26**(1), 129–42.

Hay, I.M. and M. Cope (eds) (2021), *Qualitative Research Methods in Human Geography*, 5th edition, Toronto: Oxford University Press.

Hay, I. and M. Israel (2001), '"Newsmaking geography": Communicating geography through the media', *Applied Geography*, **21**(2), 107–25.

Hay, I. and M. Israel (2009), 'Private people, secret places: Ethical research in practice', in M. Solem, K. Foote and J. Monk (eds), *Aspiring Academics*, New York: Prentice-Hall, pp. 165–76.

Hay, I. and M. Israel, M. (2022), 'Caring about research ethics in human geography', in S. Henn, K. Hörschelmann and J. Miggelbrink (eds), *Research Ethics in Human Geography*, Oxon and New York: Routledge. DOI: 10.4324/9780429507366-2

Hay, I., K. Dunn and A. Street (2005), 'Making the most of your conference journey', *Journal of Geography in Higher Education*, **29**(1), 159–71.

Hazelkorn, E. (2019). 'University rankings: There is room for error and "malpractice"'. *Elephant in the Lab*, accessed 10 January 2023 at https://doi.org/10.5281/zenodo.2592196.

Heffernan, T. (2021), 'Sexism, racism, prejudice, and bias: A literature review and synthesis of research surrounding student evaluations of courses and teaching', *Assessment & Evaluation in Higher Education*, **47**(1), 144–54, DOI: 10.1080/02602938.2021.1888075.

Heller, D. (2012), 'Higher education. Not what it used to be', *The Economist*, 1 December, accessed 30 June 2022 at http://www.economist.com/news/united-states/ 21567373-american-universities-represent-declining-value-money-their-students -not-what-it.

Hemmings, B. (2012), 'Sources of research confidence for early career academics: A qualitative study', *Higher Education Research & Development*, **31**(2), 171–84.

Hemmings, B.C. (2015), 'Strengthening the teaching self-efficacy of early career academics', *Issues in Educational Research*, **25**(1), 1–17.

Henrich, J., S.J. Heine and A. Norenzayan (2010), 'The weirdest people in the world?', *Behavioral and Brain Sciences*, **33**(2–3), 61–83.

Henville, L. (2022), 'How to structure your diversity statement for your academic job search', *University Affairs*, 17 May, accessed 11 January 2023 at https://www .universityaffairs.ca/career-advice/ask-dr-editor/how-to-structure-your-diversity -statement-for-your-academic-job-search/.

Hicken, M. (2013), 'Professors teach into their golden years', *CNN Money*, 17 June, accessed 30 June 2022 at http://money.cnn.com/2013/06/17/retirement/professors -retire/.

Hill, L.H. and S.C.O. Conceição (2020), 'Program and instructional strategies supportive of doctoral students' degree completion', *Adult Learning*, **31**(1), 36–44, https:// doi.org/10.1177/1045159519887529.

Hodgins, P. (2012), 'Make them endure, give them space: On the loss of academic cynicism', *Emotion, Space and Society*, **11**(6), 28–35.

Huopalainen, A.S. and S.T. Satama (2019), 'Mother and researchers in the making: Negotiating "new" motherhood within the "new" academia', *Human Relations*, **71**(1), 98–121.

Huysmans, R. (2020), 'Six things to do to be a better PhD supervisor', *DRH*, 7 July, accessed 18 January 2023 at https://drrichardhuysmans.com/six-things-to-do-to-be -a-better-phd-supervisor/.

IFERP (2022), 'Presenting and peaking at academic conferences – a complete rundown', 29 March, accessed 17 January 2023 at https://www.iferp.in/blog/2022/ 03/29/presenting-speaking-at-academic-conferences-a-complete-rundown/.

Imber, A. (2022), *Time Wise: Powerful Habits. More Time. Greater Joy*, Southbank, Victoria: Penguin Life.

Imes, P.R. and S.A. Clance (1978), 'The imposter phenomenon in high achieving women: Dynamics and therapeutic intervention', *Psychotherapy: Theory, Research & Practice*, **15**(3), 241–7.

Ingold, T. (2014), 'That's enough about ethnography!', *HAU: Journal of Ethnographic Theory*, **4**(1), 383–95.

International Committee of Medical Journal Editors (ICMJE) (2022a), *Recommendations for the Conduct, Reporting, Editing, and Publication of Scholarly Work in Medical Journals*, accessed 30 June 2022 at http://www.icmje.org/recommendations/.

International Committee of Medical Journal Editors (ICMJE) (2022b), 'Defining the role of authors and contributors', accessed 30 June 2022 at http://www.icmje.org/ recommendations/browse/roles-and-responsibilities/defining-the-role-of-authors -and-contributors.html.

International Professors Project (IPP) (2023), 'Professors to the World', accessed 19 January 2023 at https://www.linkedin.com/company/international-professors -project/.

Israel, M. and I. Hay (2012), 'Research ethics in criminology', in D. Gadd, S. Karsted and S. Messner (eds), *Sage Handbook of Criminological Research Methods*, London: Sage, pp. 500–514.

Irish, A. (2021), 'How to get more out of service', *Inside Higher Ed*, 3 August, accessed 18 January 2023 at https://www.insidehighered.com/advice/2021/08/03/how-use-service-bolster-your-academic-career-opinion.

Jabour, A. (2012), 'Relationship and leadership: Sophonisba Breckinridge and women in social work', *Affilia: Journal of Women and Social Work*, **27**(1), 22–37.

Jabre, L., C. Bannon, J.S.P. McCain and Y. Eglit (2021), 'Ten simple rules for choosing a PhD supervisor', *PLOS Computational Biology*, 30 September, https://doi.org/10.1371/journal.pcbi.1009330.

Jacobs, P. (2013), 'University of Iowa TA removed from class after accidentally sending nude pictures to students', *Business Insider Australia*, 25 October, accessed 30 June 2022 at http://www.businessinsider.com.au/university-iowa-ta-removed-class-accidentally-sending-nude-pictures-students-2013-10.

Jaremka, L.M, J.M. Ackerman, B. Gawronski, N.O. Rule, K. Sweeny, L.R. Tropp, M.A. Metz, L. Molina, W.S. Ryan and S.B. Vick (2020), 'Common academic experiences no one talks about: Repeated rejection, impostor syndrome, and burnout', *Perspectives on Psychological Science* **15**(3), 519–43.

Jean, V.A., S.C. Payne and R.J. Thompson (2015), 'Women in STEM: Family-related challenges and initiatives', in M. Mills (ed.), *Gender and the Work–Family Experience*, New York: Springer, pp. 291–311.

Johnson, A.M. (2011), *Charting a Course for a Successful Research Career*, 2nd edition, Amsterdam: Elsevier.

Jones, B.F. (2021), 'The rise of research teams: Benefits and costs in economics', *Journal of Economic Perspectives*, **35**(2) Spring, 191–216.

Jones, S.A. and C. Oakley (2018), *The Precarious Postdoc: Interdisciplinary Research and Casualised Labour in the Humanities and Social Sciences*, Durham University, UK: Hearing the Voice.

Kahane, D. (2011), 'Mindfulness and presence in teaching and learning', in I. Hay (ed.), *Inspiring Academics: Learning with the World's Great University Teachers*, Maidenhead, UK: Open University Press pp. 17–22.

Kara, H. (2018), 'Why and how to negotiate with academic book publishers', *HelenKara*, 6 March, accessed 16 January 2023, at https://helenkara.com/2018/03/06/why-and-how-to-negotiate-with-academic-book-publishers/.

Kawulich, B.B. (2005), 'Participant observation as a data collection method', *Forum: Qualitative Research*, **6**(2), Article 43, accessed 30 June 2022 at http://www.qualitative-research.net/index.php/fqs/article/view/466/996.

Kern, L., R. Hawkins, K. Falconer Al-Hindi and P. Moss (2014), 'A collective biography of joy in academic practice', *Social and Cultural Geography*, **15**(7), 834–51.

Kerr, E. (2020), 'How your college choice can affect job prospects', *US News*, 16 December, accessed 7 July 2022 at https://www.usnews.com/education/best-colleges/paying-for-college/articles/how-your-college-choice-can-affect-job-prospects.

Khoo, T. (2013), 'Telling research career stories – Part 1', *The Research Whisperer*, 10 September, accessed 30 June 2022 at https://theresearchwhisperer.wordpress.com/2013/09/10/research-career-stories-1/#comments.

Kim, J. (2022), 'How to have a 50-year academic career', *Inside Higher Ed*, 14 August, accessed 7 January 2023 at https://www.insidehighered.com/blogs/learning-innovation/how-have-50-year-academic-career.

Kindsiko, E. and Y. Baruch (2019), 'Careers of PhD graduates: The role of chance events and how to manage them', *Journal of Vocational Behavior*, **112**, 122–40.

Klingner, J.K., D. Scanlon and M. Pressley (2005), 'How to publish in scholarly journals', *Educational Researcher*, **34**(8), 14–20.

Knox, K. (2023), 'What does "a book" mean for tenure? Don't assume you know!', accessed 16 January 2023 at https://katelynknox.com/writing-first-humanities-book/what-a-book-means-for-tenure/.

Konkiel, S. (2014), '7 tips to supercharge your academic LinkedIn profile', *Impactstory* [blog], 22 April, accessed 30 June 2022 at http://blog.impactstory.org/7-tips-to-supercharge-your-academic-linkedin-profile/.

Konkiel, S. (2015), *The 30-Day Impact Challenge: The Ultimate Guide to Raising the Profile of Your Research*, accessed 10 January 2023 at chrome-extension://efaid-nbmnnnibpcajpcglclefindmkaj/https://blog.impactstory.org/wp-content/uploads/2015/01/impact_challenge_ebook_links.pdf.

Kreitzer, R.J. and J. Sweet-Cushman (2022), 'Evaluating student evaluations of teaching: a review of measurement and equity bias in SETs and recommendations for ethical reform', *Journal of Academic Ethics*, **20**, 73–84, https://doi.org/10.1007/s10805-021-09400-w.

Laud, R.L. and M. Johnson (2012), 'Upward mobility: A typology of tactics and strategies for career advancement', *Career Development International*, **17**(3), 231–54.

Laurance, W.F., D.C. Useche, S.G. Laurance and C.J.A. Bradshaw (2013), 'Predicting publication success for biologists', *BioScience*, **63**(10), 817–23.

Lawrence, P. (2015), 'Building great 360 feedback programs', *Training & Development*, **42**(1), 5–7.

League of European Research Universities (2023), 'Academic career maps in Europe', accessed 14 February 2023 at https://www.leru.org/academic-career-maps-in-europe.

Lee, D. (1998), 'Sexual harassment in PhD supervision', *Gender and Education*, **10**(3), 299–312.

Leighton, M. (2020), 'Myths of meritocracy, friendship, and fun work: class and gender in North American academic communities', *American Anthropologist*, **122**(3), 444–58.

Levine, A.G. (2013), 'Postdoc advancement: Marketing your value', *Science*, 22 August, accessed 30 June 2022 at http://sciencecareers.sciencemag.org/career_magazine/previous_issues/articles/2013_08_22/science.opms.r1300135.

Lewin, T. (2007), 'Dean at M.I.T. resigns, ending a 28-year lie', *The New York Times*, 27 April, accessed 30 June 2022 at http://www.nytimes.com/2007/04/27/us/27mit.html?_r=0.

Lewis, P. and W. Zelinsky (1987), 'The coffee hour at Penn State', *The Professional Geographer*, **39**(1), 75–9.

Leyshon, A. (2013), 'Why edit handbooks?', *Regional Studies*, **47**(9), 1613–14.

Lin, S. (2013), 'Why serious academic fraud occurs in China', *Learned Publishing*, **26**(1), 24–7.

Löfström, E. and K. Pyhältö (2017), 'Ethics in the supervisory relationship: Supervisors' and doctoral students' dilemmas in the natural and behavioural sciences', *Studies in Higher Education*, **42**(2), 232–47, https://doi.org/10.1080/03075079.2015.1045475.

Löfström, E. and K. Pyhältö (2020), 'What are ethics in doctoral supervision, and how do they matter? Doctoral students' perspective', *Scandinavian Journal of Educational Research*, **64**(4), 535–50, https://doi.org/10.1080/00313831.2019.1595711.

Long, J. (1994), 'The dark side of mentoring', paper presented at Australian Association for Research in Education (AARE) annual conference, Newcastle, New South Wales, accessed 30 June 2022 at http://www.aare.edu.au/publications-database.php/ 1152/the-dark-side-of-mentoring.

Lough, T. and T. Samek (2014), 'Canadian university social software guidelines and academic freedom: An alarming labour trend', *International Review of Information Ethics*, **21**, 45–56.

Lucas, U. (2011), 'Exploring the "inner" and "outer" worlds: Steps along a scholarly journey', in I. Hay (ed.), *Inspiring Academics. Learning with the World's Great University Teachers*, Maidenhead, UK: Open University Press, pp. 165–71.

Lyubomirsky, S. (2008), *The How of Happiness: A Scientific Approach to Getting the Life You Want*, New York: Penguin.

Madsen, L.D. (2007), 'A guide to NSF success', *Science*, 27 July, accessed 30 June 2022 at http://www.sciencemag.org/careers/2007/07/guide-nsf-success.

Makvandi, P., A. Nodehi and F.R. Tay (2021), 'Conference accreditation and need of a bibliometric measure to distinguish predatory conferences', *Publications*, **9**(2), 16, https://doi.org/10.3390/publications9020016.

Mallinger, M. (2013), 'Faculty to administration and back again: I'm a stranger here myself', *Journal of Management Inquiry*, **22**(1), 59–67.

Manners, B. (2016), *Retirement Ready? Plan Now to Retire Well*, Warburton, VIC: Signs Publishing.

Mantai, L. and M. Marrone (2023), 'Academic career progression from early career researcher to professor: what can we learn from job ads', *Studies in Higher Education*, DOI: 10.1080/03075079.2023.2167974.

Margolin, J.B. (1983), *The Individual's Guide to Grants*, New York: Plenum Press.

Markin, K.M. (2012), 'Plagiarism in grant proposals', *The Chronicle of Higher Education*, 10 December, accessed 30 June 2022 at http://chronicle.com/article/ Plagiarism-in-Grant-Proposals/136161/.

Marr, B. (2014), *Job Interview: Why Only 3 Questions Really Matter*, 31 March, accessed 30 June 2022 at https://www.linkedin.com/pulse/20140331030822 -64875646-job-interview-why-only-3-questions-really-matter.

Marris, E. (2004), 'NIH researchers face blanket consulting ban', *Nature*, **431**, 30 September, 497.

Martin, B. (2011), 'On being a happy academic', *Australian Universities' Review*, **53**(1), 50–56.

Martin, Q. III (2021), 'Look before you leap: Making the transition from administration to faculty', *International Journal for Academic Development*, **26**(1) 110–15.

Martin, Q. III (2022), 'From faculty to administration: Preparing the next generation of academic leaders', *Perspectives: Policy and Practice in Higher Education*, **26**(3), 109–14, DOI: 10.1080/13603108.2021.2016513.

Mascarelli, A. (2010), 'Freedom of spill research threatened', *Nature*, **466**, 29 July, 538.

Mason, M.A. and E.M. Ekman (2007), *Mothers on the Fast Track*, New York: Oxford University Press.

Mason, M.A., N.H. Wolfinger and M. Goulden (2013), *Do Babies Matter? Gender and Family in the Ivory Tower*, New Brunswick, NJ: Rutgers University Press.

Massner, C.K., L. Epling, N. Cade and R. Breckenridge (2022), 'Relational leadership: Advancing leaders in higher education through mentoring', in J. Crawford (ed.), *Leadership – Advancing Great Leadership Practices and Good Leaders*, accessed 14 February 2023 at https://www.intechopen.com/online-first/83680.

Matthews, A. (1990), *Being Happy*, New York: Penguin Putnam.

McElrath, K. (1992), 'Gender, career disruption, and academic rewards', *Journal of Higher Education*, **63**(3), 269–81.

McFadden, A. and K. Smeaton (2017), 'Amplifying student learning through volunteering', *Journal of University Teaching and Learning Practice*, **14**(3), http://ro.uow.edu.au/jutlp/vol14/iss3/6.

McGranahan, C. (2014), 'What is ethnography? Teaching ethnographic sensibilities without fieldwork', *Teaching Anthropology*, **4**, 23–36.

McKeachie, W.J. and M. Svinicki (2014), *McKeachie's Teaching Tips: Strategies, Research and Theory for College and University Teachers*, 14th edition, Belmont, CA: Wadsworth.

McNaught, K. (2015), 'The changing publication practices in academia: Inherent uses and issues in open access and online publishing and the rise of fraudulent publications', *Journal of Electronic Publishing*, **18**(3), accessed 30 June 2022 at http://dx.doi.org/10.3998/3336451.0018.308.

Merton, R.K. (1968), 'The Matthew Effect in science', *Science*, **159**(3810), 56–63.

Mintz, S.B. (2009), 'The dirty little secret of sabbatical', *Michigan Quarterly Review*, **43**(2), accessed 30 June 2022 at http://hdl.handle.net/2027/spo.act2080.0048.223.

Mintzberg, H. (1998), 'Covert leadership: Notes on managing professionals', *Harvard Business Review*, (Nov/Dec), 140–48.

Mirick, R.G. and S.P. Wladkowski (2018), 'Pregnancy, motherhood, and academic career goals', *Affilia: Journal of Women and Social Work*, **33**(2), 253–69.

Misra, J., E.L. Mickey, E.S. Kanelee and L. Smith-Doerr (2022), 'Creating inclusive department climates in STEM fields: Multiple faculty perspectives on the same departments', *Journal of Diversity in Higher Education*. Advance online publication. https://doi.org/10.1037/dhe0000402.

Mitchell, T. and J. Carroll (2008), 'Academic and research misconduct in the PhD: Issues for students and supervisors', *Nurse Education Today*, **28**(2), 218–26, https://doi.org/10.1016/j.nedt.2007.04.003.

Mongeon, P., C. Brodeur, C. Beaudry and V. Larivière (2016), 'Concentration of research funding leads to decreasing marginal returns', *Research Evaluation*, **25**(4), 396–404.

Morgan, W.R. and E.S. Wright (2021), 'Ten simple rules for hitting a home run with your elevator pitch', *PLoS Computational Biology*, **17**(3), e1008756. https://doi.org/10.1371/journal.pcbi.1008756.

Mula-Falcón, J., C. Cruz González and C. Lucena Rodríguez (2022), 'Burnout syndrome in university teachers: A review of the literature', *International Journal of Educational Organization and Leadership*, **29**(2), 33–46, doi:10.18848/2329-1656/CGP/v29i02/33-46.

Murray, D.E. (2014), '10 point guide to dodging publishing pitfalls', *Times Higher Education*, 6 March, accessed 30 June 2022 at https://www.timeshighereducation.com/features/10-point-guide-to-dodging-publishing-pitfalls/2011808.article.

Musselin, C. (2018), 'New forms of competition in higher education', *Socio-Economic Review*, **16**(3), 657–83.

National Science Foundation (2022), 'Faculty Early Career Development Program (CAREER)', accessed 23 June 2022 at https://beta.nsf.gov/funding/opportunities/faculty-early-career-development-program-career.

National Tertiary Education Union (NTEU Australia) (2015), *2015 NTEU State of the Uni Report*, July, accessed 4 May 2017 at www.nteu.org.au/stateoftheuni.

National Tertiary Education Union (NTEU Australia) (2020), *2020 Special State of the University Sector Survey. The Impact of COVID-19 on Staff Working in Public Universities*, Southbank, Victoria: National Tertiary Education Union.

Nehring, D. (2013), 'To build a successful academic career, you need to play by the rules', *SocialScienceSpace*, 6 February, accessed 1 July 2022 at http://www .socialsciencespace.com/2013/02/to-build-a-successful-academic-career-you-need -to-play-by-the-rules-but-what-are-the-rules/.

Neumann, R. (1992), 'Perceptions of the teaching–research nexus: A framework for analysis', *Higher Education*, **23**(2), 159–71.

Oakley, B. (2014), *A Mind For Numbers*, New York: Tarcher/Putnam.

Obeng-Odoom, F. (2014), 'Why write book reviews?', *Australian Universities Review*, **56**(1), 78–82.

Oberg, K. (1960), 'Culture shock: Adjustment to new cultural environments', *Practical Anthropology*, **7**(3), 177–82.

Oprisko, R. (2012), 'Superpowers: The American academic elite', *Georgetown Public Policy Review*, 3 December, accessed 1 July 2022 at http://gppreview.com/2012/12/ 03/superpowers-the-american-academic-elite/.

Orduna-Malea, E., A. Martín-Martín, M. Thelwall and E.D. López-Cózar (2017), 'Do ResearchGate scores create ghost academic reputations?', *Scientometrics*, **112**(1), 443–60.

O'Shaughnessy, L. (2012), '12 reasons not to get a PhD', *CBS Money-Watch*, 10 July, accessed 1 July 2022 at http://www.cbsnews.com/news/12-reasons-not-to-get-a -phd/.

Otis, L. (2008), 'Advice about publishing an academic book in the United States', *HSS Graduate and Early Career Caucus*, accessed 1 July 2022 at https://hssgecc .wordpress.com/dissertation-to-book/.

Pain, E. (2007), 'Getting to the top of the big pile', *Science Magazine*, 27 July, accessed 1 July 2022 at http://www.sciencemag.org/careers/2007/07/getting-top-big-pile.

Palmer, P.J. (2017), *The Courage to Teach: Exploring the Inner Landscape of a Teacher's Life*, 3rd edition, San Francisco, CA: John Wiley & Sons.

Patfield, S., J. Gore, E. Prieto, L. Fray and K. Sincock (2022), 'Towards quality teaching in higher education: pedagogy-focused academic development for enhancing practice', *International Journal for Academic Development*, DOI: 10.1080/1360144X.2022.2103561.

Patry, M. (2009), 'Clickers in large classes: From student perceptions towards an understanding of best practice', *International Journal for the Scholarship of Teaching and Learning*, **3**(2), 1–11.

Pecorari, D. (2021), 'Predatory conferences: what are the signs?', *Journal of Academic Ethics*, **19**, 343–61.

Peiperl, M.A. (2001), 'Getting 360-degree review right', *Harvard Business Review*, January, 3–7.

Perkel, J.W. (2015), 'Time management: Seize the moment', *Nature*, **517**(7535), 517–19.

Perks, L. and R. Ruffer (2019), 'On the tenure track … again', *Inside Higher Ed*, 4 December, accessed 15 February 2023 at https://www.insidehighered.com/advice/ 2019/12/04/how-successfully-move-tenure-track-position-one-institution-another -opinion.

Peter, L.J. and R. Hull (1969), *The Peter Principle: Why Things Always Go Wrong*, New York: William Morrow and Company.

Philipsen, M. and P. Bostic (2008), *Challenges of the Faculty Career for Women: Success and Sacrifice*, San Francisco, CA: Jossey-Bass.

Phillips, N. (2015), 'How Australian scientists are bending the rules to get research funding', *The Sydney Morning Herald*, 11 April, accessed 1 July 2022 at http://www .smh.com.au/technology/sci-tech/how-australian-scientists-are-bending-the-rules-to -get-research-funding-20150409-1mhrbw.html.

Pink, D.H. (2009), *Drive: The Surprising Truth About What Motivates Us*, New York: Riverhead Books.

Pitt, R. and I. Mewburn (2016), 'Academic superheroes? A critical analysis of academic job descriptions', *Journal of Higher Education Policy and Management*, **38**(1), 88–101.

Qu, Q. (2021), 'Academic job search: from failures to success', 9 June, accessed 12 January 2022 at https://qingqu.engin.umich.edu/wp-content/uploads/sites/42/2021/ 06/Job_Search.pdf.

Race, P. (2020), *The Lecturer's Toolkit. A Practical Guide to Assessment, Learning and Teaching*, 5th edition, London: Routledge.

Regan, K. (2011), 'Seeing the trees in the midst of the forest: Respecting and supporting the development of students as individuals', in I. Hay (ed.), *Inspiring Academics. Learning with the World's Great University Teachers*, Maidenhead, UK: Open University Press, pp. 135–41.

Reisz, M. (2013), 'Letters to a young academic', *Times Higher Education*, 7 February, accessed 1 July 2022 at https://www.timeshighereducation.com/features/letters-to-a -young-academic/2001292.article.

*ResearchProfessional (2023), 'Total funding awareness', accessed 17 January 2023 at http://info.researchprofessional.com/total-funding-awareness/.

ReStore (2022), 'Why develop a research team?', *ReStore@National Centre for Research Methods*, accessed 1 July 2022 at http://www.restore.ac.uk/mrp/services/ ldc/mrp/resources/teamdev/overview/.

Revell, A. and E. Wainwright (2009), 'What makes lectures "unmissable"? Insights into teaching excellence and active learning', *Journal of Geography in Higher Education*, **33**(2), 209–24.

Rhein, D. and A. Nanni (2021), 'The impact of global university rankings on universities in Thailand: Don't hate the player, hate the game', *Globalisation, Societies and Education*, DOI: 10.1080/14767724.2021.2016375.

Richards, J.I. (2012), 'Doctoral students' guide to a successful academic career', *Journal of Advertising Education*, **16**(1), 5–10.

Rogers, W. (2011), 'In the lion's den: Teaching and assessing medical ethics', in I. Hay (ed.), *Inspiring Academics. Learning with the World's Great University Teachers*, Maidenhead, UK: Open University Press, pp. 104–12.

Roiter, B. (2008), *Beyond Work. How Accomplished People Retire Successfully*, Mississauga, ON: John Wiley.

Rosa, R. (2022), 'The trouble with "work–life balance" in neoliberal academia: A systematic and critical review', *Journal of Gender Studies*, **31**(1), 55–73, DOI: 10.1080/09589236.2021.1933926.

Royal Society of New Zealand (2022), 'Information on the 2020 Marsden Fund round', accessed 21 June 2022 at https://www.royalsociety.org.nz/what-we-do/funds-and -opportunities/marsden/marsden-announcements/information-on-the-2020-marsden -fund-round/.

Rubino, D. (2022), '5 strategies to manage the hurt of student evaluations', *The Wiley Network*, accessed 19 January 2023 at https://www.wiley.com/en-us/network/

education/instructors/teaching-strategies/5-strategies-to-manage-the-hurt-of-student -evaluations.

Sage (2022), 'Help readers find your article', accessed 1 July 2022 at https://au.sagepub .com/en-gb/oce/help-readers-find-your-article.

Sale, P. (2013), 'Leaving the dark side for the light: Twelve strategies for effective transition from academic administrator to faculty member', *Administrative Issues Journal: Education, Practice, and Research*, 3(2), 1–10.

Sandiford, P.J. (2015), 'Participant observation as ethnography or ethnography as participant observation in organizational research', in K.D. Strang (ed.), *The Palgrave Handbook of Research Design in Business and Management*, New York: Palgrave Macmillan, pp. 411–46.

Sarsons, H., K. Gërxhani, E. Reuben and A Schram (2021), 'Gender differences in recognition for group work', *Journal of Political Economy*, **129**(1), January, pp. 101–47.

Schultz, K.S., M. Kaye and M. Annesley (2015), *Happy Retirement. The Psychology of Reinvention*, New York: Dorling Kindersley.

Scott, D.E. and S. Scott (2022a), 'Sabbaticals in a research-intensive university: Supports, tensions, and outcomes', in V. Handford and T.M. Sibbald (eds), *The Academic Sabbatical*, Ottawa, Canada: University of Ottawa Press, pp. 206–26.

Scott, P. (2006), 'The academic profession in a knowledge society', in U. Teichler (ed.), *The Formative Years of Scholars*, London: Portland Press, pp. 19–30.

Scott, S. and D.E. Scott (2022b), 'Sabbaticals – the gift of time! A thematic literature review', in V. Handford and T.M. Sibbald (eds), *The Academic Sabbatical*, Ottawa, Canada: University of Ottawa Press, pp. 13–38.

Seligman, M.E.P. and M. Csikszentmihalyi (2014), 'Positive psychology: An introduction', in M. Csikszentmihalyi (ed.), *Flow and the Foundations of Positive Psychology: The Collected Works of Mihaly Csikszentmihalyi*, Dordrecht: Springer, pp. 279–97.

Shah, H. (2020), 'Global problems need social science', *Nature*, 15 January, accessed 8 September 2022 at https://www.nature.com/articles/d41586-020-00064-x.

Shaw, C. (2013), 'Research funding: 10 tips for writing a successful application', *The Guardian*, 20 April, accessed 1 July 2022 at http://www.theguardian.com/higher -education-network/blog/2013/apr/19/tips-successful-research-grant-funding.

Shaw, C. and L. Ward (2014), 'Dark thoughts: Why mental illness is on the rise in academia', *The Guardian*, 6 March, accessed 1 July 2022 at http://www.theguardian .com/higher-education-network/2014/mar/06/mental-health-academics-growing -problem-pressure-university.

Sheehan, E.P., T.M. McDevitt and H.C. Ross (1998), 'Looking for a job as a psychology professor? Factors affecting applicant success', *Teaching of Psychology*, **25**(1), 8–11.

Shevlin, M., P. Banyard, M. Davies and M. Griffiths (2000), 'The validity of student evaluation of teaching in higher education: Love me, love my lectures?', *Assessment & Evaluation in Higher Education*, **29**(4), 397–405.

Sidaway, J.D. (2016), 'Scholarly publishing landscapes: A geographical perspective', *Area*, **48**(3), 389–92.

Simpson, A.B., A.D. Jolliffe Simpson, M. Soar, L.D. Oldfield, R. Roy and L.A. Salter (2022), 'The elephant in the room: Precarious work in New Zealand's universities, Auckland: Figshare, DOI: 10.17608/k6.auckland.19243626.

Smith, D.L., K.B. Rollins and L.J. Smith (2012), 'Back to the faculty: Transition from university department leadership', *Innovative Higher Education*, **37**(1), 53–63.

Smith, D.R., R. Spronken-Smith, C. Stringer and C.A. Wilson (2016), 'Gender, academic careers and the sabbatical: a New Zealand case study', *Higher Education Research & Development*, **35**(3), 589-603, DOI:10.1080/07294360.2015.1107880.

Solem, M., K. Foote and J. Monk (eds) (2009), *Aspiring Academics. A Resource Book for Graduate Students and Early Career Faculty*, Upper Saddle River, NJ: Pearson.

Sparke, M. (2013), *Introducing Globalization: Ties, Tensions, and Uneven Integration*, New York: Wiley-Blackwell.

Spiller, D. and T. Harris (2013), 'Learning from evaluations: Probing the reality', *Issues in Educational Research*, **23**(2), 258–68.

Spina, N., K. Smithers, J. Harris and I. Mewburn (2022) 'Back to zero? Precarious employment in academia amongst "older" early career researchers, a life-course approach', *British Journal of Sociology of Education*, **43**(4), 534–49, DOI: 10.1080/01425692.2022.2057925.

Spooren, P., B. Brockx and D. Mortelmans (2015), 'On the validity of student evaluation of teaching: The state of the art', *Review of Educational Research*, **83**(4), 598–642.

Stanton, J. (2014), 'SEO for CVs: Raise your academic profile', *Pulse*, 5 July, accessed 1 July 2022 at https://www.linkedin.com/pulse/20140704190341-3382219-seo-for-cvs-raise-your-academic-profile.

Starr, P. (1982), *The Social Transformation of American Medicine*, New York: Basic Books.

Stearns, P. N. (2018), 'Some historical perspectives on reference inflation', *Academe*, **104**(3), 32–6.

Stefan, M.A. (2010), 'A CV of failures', *Nature*, **468**, 467, https://doi.org/10.1038/nj7322-467a.

Sternberg, R.J. (2013), 'Self-sabotage on the academic career', *The Chronicle of Higher Education*, 29 April, accessed 1 July 2022 at https://www.chronicle.com/article/self-sabotage-in-the-academic-career/.

Stewart, M. (2014), 'Making sense of a teaching programme for university academics: Exploring the longer-term effects', *Teaching and Teacher Education*, **38**, 89–98.

Stratford, E. and M. Bradshaw (2021), 'Rigorous and trustworthy: Qualitative research design, in I. Hay and M. Cope (eds), *Qualitative Research Methods in Human Geography*, 5th edition, Toronto, ON: Oxford University Press, pp. 92–106.

Stringer, R., D. Smith, R. Spronken-Smith and C. Wilson (2018), '"My entire career has been fixed term": Gender and precarious academic employment at a New Zealand university', *New Zealand Sociology*, **33**(2), 169–201.

Stripling, J. (2010), 'Not so private professors', *Inside Higher Ed*, 2 March, accessed 8 May 2017 at https://www.insidehighered.com/news/2010/03/02/facebook.

Sutherland, K.A. (2015), 'Constructions of success in academia: An early career perspective', *Studies in Higher Education*, **42**,(4), 743–59.

Sutherland, K., M. Wilson and P. Williams (2013), *Success in Academia? The Experiences of Early Career Academics in New Zealand Universities*, Ako Aotearoa National Centre for Tertiary Teaching Excellence, Wellington, accessed 1 July 2022 at http://akoaotearoa.ac.nz/download/ng/file/group-5314/report-success-in-academia-sutherland.pdf.

Sutherland, M. (2021), 'Mount A suspends professor after investigation into complaints about blog', 7 May, accessed 16 June 2022 at https://www.cbc.ca/news/canada/new-brunswick/mount-allison-suspension-professor-1.6016047.

Teperek, M. (2018), 'How to make the most of an academic conference – a checklist for before, during and after the meeting', 16 March, accessed 17 January 2023 at

https://blogs.lse.ac.uk/impactofsocialsciences/2018/03/16/how-to-make-the-most
-of-an-academic-conference-a-checklist-for-before-during-and-after-the-meeting/.

The Conversation (2023), 16 January, accessed 16 January 2023 at: https://
theconversation.com/au.

The Economist (2010), 'The disposable academic. Why doing a PhD is often a waste
of time', 16 December, accessed 1 July 2022 at http://www.economist.com/node/
17723223.

The Economist (2015), 'Top of the class. Competition among universities has become
more intense and international', 26 May, accessed 1 July 2022 at https://www
.economist.com/special-report/2015/03/26/top-of-the-class.

Tierney, R. (2015), *The Introverted Presenter: Ten Steps for Preparing and Delivering
Successful Presentations*, Berkeley, CA: Apress.

Tower, L.E., A. Faul and J. Hamilton-Mason et al. (2015), 'Work/life fit: The intersec-
tion of developmental life cycle and academic life cycle', *Affilia: Journal of Women
and Social Work*, **30**(4), 519–32.

Trounson, A. (2015), 'University staff "donating" $1.7bn in unpaid work', *The
Australian*, 22 July, accessed 1 July 2022 at http://www.theaustralian.com.au/
higher-education/university-staff-donating-17bn-in-unpaid-work/news-story/59
2e2eb4dde2bb2fb0cfcb62d32b7ddf.

Tree, J.E.F. and J. Vaid (2022), 'Why so few, still? Challenges to attracting, advancing,
and keeping women faculty of color in academia', *Frontiers in Sociology*, Section:
Gender, Sex and Sexualities, 18 January 2022, https://doi.org/10.3389/fsoc.2021
.792198.

Trowler, P., M. Saunders and V. Bamber (2012), *Tribes and Territories in the 21st
Century. Rethinking the Significance of Disciplines in Higher Education*, New York:
Routledge.

Tulloch, B. (2012), 'Refreshing your teaching', *TDU Talk*, No. 1, 17–18.

UK Council for Graduate Education (2016), *UKCGE Launches National Supervisor
Award with Times Higher Education*, 14 April, accessed 1 July 2022 at http://www
.ukcge.ac.uk/article/ukcge-launches-national-supervisor-award-with-times-higher
-educa-301.aspx.

UK Research and Innovation (2022), *ESRC application and success rate data,
May 2018*, updated 17 March 2022, accessed 21 June 2022 at https://www.ukri
.org/wp-content/uploads/2021/10/ESRC-07102021-ESRCApplicationDataAnalysis
-May2018.pdf.

University and College Union (2022), 'University & college staff do two days unpaid
work every week', 20 June 2022, accessed 10 February 2023 at https://www.ucu.org
.uk/article/12347/University--college-staff-do-two-days-unpaid-work-every-week
#:~:text=In%20further%20education%20%2C%2093%25%20of,say%20their
%20workload%20is%20unmanageable.

University of California – Berkeley Career Center (2022), *Academic Job Search –
Letters of Recommendation*, accessed 1 July 2022 at https://career.berkeley.edu/
PhDs/PhDletters.

University of California, San Diego (undated), *The Academic Job Search Survival
Handbook Especially for Graduate Students*, accessed 1 July 2022 at https://career
.ucsd.edu/_files/GAcadJobSearchHandbook.pdf.

University of North Carolina at Chapel Hill (2023), 'Diversity statements', accessed 11
January 2023 at https://writingcenter.unc.edu/tips-and-tools/diversity-statements/.

University of Oklahoma (2023), 'Make connections and promote your work on list-servs', accessed 9 January 2023 at https://libraries.ou.edu/content/make-connections-and-promote-your-work-listservs.

University of Oxford (2022), 'Hours of work', accessed 1 July 2022 at https://hr.admin.ox.ac.uk/hours-of-work.

University of Queensland (2023), 'Three minute thesis', accessed 18 January 2023 at https://threeminutethesis.uq.edu.au/home.

Van der Heijden, I.J.M., E.M.M. Davies, D. van der Linden, N. Bozionelos and A. De Vos (2022), 'The relationship between career commitment and career success among university staff: The mediating role of employability', *European Management Review*, **19**(4), 564–80.

Vick, J.M., J.S. Furlong and R. Lurie (2016), *The Academic Job Search Handbook*, 5th edition, Philadelphia, PA: University of Pennsylvania Press.

Vitae (2022), 'Building and managing a research team', accessed 1 July 2022 at https://www.vitae.ac.uk/doing-research/leadership-development-for-principal-investigators-pis/building-and-managing-a-research-team.

Watson, A. (2021), '"Placing" participant observation', in I. Hay and M. Cope (eds.), *Qualitative Research Methods in Human Geography*, 5th edition, Toronto, ON: Oxford University Press, pp. 125–47.

Wells, T.T., C.A. Schofield, E.M. Clerkin and E.S. Sheets (2013), 'The academic job market: Advice from the front lines', *The Behavior Therapist*, **36**(2), 39–45.

Wesch, M. (2011), 'The art of loving and learning: Erich Fromm and the learning of transformation', in I. Hay (ed.), *Inspiring Academics. Learning with the World's Great University Teachers*, Maidenhead, UK: Open University Press, pp. 23–8.

Wiegel, C., S. Sattler, A.J. Goritz and M. Diewald (2016), 'Work-related stress and cognitive enhancement among university teachers', *Anxiety, Stress and Coping*, **29**(1), 100–117.

Wilbur, H.M. (2007), 'On getting a job', in A.L. DeNeef and C.D. Goodwin (eds), *The Academic's Handbook*, 3rd edn, Durham, NC: Duke University Press, pp. 123–35.

Wilcox, C. (2014), 'Lighting dark: Fixing academia's mental health problem', *New Scientist*, 10 October, accessed 1 July 2022 at https://www.newscientist.com/article/dn26365-lighting-dark-fixing-academias-mental-health-problem/.

Wiley-Blackwell (2022), 'Search Engine Optimization (SEO) for your article', accessed 1 July 2022 at https://authorservices.wiley.com/author-resources/Journal-Authors/Prepare/writing-for-seo.html.

Winefield, A.H. and R. Jarrett (2001), 'Occupational stress in university staff', *International Journal of Stress Management*, **8**(4), 285–98.

Winefield, A.H., N. Gillespie and C. Stough et al. (2003), 'Occupational stress in Australian university staff: Results from a national survey', *International Journal of Stress Management*, **10**(1), 51–63.

Wingfield, B. (2011), 'Juggling the demands of a career and motherhood: Perspectives of an academic in science', *South African Journal of Science*, **107**(9/10), Article 865.

Wolff, J. (2013), 'Academic reference inflation has set in, and everyone is simply wonderful', *The Guardian*, 29 January, accessed 1 July 2022 at http://www.theguardian.com/education/2013/jan/28/application-university-job-reference.

Wolf-Wendel, L. and K. Ward (2015), 'Academic mothers: Exploring disciplinary perspectives', *Innovative Higher Education*, **40**(1), 19–35.

Wu, L., D. Wang and J.A. Evans (2019), 'Large teams develop and small teams disrupt science and technology', *Nature*, **566**, 13 February, 378–82.

Yates, D. (2011), 'Brief diversions vastly improve focus, researchers find', *Illinois News Bureau*, 8 February, accessed 1 July 2022 at https://www.sciencedaily.com/releases/2011/02/110208131529.htm.
Zahorski, K.J. (1994), *The Sabbatical Mentor: A Practical Guide to Successful Sabbaticals*, Boston, MA: Anker Publishing.

Index

'The book's new edition revisits and builds on the insightful and actionable advice previously given in the already solid first edition. Notably, it adds more nuance to its content, which will make it even more relevant to academics outside of higher education institutions located in English-speaking countries.'
Iván Farías Pelcastre, University of Birmingham, UK

'In the context of increasingly challenging and precarious times in higher education, this highly readable 2nd edition offers valuable and insightful advice based on experience and research for lecturers at any stage of their career to reflect upon as they seek to navigate and sustain rewarding and balanced academic careers.'
Ruth Healey, University of Chester, UK

'Written as an accessible and thoughtful guide, How to be an Academic Superhero is an essential resource for navigating the many stages of an academic career. From the pre-Ph.D. school selection stage through tenure and retirement, Iain Hay exposes the frequently hidden pathways and challenges of an engaged and successful academic career by emphasizing the importance of planning and imagining one's individual trajectory while also highlighting the importance of maintaining broader life balance.

How to be an Academic Superhero provides relevant examples, current resources and a concise set of strategies for successfully navigating each career stage. Although much is written about early career stages, many fewer resources exist for traversing mid-and-later career opportunities and challenges. Iain Hay leverages his deep experiences across multiple positions in the academy and clearly and concisely distils the essential elements of a well-rounded academic career.'
Holly Barcus, Macalester College, USA

'An academic career is an increasingly challenging one, and professional success clearly requires a truly vocational level of commitment. In this comprehensive work, Professor Iain Hay, himself a decorated academic superhero, provides a comprehensive and practical guide to realizing excellence in the multiple and complex roles that an aspiring academic must fulfill.'
Michael Meadows, Nanjing University, China